100 BEST BOOKS BY TITLE

- ☐ The 1-Page Marketing Plan 146
- ☐ The 4 Disciplines of Execution 194
- ☐ The 7 Habits of Highly Effective People 100
- ☐ The 22 Immutable Laws of Marketing 149
- ☐ Atomic Habits 98
- ☐ Badass 126
- ☐ Becoming the Evidence-Based Manager 185
- ☐ Blindspot 31
- ☐ Building a Storybrand 2.0 148
- ☐ Captivate 138
- ☐ The Catalyst 136
- ☐ The Challenger Sale 155
- ☐ Co-Active Coaching 241
- ☐ The Coaching Habit 243
- ☐ Connected 213
- ☐ The Conversation 236
- ☐ Creating Your Best Life ... 75
- ☐ Crossing the Chasm 130
- ☐ Crossing the Unknown Sea 59
- ☐ Crucial Conversations ... 227
- ☐ The Defining Decade 68
- ☐ Designing Your Life 57
- ☐ The Desire Map 76
- ☐ Difficult Conversations ... 231
- ☐ Drive 84
- ☐ The Effective Executive ... 105
- ☐ Fierce Conversations 229
- ☐ Financial Intelligence 187
- ☐ Finding Your Own North Star 54
- ☐ The First 90 Days 64
- ☐ The Five Dysfunctions of a Team 190
- ☐ Full Catastrophe Living ... 19
- ☐ Get Everything Done ... 107
- ☐ Getting Things Done 109
- ☐ Give and Take 221
- ☐ The Go-Giver 223
- ☐ Good Habits, Bad Habits 95
- ☐ The Good Life 212
- ☐ Good to Great 196
- ☐ Great at Work 12
- ☐ I Will Teach You to Be Rich 45
- ☐ Immunity to Change 166
- ☐ Influence 134
- ☐ The Inner Game of Work ... 17
- ☐ The Jobs to Be Done Playbook 128
- ☐ Keep Going 118
- ☐ The Leadership Challenge 173
- ☐ Leading Change 168
- ☐ Leading from the Middle ... 183
- ☐ Let Your Life Speak 56
- ☐ The Little Red Book of Selling 153
- ☐ Made to Stick 140
- ☐ The Magic Lamp 81
- ☐ The Making of a Manager ... 182
- ☐ Managing Transitions ... 164
- ☐ Measure What Matters ... 78
- ☐ Million Dollar Weekend ... 70
- ☐ The Mindful Athlete 22
- ☐ The Mindful Coach 244
- ☐ Mindfulness 24
- ☐ Mindset 6
- ☐ The Miracle Morning ... 72
- ☐ Moneyball 206
- ☐ New Sales. Simplified. ... 157
- ☐ Nonviolent Communication 233
- ☐ Now, Discover Your Strengths 41
- ☐ The ONE Thing 111
- ☐ Orbiting the Giant Hairball 116
- ☐ Peak 8
- ☐ The Personal MBA 66
- ☐ Personality 37
- ☐ The Power of Vulnerability 215
- ☐ The Practice 120
- ☐ Predictably Irrational ... 29
- ☐ The Progress Principle ... 88
- ☐ The Project 50 114
- ☐ 48
- ☐ 39
- ☐ 179
- ☐ 224
- ☐ Making Marriage Work ... 217
- ☐ The Simple Path to Wealth 50
- ☐ Six Thinking Hats 33
- ☐ The Speed of Trust 175
- ☐ The SPIN Selling Fieldbook 160
- ☐ Talent 200
- ☐ The Talent Code 10
- ☐ Tiny Habits 97
- ☐ Total Leadership 177
- ☐ Traction 192
- ☐ The Ultimate Question 2.0 124
- ☐ When Things Fall Apart ... 170
- ☐ Who 202
- ☐ Work Rules! 204
- ☐ Your Brain at Work 27
- ☐ Your Money or Your Life ... 46

100 BEST BOOKS
FOR WORK & LIFE

TO JACK COVERT,
FOR GIVING ME A CHANCE.

TO RAY BARD,
FOR TRUSTING IN ME.

100 BEST BOOKS FOR WORK & LIFE

TABLE OF CONTENTS

START HERE: A PATH TO BETTER 1

SECTION ONE: YOU 4
CHAPTER 1	**BETTER**	5
CHAPTER 2	**MINDFULNESS**	15
CHAPTER 3	**THINKING**	26
CHAPTER 4	**PERSONALITY**	36
CHAPTER 5	**MONEY**	44
CHAPTER 6	**PURPOSE**	53

SECTION TWO: PROGRESS 62
CHAPTER 7	**STARTING**	63
CHAPTER 8	**GOALS**	74
CHAPTER 9	**MOTIVATION**	83
CHAPTER 10	**HABITS**	93
CHAPTER 11	**FOCUS**	103
CHAPTER 12	**CREATIVE WORK**	113

SECTION THREE: **GROWTH** 122
CHAPTER 13	**CUSTOMERS**	123
CHAPTER 14	**INFLUENCE**	133
CHAPTER 15	**MARKETING**	145
CHAPTER 16	**SALES**	152

SECTION FOUR: **LEADING** 162
CHAPTER 17	**CHANGE**	163
CHAPTER 18	**LEADERSHIP**	172
CHAPTER 19	**MANAGING**	181
CHAPTER 20	**TEAMS**	189
CHAPTER 21	**HIRING**	199

SECTION FIVE: **CONNECTION** 210
CHAPTER 22	**RELATIONSHIPS**	211
CHAPTER 23	**GENEROSITY**	220
CHAPTER 24	**CONVERSATIONS**	226
CHAPTER 25	**COACHING**	238

ACKNOWLEDGEMENTS	248
CREDITS	250
COPYRIGHT	251
INDEX	252
ABOUT	264

START HERE
A PATH TO BETTER

"The more that you read, the more things you will know. The more that you learn, the more places you'll go."
—Dr. Seuss, *I Can Read with My Eyes Shut!*

THIS BOOK IS FOR PEOPLE WHO WANT TO GET BETTER.
The purpose of *100 Best Books for Work and Life* is to help readers find the best books to help them get better. Think of this book as a map—a guide that highlights the most valuable destinations and shows how they connect. It's designed to help you navigate the journey, but the journey itself is yours to take.

I believe we are all on a path to be better. This book is for anyone ready to invest in that path. Sometimes better is just getting up in the morning and doing something that you feel will help—meditating for thirty minutes or walking to the park and back. Maybe it's reading this book in the quiet hours before everyone around you awakens. Better can also be finding the right person to hire for your team. Or being skillful in a conversation you need to have with someone important in your life. Better is often seen even more clearly in others around us and gives us something to aspire to.

THIS BOOK HELPS YOU FIND THE BOOKS YOU NEED.

Each year, there are tens of thousands of new titles published to help readers improve their work lives and personal lives. Titles from the categories of business and self-help fill entire sections of bookstores. Sorting through all of those titles is a daunting task, even for the most devoted readers.

The books contained in *100 Best Books* show the reader a problem *and* offer a solution. Self-help books tend to focus more on the problem. Business books emphasize the solution. Both approaches are helpful; especially when the broader genre is really "how to get better," no matter what shelf they might be found on in the bookstore.

THIS BOOK USES THREE FACTORS FOR ITS SELECTIONS.

First, these books challenge conventional thinking. While many great books offer straightforward solutions, the most impactful ones reframe the problem itself. By presenting a fresh perspective, these books invite readers to reconsider their assumptions and, in doing so, uncover more meaningful solutions.

Second, these books excel at tackling the most common obstacles we face in both work and life. While bookstores scatter these titles across various categories, this book organizes them into twenty-five essential topics—focus, influence, leadership, relationships, money, mindfulness, and more. Each chapter contains three to five of the best books on the topic. My hope with each chapter is that you will find an approach that resonates with your situation and other books that broaden your understanding of the journey ahead.

Third, these books are approachable. The selections in the *100 Best Books* avoid dense, overly academic writing. Insight only matters if it's understandable and applicable—especially when time is limited. This collection of authors excels at making complex ideas clear and practical, ensuring their insights are available to a broad audience.

THIS BOOK IS MEANT TO BE USED.
Let me suggest how you might get started using *100 Best Books* today:

1. Take a moment and think about your three biggest priorities in all aspects of your life. My guess is you'll know what they are immediately.
2. With those in mind, turn to the front of the book and look down the chapter list. As you skim the books in each chapter, you'll naturally stop at a group of books that resonate with you.
3. Turn to that chapter immediately and start reading.

Each review has a similar format. The review opens with a quote from the author that is meant to set the stage. The body of the review contains the key concepts in the book and why they matter to the topic at hand. The end of each review has a conclusion that presents even more utility from the book. This last element might be a set of reflection questions from the author, a summary of a key framework, or a closing thought that lands a key lesson. Most chapters in *100 Best Books* can be read in about ten minutes, and at the end of that time, you will already have some ideas of how to do better on your biggest priorities.

To make the book even easier to use, you'll find an alphabetical list of all the book titles on the endsheets in the front and back of the book. The index is another great tool, helping you see where authors, books, and key topics appear throughout *100 Best Books for Work and Life*.

THIS BOOK IS A GIFT TO YOU.
Thank you for picking up *100 Best Books for Work and Life*. I wrote this for you. The whole project took four years to complete. I stayed with it because I love books and I am passionate about sharing all the wisdom they have to offer.

My hope is that this book is helpful for you as you walk down your path to getting better.

Todd Sattersten
todd@bardpress.com

P.S. There are more resources at bardpress.com/100best. You will find more recommendations and interviews. Be sure to check it out!

SECTION ONE
YOU

**BETTER
MINDFULNESS
THINKING
PERSONALITY
MONEY
PURPOSE**

CHAPTER 1
BETTER

"It's what you learn after you know it all that counts."
—John Wooden

Your self-help shelf is filled with books telling you that you can get better. Most are filled with over-quoted truisms and inspirational stories of people that have overcome adversity. We are told to surround ourselves with positivity and good vibes. It can feel like good things will just manifest from our thoughts. Thoughts do matter, but differently than we might think.

Researchers have confirmed that we can get better. Carol Dweck has shown that believing you can change changes your belief about what is possible. Anders Ericsson's work points toward an almost limitless possibility for improvement through practice. And Daniel Coyle reports from an even wider range of sources how talent can be cultivated and grown.

Mindset: The New Psychology of Success
by Carol Dweck

"It's for you to decide whether change is right for you now. Maybe it is, maybe it isn't. But either way, keep the growth mindset in your thoughts. Then, when you bump up against obstacles, you can turn to it. It will always be there for you, showing you a path into the future."

BILLY BEANE has gained icon status for his pioneering work as the general manager of the Oakland A's and for using statistics to recruit undervalued talent. His story was chronicled by Michael Lewis in *Moneyball*, and he was played by Brad Pitt in the movie version of the story. Beane was also a stand-out athlete in college and played in MLB, but he never lived up to early expectations. Carol Dweck argues that his difficulties as a player and his innovative success as a manager can be tied to the mindset he brought to each part of his career.

Dweck's theory is very simple: some people don't think they can change, while others think they can. Take a moment and think about that for yourself. Do you believe that you can change? Do you think that intelligence is a known quantity that goes unchanged over a lifetime? That fixed mindset, as Dweck calls it, might show up in smaller ways. How about this: Do you think you can change the quality of your relationship with your partner? Or your child? Or your parents? What about your relationship with your boss?

Now, fixed mindsets can manifest in many ways. For Beane, it became difficult to compete the further he advanced as a player. He believed his natural talent would carry him; as a scout described it, "Billy was of the opinion that he should never make an out." With fixed mindsets, we can never admit our deficiencies or work to correct them. That failure of admission can look like resistance or superiority—as famed basketball coach John Wooden said, "You aren't a failure until you start to blame."

Now, if we believe we can change, then we believe we can grow. Dweck says, "When we teach people the growth mindset, with its focus on development, these ideas about challenge and effort follow."

And she sees it everywhere. Dweck points to the selfless, ever-improving quality of Level 5 leadership in Jim Collins's *Good to Great* framework. She sees it in schoolteachers like Marva Collins who challenges four-year-olds who start in September to be reading by Christmas. Dweck sees it as the goal of any relationship to encourage the other's development and for them to do the same for you. In Beane's case as general manager, he saw something that he couldn't see as a player—that mindset mattered more than talent—and he's gone on to field competitive teams for years with that insight.

What seems obvious is full of nuance, too. Praise is a reward in any social relationship; for example, we are often quick to tell a child how smart they are. Dweck found over and over that praising a child's intelligence reinforces a fixed mindset, harms their motivation, and harms their ongoing performance because it leaves them unprepared for failure and setbacks. And the tricky part is that kids love that kind of direct praise. We all do. The reality is that effort is what makes people smart and talented. That is the activity we need to praise and reward.

Malcolm Gladwell has a theory that we hold up geniuses as a society. We marvel at their talent and the seeming effortlessness of it. "People with the growth mindset, however, believe something very different," Dweck says. "For them, even geniuses have to work hard for their achievements. And what's so heroic...about having a gift? They may appreciate endowment, but they admire effort, for no matter what your ability is, effort is what ignites that ability and turns it into accomplishment."

EFFECTIVE FEEDBACK THAT ACKNOWLEDGES CHALLENGES AND CONFRONTS MISTAKES:

- "Thank you for taking the initiative on that."
- "Thanks for seeing that difficult task through. I know it was really hard."
- "Thank you for struggling and learning something new. It really helped."
- "Thank you for being undaunted by the setbacks we had on that project."
- "I appreciate you being open to and acting on the feedback you got."

Peak: Secrets from the New Science of Expertise
by Anders Ericsson and Robert Pool

"In pretty much every endeavor, people have a tremendous capacity to improve their performance, as long as they train the right way. If you practice something for a few hundred hours, you will almost certainly see great improvement...but you have only scratched the surface. [H]ow much you improve is up to you."

MY GUESS IS that you probably don't know who Anders Ericsson is, but if I mentioned "the 10,000-hour rule" popularized by Malcolm Gladwell, you'd immediately know his work. What's even more interesting is how poorly that pop culture reference both misrepresents and underrepresents the depth of Ericsson's work. If I put on my book publisher hat, I have to say that the title of the book also masks his insights. Let's see if we can start to correct all that.

Ericsson spent his whole life studying what makes people the best in their field. His first research was with Steve Faloon, an undergraduate student he recruited for a study on memory. Each day, Ericsson and Faloon would practice to see how many digits Faloon could recall from a single string spoken to him. By the end of two hundred sessions over a two-year period, Faloon could repeat back eighty-two digits, which broke all previous records.

This is the first important finding in Ericsson's research: There appears to be no limit to the ability to improve. Rajveer Meena of India can recite seventy thousand digits of pi. Barbara Blackburn, the current American record holder, can type 212 words per minute. Jan Kareš of the Czech Republic performed 4,654 pull-ups in twelve hours. In 2019, Nirmal Purja of Nepal climbed fourteen mountains over eight thousand meters tall in six months and six days. The previous record was seven years and 310 days.

The next finding is that talent is overrated. It may be important in giving people motivation when they are first starting out, but practice wins over time, every time. Savants of all types develop their skills the same way other experts do. Ericsson told Larry King in

2016, "This idea that somebody more or less discovers, suddenly, that they're extremely good at something, I've yet to find even a single example of that type of phenomenon."

That just leaves us with practice. One of Ericsson's landmark research projects was with violinists at the Berlin University of Arts. In the school, Ericsson worked with musicians who would go on to be the best in the world. He controlled the training the musicians received. The choice of violinist as subject was also clever, because the standards for skills and techniques were well established for decades. The single factor that separated average players from the best players was hours of practice. The best players put in almost twice the number of hours of the average player (7,410 hours versus 3,420 hours). Ericsson further confirmed this with violinists playing in orchestras in Berlin and found those players practiced over seven thousand hours a year. "We found no shortcuts and no 'prodigies' who reached an expert level with relatively little practice," the authors write.

Now, the kind of practice that makes people world-class experts has particular qualities. Feedback is essential, which means solely gained experience is not particularly effective at building expertise. Deliberate practice, as Ericsson calls it, also pushes one out of their comfort zone. The Navy built the Top Gun school in 1968 to put pilots through daily live-action dogfights against top-notch instructors and immediately followed up with after-action reviews to assess performance and prepare for the next day. Make mistakes. Correct mistakes. Learn new skills.

There's so much more. Great instructors play an important role. Focusing on effort produces real benefits. We need objective standards for success in a wider range of fields. Doing always beats knowing. And the mindset that you can continue to improve is essential.

CLOSING WORDS FROM ERICSSON:
"Imagine a world in which doctors, teachers, engineers, pilots, computer programmers, and many other professionals hone their skills in the same way that violinists, chess players, and ballerinas do now. Imagine a world in which 50 percent

of the people in these professions learn to perform at the level that only the top 5 percent manage today. What would that mean for our health care, our educational system, our technology?"

The Talent Code: Greatness Isn't Born. It's Grown.
by Daniel Coyle

"Skill is insulation that wraps neural circuits and grows according to certain signals."

IN READING *The Talent Code*, you get a different telling of what makes people get better. Daniel Coyle is a writer who brings a journalistic approach to the story of getting better. He connects the dots and more of them. His reporting from research labs and training centers around the world enriches the topic.

Every thought, feeling, or movement we have is an electrical signal that travels along a path of neurons in our brain. As a path gets more traffic, the brain starts to notice, and it reinforces those paths by wrapping them with a substance called myelin. The more those paths fire, the more they are wrapped. Speeds along those paths slowly increase from two miles per hour to two hundred miles per hour. It turns out our brains build skills the same way our muscles build strength—through repetition.

To properly build those pathways, we need the deep practice that Anders Ericsson suggests. The amazing talent in Florence, Italy, during the Renaissance is explained by the craft guilds and their apprenticeships, which children started in as early as six years old. Small skills, like the way to hold a chisel or perhaps a tennis racket today, are acquired and connected to other skills in small chunks. Coaches will often slow down the action to make it easier to see the errors in those tiny segments. And then you repeat, over and over, with careful attention to notice the gap between the target and the attempt. Those repetitions build the myelin-covered pathways.

These future experts need motivation to keep practicing. There are many sources that can provide a spark. Telling someone they share a birthday with a mathematician will cause them to work 65 percent longer on a sample problem. In his own study, Coyle declares that children later in the birth order occupy more slots as the world's fastest sprinters and top NFL running backs. In Knowledge Is Power Program Public Schools, students are told to focus on the fact that they will go to college. Researcher Gary McPherson found that asking young musicians about how long they planned to pursue their new craft predicted how fast they progressed. Those who expressed long-term commitment ("all my life") progressed 400 percent more than those who made a short-term commitment ("for this year"). Powerful ignition comes from some internal push that says, "Better get busy!"

In Coyle's model, great teachers are the last component of superior skill building. Great teachers were often aspiring talents that didn't reach the highest level and went on a quest to understand what makes great talent. These coaches see each student's unique feedback needs and are incredibly perceptive to those needs. And they use the techniques that we've covered in this chapter. "Seek small improvement one day at a time," wrote UCLA coach John Wooden. Vocal coach Linda Septien delivers corrections in quick chunks—"check back, tongue tighter, yawn muscles." Tom Martinez, the personal coach of former NFL quarterback Tom Brady, stresses the importance of getting to know the student to better understand how to best work with them.

Coyle quotes Anders Ericsson as saying, "There is no cell type that geniuses have that the rest of us don't." If there is anything I want you to take away from this chapter, it is that. Getting better is available to all of us with the right mindset, practice, and people giving us feedback.

TALENT TIPS FROM COYLE'S FOLLOW-UP BOOK *THE LITTLE BOOK OF TALENT:*

- Choose spartan over luxurious: Simple, humble spaces help focus attention on the deep-practice task at hand.
- Take your watch off: Instead of counting minutes or hours, count reaches and reps.

- Pay attention immediately after you make a mistake: Look straight at mistakes and see what really happened, and then ask yourself what you can do next to improve.
- Shrink the space: Toyota trains new employees by shrinking the assembly line into a single room filled with toy-sized replicas of the equipment and found it was more effective than training on the actual production line.
- To learn from a book, close the book: Writing a summary forces you to figure out the key points (one set of reaches), process and organize those ideas so they make sense (more reaches), and write them down on the page (still more reaches, along with repetition).

Great at Work: How Top Performers Do Less, Work Better, and Achieve More
by Morten Hansen

"It turned out that our seven work-smart practices went a long way toward explaining differences in performance. In fact, they accounted for a whopping 66 percent of the variation in performance among the 5,000 people in our dataset."

MORTEN HANSEN'S RESEARCH could appear in any number of chapters here. I decided to put *Great at Work* in this first chapter to show that investing in a better version of yourself can be measured and that research shows a dramatic improvement in performance and well-being. Many of these practices are covered again in full chapters with more titles later in this book. For now, let's consider how Hansen sees our path to better.

That path starts with "Do Less, Then Obsess." Any number of bestsellers in the last decade have encouraged us to reduce the number of priorities we are working with and focus on the important things. Hansen is very clear that this is only half of the equation. Taking that time gained and obsessing about the few most vital issues is what sets top performers apart. Hansen is often asked, "How many tasks can I remove, given what I must do to excel?" His response is, "As few as you can, as many as you must."

The next lever is being more effective in your work. Look at activities through the lens of the value it creates for others. Get rid of fluff. Dedicate more effort to high value. Provide more value. Look for new activities that create new value. That probably sounds like a lot of "value," but all he's asking is how much you're helping others. Hansen is encouraging us to look at both sides of Peter Drucker's famous adage—do things right *and* do the right things. We then apply learning loops to try out new approaches to doing the work, as we look for "small, concrete actions you [can] take on a daily basis to improve a skill."

Hansen writes that high performers pursue two ends. They seek pursuits that ignite their passion, but relying solely on passion, as a singular measure, can lead to heartache and isolation. The research also notes that deep passion for one's job can lead to too much engagement and poor work-life balance. Passion is best paired with purpose. By introducing purpose, we add the pursuit of what contributes to the well-being of others. It might be tempting to think we can't have both passion and purpose. Hansen's research again proves the contrary. He found people across the dataset who reported being passionate about their jobs (with no job type being rated below 10 percent) *and* who felt purpose through their contribution to society. Among construction workers, 28 percent report feeling a deep purpose for the work they do.

I have mostly highlighted the individual practices from the first half of the book. The whole second half of the book focuses on practices that higher performers use when they engage with others. High performers become forceful champions for the change they want to see in the world, using emotional appeal and persistence that addresses concerns. They encourage groups to vigorously debate topics *and* unite around the decision once it has been made. High performers also collaborate in a balanced way that emphasizes value for them and the organization, ensures resources are committed for success, and shares rewards for the results rather than the activities.

FINDING PASSION BEYOND THE WORK ITSELF:
- Could it be joy in the tasks you are doing?
- Could it be excitement from succeeding?
- Could it be the thrill of unleashing your creative energy?
- Could it be from being with the people you work with?
- Could it be from the delight of learning and growing?
- Could it come from the elation of a job well done?

CHAPTER 2
MINDFULNESS

"Our life is what our thoughts make it."
—Marcus Aurelius, *Meditations*

Dōgen Zenji, the founder of Zen Buddhism in Japan, said, "To study the Way is to study the Self. To study the Self is to forget the Self." Emotional intelligence, self-awareness, and now mindfulness all name that same effort. We observe ourselves and see where we are getting in our own way. We notice all the stories we tell ourselves, all the voices in our heads judging what we just did or what we'll say next. We need to put all that down.

Why? It hurts. Wanting things to be different hurts. Blaming others hurts. Worry hurts. There can be painful confusion over what we think is happening and what is real in each moment of our day. Those habitual thought patterns and lived memories influence our perceptions of a boardroom meeting or dinner table conversation.

Ellen Langer's definition of mindfulness is "the simple process of actively noticing new things." Empathy is a forgetting of self, an attempt to put down our engrained perspectives and see another's point of view. Compassion is even more active as we act to relieve hardship and suffering, which is impossible if we hold preconceived notions about a person or a situation. The most important person you might help with less "self" is *yourself*.

The Inner Game of Work: Focus, Learning, Pleasure, and Mobility in the Workplace
by Timothy Gallwey

"It is only when we are giving our full attention to what we are doing that we can bring all of our resources to bear effectively. Why? Because when we are giving full attention, self-interference is neutralized. In the fullness of focus, there is no room for...fears and doubts."

TIMOTHY GALLWEY'S *The Inner Game of Tennis* is a classic book that came out in 1974 and is still recommended by coaches to players. Gallwey was a national hard court tennis champion and working as a tennis pro, when he came in touch with the teachings of the Maharaj Ji, a family of Indian spiritual leaders. That experience forever changed how he played and how it taught others to play.

There is little spirituality to Gallwey's approach. He merely says that we are easily distracted by our egos, or what he calls "Self 1." We judge our performances. We take feedback personally rather than accepting the helpful observations. Gallwey keenly notes that coaching, in its most common forms, complicates and actually encourages negative self-talk in students. His answer is to quiet the criticisms and allow "Self 2" to naturally take charge. Gallwey's description of Self 2 is indirect. He says, "Inherent in it is an inner intelligence that is staggering."

As the popularity of his approach grew, Gallwey wrote several books in the Inner Game series around golf, skiing, and music, but the real traction he experienced was in business organizations. Executives would visit him to take a tennis lesson and then ask if he could come teach the same ideas to their employees. It would be almost twenty-five years before Gallwey would write a book directly for the workplace, and I recommend *The Inner Game of Work* for a couple of important reasons.

The Inner Game of Tennis will forever be Gallwey's most popular work, and if you are drawn to it, read it. The challenge is that the reader has to translate the material from the world of sports into their personal and professional lives. Some can do that, but writing with a focus on organizational challenges gives *The Inner Game of Work* a more relevant context. What also often happens with authors of multiple books is that the author gets better over time at describing the problem and their solutions. That's the case here.

The topics that Gallwey addresses appear in other books. He talks about conformity when describing the factors that keep us from believing we can change and grow, as Carol Dweck does. The opening quote of this review on focus could be from *The ONE Thing*. Gallwey, though, highlights a different cause for our difficulty with these important issues. He acutely details how we get in our own way. While other books would ask us to change a belief or just build a new habit, Gallwey would ask us to listen more closely to the story we are telling ourselves when we bump up against a challenge. "Before you go about changing something, increase your awareness of the way it is."

When Gallwey specifically talks about awareness, he says the goal is to get the clearest possible picture of reality. He suggests that we look for what stands out and for what doesn't. Besides clarity, our job is to be distinct. He tells the story of working with the Houston Symphony and noticing the trouble a tuba player was having with his upper notes. The tubist said his tongue often felt dry and thick. Gallwey told him to play a selection again and just focus on changes in the moisture. Gallwey admits to no real knowledge of music, but he knew his coaching helped when the entire observing orchestra gave the performance a standing ovation. Gallwey says, "Remember, awareness itself is curative."

QUESTIONS THAT HELP CREATE AWARENESS:
- What stands out?
- What do you understand? What don't you understand?
- How would you frame the underlying problem?
- What's been working and not working?

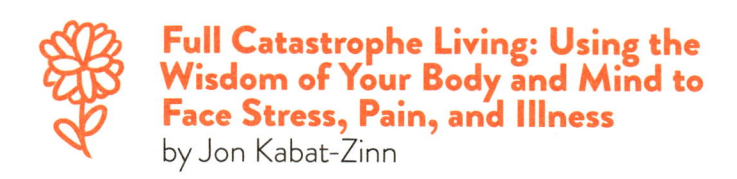

Full Catastrophe Living: Using the Wisdom of Your Body and Mind to Face Stress, Pain, and Illness
by Jon Kabat-Zinn

"Simply put, mindfulness is moment-to-moment non-judgemental awareness. It is cultivated by purposefully paying attention to things we ordinarily never give a moment's thought to. It is a systematic approach to developing new kinds of agency, control, and wisdom in our lives, based on our inner capacity for paying attention and on the awareness, insight, and compassion that naturally arise from paying attention in specific ways."

JON KABAT-ZINN'S original editor for *Full Catastrophe Living* thought the title might detract readers from picking up the book. I have two concerns here: First, as a publishing professional who has been an agent, an editor, and a publisher, I agree with the original editor. Kabat-Zinn's next books *Wherever You Go, There You Are* and *Coming to Our Senses* both employ more reader-receptive positioning. Second, I am concerned you will skip this recommendation and pick up one of those other books, thinking they were better suited to you. Please don't. Don't let the sixty-five-page introduction or the six hundred pages of text or the eleven pages of book recommendations in the appendix make you think this book is too much. It's not.

One of the leading title alternatives was *Paying Attention: The Healing Power of Mindfulness*. Kabat-Zinn is a biomedical researcher by training, and from the very beginning of his work, he was drawn to bringing his meditation and yoga practices into the medical setting. He believed patients and caregivers could be deeply helped by these techniques. The book is about the eight-week class that is the basis of mindfulness-based stress reduction (MBSR), opening with Kabat-Zinn starting a new session. Founded in the medical environment, MBSR focused more on health outcomes, was encouraged to support the benefits of the technique with follow-up research, and was built to teach a wide range of individuals.

"The interesting thing about this work is that we don't really do anything for them," Kabat-Zinn writes. "If we tried, I think we would fail them miserably. Instead we invite them to do something radically new for themselves." This work with awareness is a personal one. Someone else can't eat or exercise for you. Practicing mindfulness requires the same internal commitment. For the class, participants meet once a week for eight weeks. The three-hour session covers mindfulness techniques, group sharing of their experiences, and practice. Between classes, instructors ask participants to spend one hour a day on building awareness.

Three practices make up the teachings of MBSR. The first practice is body scanning, a technique that re-establishes contact with the body and simultaneously develops both concentration and flexibility to shift one's attention. The emphasis is tuning into all sensations—whether sharp and painful or dumb and absent. Body scanning is the primary practice in the opening weeks of class because it can be done lying down for longer periods of time and accommodates the widest range of participants.

Hatha yoga is the second practice. Kabat-Zinn describes it as consisting of "gentle stretching, strengthening, and balancing exercises, done very slowly, with moment-to-moment awareness to breathing and of the sensations that arise as you put your body into various configurations known as 'postures.'" He also points out that this practice suits many people who prefer movement and that movement can be a powerful and subtle practice to challenge beliefs that become fixed on being "out of shape" or "too old." Remembering that MBSR evolved in a health care environment, Kabat-Zinn advocates for the strengthening and stretching of muscles and joints to help create a full range of motion and greater state of balance.

Seated meditation is the third practice. Kabat-Zinn says, "It helps...to adopt an erect and dignified posture, with your head, neck, and back aligned vertically." He encourages students to keep returning back to the breath. "Treat all of your thoughts as if they are of equal value," he says. Over the course of the eight weeks, participants increase their sitting time from ten minutes to forty-five minutes. In addition to breath, there are exercises that bring the focus to the body, sound, thoughts and feelings, and finally choiceless awareness.

The first 160 pages of this book hold the best instructions I have found for building a mindfulness practice. The rest of the book has chapters that cover specific topics ranging from physical pain to anxiety to the many forms of stress. Kabat-Zinn writes as a teacher who anticipates your questions and an instructor who lays out the steps to incorporating this work into your life. The book is supplemented by audio-based guided meditations that are narrated by Kabat-Zinn and available for download as files or as a phone app. If you are considering starting a mindfulness practice, I wholeheartedly encourage you to get these resources.

SEVEN PILLARS OF MINDFULNESS PRACTICE:
1. **Non-judging:** Notice the judging quality of the mind and simply observe what is unfolding, including your reactions to it.
2. **Patience:** Be completely open to each moment, accepting its fullness, knowing that things can only unfold in their own time.
3. **Beginner's mind:** Be receptive to new possibilities and what gets us stuck in our rut of experience.
4. **Trust:** Cultivate trust in yourself so it will be easier to trust other people and see their basic goodness.
5. **Non-striving:** The best way to achieve goals is to back off from striving for results and instead starting to focus on seeing and accepting things as they are.
6. **Acceptance:** See things as they are right now, in the present moment. This is a form of healing.
7. **Letting go:** Being willing to look at the ways we hold on ultimately shows us a lot about everything we freely let go of.

The Mindful Athlete: Secrets to Pure Performance
by George Mumford

"Life is a marathon. We go and go, others running alongside us. In order to run this marathon, we need to train in the same way any other athlete trains to compete effectively in a sport. Without awareness and clear intention, we may start off too slowly, not finishing the race in a timely manner. Without diligence and practice, we may go too quickly, burning out before we get what we want and becoming disabled or quitting before we make it to the finish line."

WHEN YOU THINK of mindfulness, what image comes to mind? I picture someone sitting quietly, eyes closed, breathing softly. Maybe it's cool, with a soft breeze and birds chirping. But can you imagine that same person undisturbed at a busy intersection with cars honking their horns? Or in a room with a one-year-old child crying in distress? What does that person look like sitting courtside during an NBA playoff game? Mindfulness isn't just about calm settings—it's about expanding our awareness, noticing our reactions, and bringing that into the chaos of everyday world.

As George Mumford describes mindfulness early on in the book, he invokes Mihaly Csikszentmihalyi's flow state. He shares descriptions from NBA all-star Bill Russell and professional rower Craig Lambert like "it was almost like we were playing in slow motion" and "the boat seemed to fly over the water, and a lot of the effort disappeared from the stroke." The ease that these athletes describe is the same that Gallwey and Kabat-Zinn are describing in their books. The setting, though, is active, and these individuals find moments where they connect differently to the physical and emotional demands put on them. Mumford quotes Joseph Campbell as saying, "The athlete who is in championship form has a quiet place in himself."

In *The Mindful Athlete,* Mumford freely uses Buddhist philosophy and terminology to teach the reader how to find that place. The structure of the book is based on the Buddha's Eightfold Path. He quotes the Buddha, Thich Nhat Hanh, and Sharon Salzberg alongside Bruce Lee and Arnold Schwarzenegger. Mumford describes the five hindrances—sensual desire, ill will, sloth, worry, and doubt—and follows with stories of soccer star Zinedine Zidane, baseball pitcher Steve Bass, and golfer Tiger Woods who fall victim to their hindrances. That free-range approach appeals to me.

Mumford himself writes, "That 'intrinsic wholeness' serves you wherever you are and in whatever you're doing. Everything is connected." As we build awareness, it gets harder and harder to ignore that connectedness, that wholeness, that everythingness. His quote from Jack Kornfield deserves full sharing:

"You know, this idea of 'Be Here Now' and so forth, it sounds good. It's not so good. It isn't because of what happens when you're here now. Has anybody looked? Pain, boredom, fear, loneliness, pleasure, joy, beautiful sunsets, wonderful tastes, horrible experiences, people being born, people dying, light, dark, up, down, parking your car on the wrong side of the street, getting your car towed; all those things. For if you live here, it means that you have to be open to what Zorba called 'the full catastrophe.' Sometimes we don't want that. Right effort is the effort to see clearly."

So much gets in the way. Our egos get in the way. Our craving for a different outcome continues the suffering. Our judging something as good or bad keeps us from seeing events as things that just happened. That seeing clearly is built through the important work of cultivating awareness.

MUMFORD'S FIVE SPIRITUAL SUPERPOWERS:

1. **Mindfulness:** What's in and on your mind determines how well you perform.
2. **Concentration:** When the body and mind are quiet, there is a synergy that feeds pure performance.
3. **Insight:** Practice abandoning thoughts and belief systems.
4. **Right effort:** Every mindful moment off the courts, no matter how small, improves your game on the courts.
5. **Trust:** Pure performance is, ultimately, a leap of faith. What else can be let go? What else can you strip away?

Mindfulness – 25th Anniversary Edition
by Ellen Langer

"Every idea, person, or object is potentially simultaneously many things depending on the perspective from which it is viewed. A steer is a steak to a rancher, a sacred object to a Hindu, and a collection of genes and proteins to a molecular biologist."

ELLEN LANGER brings another perspective to mindfulness. First, she treats it as a phenomenon that touches every aspect of our lives. Prejudice, creativity, burnout, aging, and addiction all can be influenced by Langer's approach to mindfulness. We see from her motivation research that while efficient processes help build habits, they can also stifle autonomy and creativity. Second, she is a prolific researcher who finds simple, straightforward ways to test her theories. At points, there are so many examples in her book that confirm her findings that it is difficult to process just how much her work forces us to think differently.

Langer starts with the cost of not being mindful. As a simple experiment, she sent an interoffice memo to other university departments. The only text on the memo was "Return this memo to Room 247." 90 percent of recipients mindlessly returned the memo without a second thought. She writes, "Mindlessness, as it diminishes our self-image, narrows our choices, and weds us to single-minded attitudes." We might attribute a current difficulty to a single cause, which then limits potential solutions and induces a deeper loss of control over the difficulty.

There are many more insights that we can employ toward improving mindfulness. Take categories. Broad global categories like progressive/conservative and hot/cold carry with them a schematic of inherent meanings that bypass seeing a situation in other ways. Assign labels to a random group and the "assistants" will perform worse than the "bosses." Tell hotel maids that their daily work is "exercise" and they start to lose weight. When asked to describe someone you dislike in greater detail, Langer writes that "eventually there will be some quality we appreciate."

The counter-measure to the confinement of categories is to find ways to be open to new information and consider multiple interpretations of a situation.

In the latter half of the book, Langer spends an entire chapter on how mindfulness might be exercised for better outcomes in the workplace. She starts with the problems that arise from ignoring subtle changes or weak signals in your team or the marketplace. Langer attributes this to mindlessness, an attachment to assuredness that past behavior will predict future performance. "Deviations from some habitual way of working are less problematic if there is tolerance for uncertainty and no rigidly set method in the first place," she writes. "The deviations then become simply elements of the present situation." Can you imagine yourself as a manager displaying confidence but also uncertainty with your employees in an effort to give them more freedom in how a task might be accomplished? The act of asking questions is another way to honor uncertainty and be mindful of the present context.

Langer tells the story of an elderly woman at a nursing home who wanted to make her own peanut butter sandwich in the kitchenette rather than eat in the dining room. Management's response was to ask, "What if everyone wanted to do that?" Through their point of view, this was a problem, a threat to the certainty of the institution's policies. But with just a small shift in framing, all sorts of new mindful interpretations arise. Could that save food costs at the home? Could that give residents a little more autonomy and improve their health (something that matched Langer's experiments when giving residents houseplants to care for)? "At the very least," she writes, "it would have been useful information for the chef."

FROM THE INTRODUCTION OF THE BOOK'S TWENTY-FIFTH ANNIVERSARY EDITION:

"The more we realize that most of our views of ourselves, of others, and of presumed limits regarding our talents, our health, and our happiness were mindlessly accepted by us at an earlier time in our lives, the more we open up to the realization that these too can change. And all we need do to begin the process is to be mindful."

CHAPTER 3
THINKING

"Knowing how to think empowers you far beyond those who know only what to think."
—Neil deGrasse Tyson

Books about thinking used to be a tough sell to readers. Times have changed. In this chapter, I want to share a small set of titles that might help see what brain research and laboratory experiments have uncovered over the last thirty years. You'll benefit from understanding how much energy it takes to create priorities, how often we make decisions that are to our detriment, and how difficult it can be to see the blind spots that we have. Consider this just a start to the work you can do in this area.

Your Brain at Work: Strategies for Overcoming Distraction, Regaining Focus, and Working Smarter All Day Long
by David Rock

"One of the first things to discover upon exploring the brain is just how much it appears to be like a machine. So much of your mental activity is automatic, driven by forces out of your control, often in reaction to predefined goals, such as maintaining status or certainty. The realization that we are so automatically driven can be frightening to some, but if that is where the story ended, you would be missing a key aspect of being human."

I LOVE ALL THE BOOKS in *100 Best Books*, but if you asked me to pick one book that I wished everyone would read, that book would be *Your Brain at Work*. It is remarkable how much we have learned about how the brain works in the last thirty years, and even more remarkable is the work that has been done to apply this research to achievement, happiness, and well-being. Here is where the opportunity lies. In this review I will focus on one area where we might improve.

Prioritizing is tough work, more difficult than we realize, as we balance five different cognitive activities. First, we often start with *understanding* new information by comparing it with what we already know about the world. This requires us to *recall* memories and *memorize* new information to build an ever-wider store to draw from. Then, we need to *decide* what to do by comparing options to one another. And all the while, we have to *inhibit* external and internal distractions that keep us from our work.

These five functions are all critical to thinking and are managed by the prefrontal cortex. The prefrontal cortex sits right behind the forehead, is less than a quarter centimeter thick, and accounts for less than 5 percent of the human brain. Yet that thin layer is where our conscious thought takes place. The comparison David Rock uses is that the prefrontal cortex is like a stage with a performance going on and you are watching from the balcony. He writes, "We have three limitations: The stage takes a lot of energy to run, it can hold only a handful of actors at a time, and these actors can play only one scene at a time." We undervalue the limitations each one of those presents, often to our detriment.

The countermeasures that Rock suggests are ones suggested by other scientific research, but in the context of work we have the opportunity to appreciate them more. From the willpower research, a dose of glucose is surprisingly effective at improving memory and counteracting sluggish thought. From the world of productivity, writing down priorities to let the piece of paper hold the options lowers the brain's energy consumption. This technique also gives the opportunity for the brain to evaluate and compare each option individually. To use Rock's stage metaphor again, this lets the right actors enter the performance when they are needed. Finally, simplify the ideas you are working with—connect new ideas to existing ones, descriptions with four words are better than those with fourteen, and images are even better than words. For the process of writing this book, I unknowingly used Rock's advice by letting that stack of books on the office table hold my upcoming writing priorities, so I could stay focused on the current review.

This only partially summarizes one section of *Your Brain at Work*, however. Rock gives equal attention to how emotions impact the quality of our thinking and how we might use what we know about the brain's workings to help others change their worldviews. He is also very effective in showing how these topics intersect with themes of work and life. Each chapter starts with a short story about Emily and Paul, a married couple, and how one of them is working with a work-related issue. Quickly, we see how professional difficulties lead to problems in their marriage and in their relationships with their children. Rock then talks about the challenge from the perspective of brain science. He ends each chapter by retelling the opening story and showing how differently the scene might unfold with a more self-aware person.

MORE BRAIN INSIGHTS FROM ROCK:
- "Sticks and stones may break my bones, but names will never hurt me" is not true! Social pain is felt in the same parts of the brain as physical pain. And the brain remembers social pain much longer and more intensely than physical pain.

YOU: **THINKING**

- Researcher Mark Beeman could predict the ability of someone to have breakthrough insights on a problem by measuring their level of internal self-awareness, which highly correlates to the ability to change their thinking.
- Notice your constant emotional responses to stimulus in the world. Happiness, curiosity, and contentment are *toward* responses. Anxiety, sadness, and fear are *away* responses. Goals are also more likely to be successful with a positive *toward* framing.
- When faced with a challenge, focus on the outcome, not the problem. This decreases *away* emotions, primes the brain to look for information related to the outcome, and increases the chances of dopamine-induced insights.

Predictably Irrational: The Hidden Forces That Shape Our Decisions
by Dan Ariely

"What did our experiments suggest? It may be that our models of human behavior need to be rethought. Perhaps there is no such thing as a fully integrated human being. We may, in fact, be an agglomeration of multiple selves."

I WONDERED if going back to read *Predictably Irrational* would invoke the same reaction I had a decade ago when it was originally released. The findings from the field of behavioral economics are well reported. The experiments conducted by Dan Ariely and his colleagues around the world have become oft-repeated anecdotes and easy starters for cocktail conversations. At first, the results of these often simple experiments seemed to illuminate errors in the human code base. Over time, I feel like the acceptance for these particularities has grown, and a new willingness to examine the varied nature of our decision-making has taken root. And still, Ariely's findings surprise me.

Ariely doesn't offer some single explanation for his unexpected findings. He does say that the completely rational actor from the traditional point of view of economics doesn't exist. We are not computers that equally assess all the options presented and proceed with clear repeatable actions. Our errors are also "neither random or senseless—they are systematic and predictable. We all make the same types of mistakes over and over, because of the basic wiring of the brain," writes Ariely.

In one example, Ariely describes how ownership sways our view of value. His experiment leads him to ask students at Duke University the value of tickets to basketball games. Obtaining tickets is difficult, requiring students to literally camp outside the arena and wait for randomly timed air horns to claim their prize. Not everyone gets tickets. Ariely asks those who didn't get tickets how much they would pay, and the average price is $170. When Ariely asks the lucky students with tickets how much they would be willing to sell their tickets for, he finds the average price is $2,400. Ownership skews our view. Homeowners selling their houses often want more money than prospective home buyers want to pay. Ariely and Mike Norton call this the IKEA effect. The more you invest in the creation of something, whether assembled furniture or a co-created business proposal, the more ownership you feel for the work. The more we invest, the more we fear the loss of it.

Ariely has experiments that affirm the advice from other chapters in the book. Goals and deadlines definitely produce better outcomes, whether the deadline is chosen for us or we make our own commitment to completion. Without that anchor, we are easily swayed. This same shortsightedness presents itself when we are given a set of options. Our inclination is to keep our options open as long as we possibly can. We'll even ignore the actual benefit of the option as we overvalue the possibility of keeping more paths open.

These forces of emotion, social norms, and relativity have outsized impacts on the quality of our decisions. Ariely writes, "Our natural tendency is to vastly underestimate or completely ignore this power." Novice and expert alike can be drawn into these unseen forces that affect our choices. This is not about intelligence, competency, or skill. The lesson is building more awareness for the potential pitfalls in our own decision-making.

ONE MORE THOUGHT FROM ARIELY:

"Most people don't know what they want unless they see it in context. ... We don't even know what we want to do with our lives—until we find a relative or a friend who is doing just what we think we should be doing. Everything is relative."

Blindspot: Hidden Biases of Good People
by Mahzarin Banaji and Anthony Greenwald

"Blindspots hide both discriminations and privileges, so neither the discriminators nor the targets of discrimination, neither those who do the privileging nor the privileged, are aware. No small wonder that any attempt to consciously level the playing field meets with such resistance."

SEEING FLAWS in our decision-making is slippery work. Angry partners or a string of lost deals can provide information that is hard to ignore. Friends and colleagues can also be a source of more compassionate feedback. Just paying more attention to smaller cues in conversations creates additional moments for potential self-reflection. All of these examples (and many more from other works featured in *100 Best Books*) illustrate how we might be consciously aware of problematic behavior. But what about situations where we are less aware of our actions and the underlying influences?

Mahzarin Banaji and Anthony Greenwald have been studying biases around decision-making for more than three decades. I'll let them describe their work further: "Our work has led us to think about single ordinary instances—a smile or a suspicious look, a bank loan approved or rejected, a decision to stop and search, to promote or let go, to investigate with further medical tests or not. Each individual act involves but a single decision that one mind makes about another, and it is here that we must look for mindbugs."

"Social mindbugs" is the term they use for the mental shortcuts we use to make decisions about others. We are often put into situations where we need to quickly assess compatibility and trustworthiness of those around us. The trouble is that those assessments are often poor estimations of those individuals. What's even more problematic is how difficult it can be to see those biases from a lifetime of cultural norms that subtly influence our in-the-moment decision-making.

You might be familiar with Banaji and Greenwald's research with the Implicit Association Test. The test assesses people as they make different mental associations between pairs of things and looks at how much time it takes for them to make those connections. They start by showing that pairing flowers with pleasant-meaning words is easier than making those same positive associations with insects. From there, the researchers present more pairings.

Readers are asked to pair photos of Black faces and White faces with pleasant words. The challenging part of this pairing test is the results consistently show that people take more time to associate Black faces with pleasant words. The results are so shocking for some people that the authors specifically caution readers to think about whether they want to take the test and have their perspectives challenged. Banaji and Greenwald have done follow-on research to show that the Implicit Association Test further predicts exclusionary behavior in later situations.

As you are processing the implication of all that, consider another whopper: Test results are often similar for the advantaged group and the disadvantaged group. Yes, Black people can have just as hard a time making positive associations with Black faces as White people can. And yes, I, like 75 percent of Americans who took the test, showed an automatic preference for White faces in my test results.

What Banaji and Greenwald's research says about race has gotten the most coverage, but equally important is the variety of other mental associations they have identified with implicit association. "We now have ample evidence," the authors write, "of the dissociation between reflective egalitarianism and automatic preferences in attitudes involving race, sexual orientation, and age as well as skin color, body weight, height, disability, and nationality." Testing that now operates in thirty-nine countries and twenty-four languages shows similar results. The number of studies that are cataloged in the book were, at times, too much to process.

I can only say this is some of the most fascinating research that I have read on the topic of decision-making, and that the most likely ways you will discriminate against another person are small and barely noticeable. It might be whether you let someone go in line in front of you at the grocery store. In considering a set of job offers, you might favor working for a man over a woman and not even realize it. We all have biases and thus the opportunity to look a little harder for them.

WAYS TO COUNTERACT OUR IMPLICIT BIASES:
- Some symphonies instituted "blind auditions" for their groups by obscuring the musicians behind a piece of cloth. After the change, the number of female musicians hired rose from 20 percent to 40 percent.
- Mahzarin created a rotating set of images for her computer's screensaver that show counterstereotypes—a short bald man as a CEO or a construction worker feeding her baby—in order to expand her mental associations.
- Professor Sapna Cheryan added typically feminine decor to a computer science classroom to strengthen associations between women and careers in technology.

Six Thinking Hats
by Edward de Bono

"The main difficulty of thinking is confusion. We try to do too much at once. Emotions, information, logic, hope, and creativity all crowd in on us. It is like juggling with too many balls."

YOUR BRAIN CAN'T MULTITASK. The books in Chapter 11, "Focus," make that case and show ways for you to stay on track. Edward de Bono wants you to recognize this same problem when you are thinking with others. His approach is to be clear about what kind of thinking you are engaged in.

Western-style communication is largely built around who can make the best argument through criticizing and discrediting the counterargument. This keeps the scope of the conversation narrow. Participants spend all their time justifying their position rather than composing the best solution from all of the available information and perspectives. Focusing a group's attention in a single direction saves time, removes ego, and gives the opportunity for all participants to fully explore alternate approaches.

De Bono describes six modes of thinking that illuminate different perspectives that are equally important in constructing a map of possibility. Each mode is a "thinking hat," and when a hat is "on," the group's thinking is pointed in a specific direction to gather as much perspective as possible. The Six Hats framework keeps thinking moving in one direction and provides a clear mechanism to switch to a new thinking type when needed.

HERE ARE THE SIX HATS AND THEIR DESCRIPTIONS:

- **The White Hat:** Just the facts and figures. They can be true or believed to be true. Always true? Been known to happen? Explore the degree of truth, the circumstances when the fact is true, and to whom it is true. This hat is all about information.
- **The Red Hat:** The place for feelings. No justification is needed. We need a place to freely share intuitions and doubts without judgment. We start to see our values. No need to guess anymore what others feel—all decisions in the end are emotional ones.
- **The Black Hat:** Caution and carefulness. This is the most used and most important hat. We want to make sure we don't make mistakes and we point out the weakness so the weakness can be solved. We use logic here to find possible danger, obstacles, and problems. Keep criticism here in the Black Hat.
- **The Yellow Hat:** Optimism and positivity. Elevate value in the same way we see danger. Again, we use a spectrum of proven to remote possibilities. This is the realm of generation and proposals and suggestions, even speculation about what might be possible.
- **The Green Hat:** Exploring creative possibilities. This is for new ideas and new ways of looking at things, and it's based on finding a better way. Use movement forward as the objective. Provoke!

Break through the current patterns. Seek alternatives to the current approach.
- **The Blue Hat:** Thinking about thinking. Someone wears this hat throughout the process. Organize the approach. Process-check the discussion to keep the group focused on the hat they are exploring. Facilitate the session and ask for the outcome. Record the thinking that took place.

CHAPTER 4
PERSONALITY

"Personality has power to uplift, power to depress, power to curse, and power to bless."
—Paul Harris

Psychologists call behaviors that are persistent and unique in individuals "traits." As far back as the Greeks, there has been a quest to find a way to explain why we do what we do. You have undoubtedly taken assessments like the Myers-Briggs, DISC, Kolbe A, and HBDI tests. Daniel Nettle says in the opening to his book, "Personality psychology has, until recently, had a rather low status compared to other branches of psychology. It has been perceived as based on flimsy evidence, internally divided, and far removed from the hard science end of psychology. There may once have been some justice in these views, but I believe that things have changed. In fact, a renaissance is underway in the study of personality." In this chapter, we'll look at a variety of approaches and perspectives on the topic of personality. Maybe we can understand more about ourselves and others in our lives.

Personality: What Makes You the Way You Are
by Daniel Nettle

"We have the freedom, the power, and indeed the responsibility to use our minds to seek out the good niches that are right for [our personalities], and to avoid the ones that are bad. It is also a matter of understanding the trade-offs inherent in certain choices."

PSYCHOLOGISTS have long proposed a set of traits that appeared in humans. In the 1990s, researchers narrowed the list to five traits that explain the most important aspects of behavior. The strongest evidence for the "five factors" is their ability to accurately assess the traits and their consistency over long periods of time. Many other assessments like Myers-Briggs fail in this regard. Daniel Nettle has written a great book that describes each trait in chapter length and shows how the research confirms them in both a biological sense and an evolutionary sense.

Let's start with openness, the least understood factor. Broadly, it measures our ability to make mental connections among different domains. This capacity is most associated with artists of all types, but what we might describe as intelligence in the sciences is likely the same quality. People who score highly in openness are "drawn to consume complex, multiple-meaning representations" and experiment with different pursuits. On the extreme, people might hold controversial beliefs or report unusual experiences like visions or sounds, with schizophrenia being at the edge of this spectrum.

Conscientiousness at its core is about impulse control. The famous marshmallow test measures this ability to resist temptation and forgo immediate benefits. Addictions of all types are suffered by people who score low on conscientiousness. In the realm of work, this factor consistently predicts occupational success. People who score highly set goals and stay with them, and are better able to work autonomously. Order and planning are highly valued in the modern world, but we might also imagine how the low impulse control often associated with ADHD could be valued in other environments.

Extraversion is interesting because our traditional definition of boisterous folks who love being around people isn't quite right. As a factor of personality, Nettle writes that "extraversion is variation in the responsiveness of positive emotions." An even better explanation is that people who score highly on extraversion are more affected by the neurotransmitter dopamine and report stronger physiological effects to the chemical. So, stimulus that the brain interprets as being a reward, like achievement, success, or romance, is going to be more strongly felt by extraverts and therefore more strongly pursued, sometimes to the point of detriment.

Agreeableness in the five-factor model is closely associated with the attention we give to others' emotions and how we let it shape our responses. "High scorers are described as cooperative, trusting, and empathetic, whilst low scorers are cold-hearted, hostile, and non-compliant," Nettle writes. The latter part gets most of our attention when others are hostile or cold in our interactions. Low scores in agreeableness actually improve chances of success in creative fields, while high scores are a negative predictor of salary levels. This leaves an open question around the evolutionary importance of agreeableness, but when modeled, a mixed equilibrium appears that balances others and self.

That leaves us with neuroticism, for which Nettle provides a great comparison: "Neuroticism is to negative emotion as extraversion is to positive emotion." Negative emotions like fear, guilt, shame, anxiety, and sadness can all serve as signals for things that we should avoid. High scores in neuroticism signal that individuals are hypervigilant to threat, and research shows those highly engaged states negatively affect attention and decision-making. Phobias and mood disorders are highly predicted by these trait scores. Adrenaline and cortisol are overproduced and serotonin is underproduced, which exacerbates negative emotions. At the same time, high scores also connect with good planners and people who can often better see the reality of their situation.

As with all five traits, low or high scores don't necessarily indicate good or bad outcomes. These are traits that have arisen to help humans survive and thrive. Our job is to see how our personality can support the outcomes we want to achieve.

TAKING THE TEST YOURSELF:

The ten-question Newcastle Personality Assessor or 120-item IPIP-NEO Personality Inventory are both based on scientific research and can both be easily found with an internet search. Take one or both tests yourself and see what you can learn from them!

....

Quiet: The Power of Introverts in a World That Can't Stop Talking
by Susan Cain

"The secret to life is to put yourself in the right lighting. For some it's a Broadway spotlight; for others, a lamplit desk. Use your natural powers—of persistence, concentration, insight, and sensitivity—to do work you love and work that matters. Solve problems, make art, think deeply."

THERE'S A NOTE at the end of *Quiet* where Susan Cain says that she created her own definitions to center the book. Cain says she chose to compare the cultural tropes of introversion and extroversion, though what we commonly cast into these two categories confuses definitions and doesn't hold up to more recent scientific research (see the prior review). It's hard to put down the dichotomy of the gregarious, assertive, and risk-taking when seen next to the calm, modest, and sensitive among us. Even with the choice of familiar, traditional definitions, Cain composes a provocative weaving of science and personal stories to illuminate new understandings about these well-worn preferences for how we want to interact with the world and each other.

Cain prefers a definition of a "rich inner life" when she describes introversion, and she opens the book with a wide survey about how introversion has been discounted in American culture. Cain uses Dale Carnegie and Tony Robbins as promoters of personality and extroverted perceptions. Rather than another possibility for being in the world, introversion became synonymous with insecurity and social anxiety. She visits Harvard Business School and observes classroom case studies that reward quick and witty answers, alongside after-hours socializing, that leave this partially introverted writer exhausted by the descriptions. Cain quotes a fifth-grade public school teacher in Manhattan who sums up the cultural impact on teaching: "People's respect for others is based on their verbal abilities, not their insight or originality. … It's elitism based on something other than merit."

So where does that leave introversion's preference for quiet, pensive solitude? Well, it depends on what we value. "Extroverts get better grades than introverts during elementary school," says Cain, "but introverts outperform extroverts in high school and college. At the university level, introversion predicts academic performance better than cognitive ability." Other research highlighted by Cain and other authors here in *100 Best Books* shows more introverted advantages, from Jim Collins's quiet, humble manner of Level 5 leaders to Anders Ericsson's deliberate practice that requires focused solitude. On the quirky end, introverts function better when sleep deprived, according to military researchers. I really like one description in *Quiet* that says introverts' approach is by "water rather than fire."

Introverts will have an overarching tendency to slow down in response to risk in their environment. Biologists believe this exists as a genetic feature in all animals and have so far specifically identified it in over a hundred species, from fruit flies to Trinidadian guppies. Researchers believe a preference toward first inspecting versus responding is a means of self-preservation. "Shy" animals avoid more predators and survive by foraging less often but more widely for food. When Cain interviewed Wall Street professionals after the 2008 stock market collapse, some attributed poor systematic decision-making to a skewed selection of traders who favored an extroverted "just do it" approach over an introvert's "watch and wait."

The message here is that there is a role for both introversion and extroversion in our lives, and it is likely that we are deeply involved with our opposite as partners or children. My favorite description from Cain is where she describes research that put opposite pairs into one-on-one conversations: "Introverts talking to extroverts chose cheerier topics, reported making conversation more easily, and described conversing with extroverts as a 'breath of fresh air.' In contrast, the extroverts felt that they could relax more with introverted partners and were freer to confide their problems. They didn't feel pressure to be falsely upbeat." Many thanks to Cain for speaking up for the quiet among us.

INTROVERTS WILL DO BETTER WHEN:
- They experience lectures, independent projects, and downtime in learning environments.
- They are praised and supported in their deep, individual passions and are helped in finding others with similar interests.
- They are asked to write down their ideas first before discussing them in a group.
- They meet people in friendly contexts versus competitive ones.
- They are given tasks that involve imagining things, recalling events from their past, and making "what if" plans about the future.

Now, Discover Your Strengths
from Gallup

"1. Each person's talents are enduring and unique. 2. Each person's greatest room for growth is in the areas of their greatest strength."

HERE'S THE PITCH: There are lots of things you can do in life. Do the things you are naturally good at, because getting better at them will be easier and you will love your life. Gallup, Inc., reports that "more than six out of ten employees feel they are miscast," and the company has built an empire around helping people find the roles they fit into. Gallup calls them strengths, and their definition is very specific: "consistent near-perfect performance in a given task."

To connect this to other themes in *100 Best Books*, Gallup research indicates that reaching high proficiency in your strengths comes through the combination of talent, knowledge, and skills. Talent is the innate component: "any recurring pattern of thought, feeling, or behavior" formed from the neural pathways in the brain that simply have stronger connections. Knowledge is acquired in two ways—factual (10 x 10 = 100) and experiential ("I see people love reading lists").

Self-awareness also generates a kind of knowledge that helps us see what we are good at and what we enjoy. Skills are the steps that lead to the completion of specific tasks. In Gallup's view, skills are soulless without the underlying talent, a perspective that puts them in conflict with Anders Ericsson's theory of deliberate practice.

All of Gallup's research comes together in the CliftonStrengths assessment. They say their goal is to "find where you have the greatest potential for a strength." In forty minutes and 177 questions, their testing generates a ranked list of your top five strengths out of a potential list of thirty-four. The book provides a cursory description of each strength. The assessment goes even further to personalize the feedback based on your choices to their paired statements.

The book then provides a chapter of frequently asked questions for the newly assessed. Are there obstacles to building your strengths? Yes, your fear of failure and Western society's focus on correcting weakness. Is there a significance to the order? Not really, because the important part is identifying your dominant strengths. Can I develop new strengths if I don't like the ones I have? No, but you can focus on new knowledge and skills to take your life in other unexpected directions using the talents you have. Gallup writes, "In a study of more than 20,000 people who love their jobs, we found that people with similar strengths profiles were often very happy in very different roles. Likewise, we found that many people with the same job managed to thrive despite having very different strengths profiles."

The remainder of the book turns in a sharper direction toward managers and executives. There is a chapter about managing others using their strengths, including a set of suggestions for each strength. The final chapter is about building a strengths-based culture, and the latter half takes an even sharper turn toward human resource planning around hiring, performance, and development. They do share several lists of questions to help with measuring employee engagement, customer satisfaction, peer impact, and managerial effectiveness. If you are wondering about all the effort, Gallup's research shows that people who have a chance each day to do what they do best "claimed fewer sick days, filed fewer workers' compensation claims, and had fewer accidents on the job." Imagine how many are just happier doing work they love.

GALLUP'S FOUR LARGER STRENGTHS-BASED DOMAINS THAT CONNECT TEAMS:

- **Executing:** Focus on how to make things happen or get things done.
- **Influencing:** Help reach broad audiences and sell the team's ideas.
- **Relationship building:** Help encourage individuals and keep teams together.
- **Strategic thinking:** Help teams stretch their thinking and make better decisions.

CHAPTER 5
MONEY

"Money is a great servant but a bad master."
—Francis Bacon

A collection of books about work and life requires a chapter on money. For a long time, I held a dim view of this category, because all the books said the same thing: "Spend less than you earn!" In recent years, authors have gotten more sophisticated in their teachings. Many people, including very successful high earners, find it difficult to live within their means. Our relationship to money mimics our relationship to safety, success, and desire. In this chapter, there is a story of a person who retired at age thirty by making different choices. Another author makes the rock-solid case for the "buy and hold" strategy using index funds to create freedom. The other two authors show how we can use positive emotions to manage our money in a way that fits our life.

I Will Teach You to Be Rich: No Guilt. No Excuses. No BS. Just a 6-Week Program That Works
by Ramit Sethi

"Do you notice how so many money experts use words like 'worry,' 'fear,' and 'guilt'? How they start their advice by telling you all the things you can't do with your money? They're all playing defense. I have a different approach."

YOU MIGHT NOTICE that the books across this collection tend to have a strong point of view. Ramit Sethi also has a strong point of view. When it comes to money, he says we get caught up too easily in chasing the wrong details. We have unhelpful scripts about money running in our head that we picked during our childhood or by listening to CNBC too much (likely both). We aren't willing to have tough conversations. Money is no different than almost every other part of our life.

I think there are two ways to read *I Will Teach You to Be Rich*. The first is as someone who has never thought about the basics of personal finance. Maybe you just got your first job and are handling money for the first time. You have income. There are expenses of all types. You are paying taxes. You have bank accounts and credit cards. People say you should save and put money away for retirement. And if there is money left over, what do you do with it?

Sethi makes it all simple. You spend a week on six important items and have your finances organized a month and a half later. It's worth a week to look at the credit cards you have, determine if they are right for you, and maximize their benefits. Come up with a plan to get rid of your credit card debt. It is worth another week to figure out which banks offer no-fee checking accounts and savings accounts that actually pay interest. You'll want the accounts to fund other investment accounts. Sethi hates budgeting and proposes looking at spending. Know the fixed costs. Deposit money into your savings accounts next. And then spend the rest guilt free by knowing what is important to you (for me it is books and collecting one style of discontinued Patagonia sweaters) and being fiercely frugal in almost every other spending segment (we own one car). And then you automate it all so it happens without your effort or (un)conscious interference.

The second way you might read this book is as a check-up on your finances. Are you using bank accounts that don't have fees? Are you using the credit cards that best match the benefits you can use? Have you checked your credit score lately? When I did, I found that one agency was pinging my credit report every day and costing me ten to twenty points on my score. Have you analyzed your expenses lately? If you have mutual funds, do you rebalance your asset allocations every year? All the reminders encourage both overdue action and honesty about where you should simplify further.

I should also say the voice, layout, and language of this book cater to Millennials and Gen Z. The chapter sections are short. There are lots of sidebars. Every page seems like it has a testimonial from a prior reader who took action and benefited greatly. It is impossible to avoid the proof points. For some readers, this approach helps them move through it quickly and get what they need to benefit from its content.

AUTHORS THAT SETHI RECOMMENDS:

- Dan Solin has several books under *The Smartest _____ Book You'll Ever Read* banner, where he tackles money, investing, retirement, and 401(k)s. He also has a strong newsletter.
- Ron Lieber is the money columnist for *The New York Times*. His books *The Opposite of Spoiled* and *The Price You Pay for College* are both outstanding books for parents.

Your Money or Your Life: 9 Steps to Transforming Your Relationship with Money and Achieving Financial Independence
by Vicki Robin and Joe Dominguez

"If someone thrust a gun in your ribs and said those words, what would you do? Most of us would turn over our wallets. The threat works because we value our lives more than we value our money. Or do we?"

YOUR MONEY OR YOUR LIFE is a hard book to pin down. There isn't one big idea carefully laid out in a "don't do this, do that" format. The questions that Vicki Robin and her late co-author Joe Dominguez are asking require the same considerations as the books in Chapter 6, "Purpose," and Chapter 2, "Mindfulness." The authors ask for deep consideration that questions the personal and cultural assumptions most of us don't even notice.

Some of you might know this book as the source for the Financial Independence, Retire Early (FIRE) movement. This is exactly what Dominguez did by working on Wall Street for a decade, living frugally, and investing his savings in the high-interest US treasury notes of the time. He retired when he was thirty. The FIRE movement grew out of that same philosophy of maximizing the space between income earned and expenses paid. With those savings, you invest to earn new income, and as that investment income nears and then exceeds your recurring expenses, you have many more options for how you spend your time. FIRE really emphasized the practicality of maximizing income, minimizing taxes, and successfully investing, but I think there is more to pay attention to within this book.

The authors encourage a deeper look at how we both earn and spend our money. On the earning side, they equate money to "life energy." That might sound too new age for some, but consider how many hours over weeks and months you're spending to acquire your income right now. The trick is to put down whatever identity you have about the work or the job or the position and just think hard about whether it is a good exchange. Could there be ways to earn more? Could there be approaches to earn income in different ways? Maybe earning income is a focus for a season in your life and priorities shift away in other seasons. The time we have and the energy available is finite. Let's be thoughtful about how we use it.

On the spending side, the authors encourage a variety of ways to build similar awareness for our spending. They ask readers to start equating purchases with the amount of life energy required to buy them. They ask readers to create a detailed analysis of every penny that leaves your pocket. This exercise, while tedious at first, lets us recognize the varying levels of attentiveness we bring to the money we spend. It's one thing to look at your grocery bill, and it is another to notice all the items that left the store with you, whether they were on your original list or not. A job itself needs money in the form of things like transportation, clothes, and childcare. The objective is just to know where all of your life energy is going and consider those choices.

Remember the whole point is financial independence— "independence from needing money to meet my needs." When we change both sides of the equation, we create opportunities to approach life differently.

MORE GREAT MONEY QUESTIONS TO CONSIDER:
- Describe your relationship with money in five words or less. Why did you choose those five words?
- What are your top priorities and how does your spending support them—or not?
- What does "enough" mean to you?
- What might change if you could know what others—a friend, date, boss, or stranger—earn?
- Talk about one thing that you own that you love. What do you ove about it?
- If you didn't have to work for a living, what would you do with your time?

The Psychology of Money: Timeless Lessons on Wealth, Greed, and Happiness
by Morgan Housel

"We think about and are taught about money in ways that are too much like physics (with rules and laws) and not enough like psychology (with emotions and nuance)."

BY NOW, you have probably noticed the formula for every review in this book: The world works some way, we have a hard time thinking about it that way, and here is a new way of thinking to help. The key word is *thinking*. Morgan Housel's book is all about how we think about money.

The first part to understand is that our difficulties with money are not really about money. Money is just a medium of exchange. We have one (or more) ways of earning money and many more ways of spending it. Both sides of that equation are functions of thinking—choices made, desires fulfilled. We could make the same analogy using the time we are given each day—choices are made, wants are satisfied. With both time and money, we struggle with feeling like we never have enough. Housel writes in several different ways that if we don't find the place of enough that we'll be whipped around by comparing ourselves to others and setting ever higher anchors for what is acceptable for our lifestyle. Housel also reminds us that "there are many things never worth risking, no matter what the potential gain."

In the space between what we earn and what we spend is what we save. That money left over is the first ingredient for how wealth is created. The next ingredient is time—having the mental capacity to keep that money invested in the same place for long periods of time. Our desires for the better returns, promised by talking heads in the financial media, causes us to chase better opportunities in yet another investment. The belief that we can time when to sell and when to buy again almost undoubtedly spoils the recipe for the returns that create wealth.

Housel also notes that the financial environment we grew up in creates filters for how we perceive risk in the present moment. That history clouds our view for seeing the power of compounding over the long term. He suggests a different filter to help: Invest in what you love, whether it is an investment strategy or a particular investment. He writes, "If you view it as the thing providing the endurance necessary to put the quantifiable odds of success in your favor, you realize it should be the most important part of any financial strategy."

We might measure the success of our savings and investing by how our net worth grows over time, but here again we are measuring the medium and not the means it creates. Housel, like every author in this chapter, says, "Flexibility and control over your time is an unseen return on wealth." He invokes freedom and independence. You could also say, as Housel does, that wealth provides a margin of error in a world of unpredictable odds, whether it's knowing what the average stock market return will be over the next ten years or if the business you work for or own will adapt to the next phase of industry innovation. Another reason for financial flexibility is "that people are poor forecasters of their future selves." Housel writes and draws on research from Daniel Gilbert that shows people from ages eighteen to sixty-eight underestimate how much they will change in the future. Not knowing who we will be or what mistaken behaviors we'll be drawn into is enough of a reason to *think* about how you *think* about money.

THREE CRYSTAL-CLEAR PIECES OF ADVICE FROM HOUSEL:
1. "The biggest single point of failure with money is a sole reliance on a paycheck to fund short-term spending needs, with no savings to create a gap between what you think your expenses are and what they might be in the future."
2. "If you have flexibility, you can wait for good opportunities, both in your career and for your investments. You'll have a better chance of being able to learn a new skill when it's necessary. ... The ability to do those things when most others can't is one of the few things that will set you apart in a world where intelligence is no longer a sustainable advantage."
3. "There are few financial variables more correlated to performance than commitment to a strategy. ... The historical odds of making money in U.S. markets are 50/50 over one-day periods, 68% in one-year periods, 88% in 10-year periods, and (so far) 100% in 20-year periods."

The Simple Path to Wealth: Your Road Map to Financial Independence and a Rich, Free Life
by J. L. Collins

"You can't pick winning stocks. Don't feel bad. I can't either. Nor can the overwhelming majority of professionals in the business."

THIS IS THE KIND OF BOOK where the title really does communicate what is inside. J. L. Collins describes a simple, straightforward process for long-term financial success. Here it is: "Spend less than you earn—invest the surplus [in index funds]—avoid debt." That's it. If you already know that, believe that, *and* practice that, you can skip this one. But I am including *The Simple Path to Wealth* in this book because too many people still don't do these three things.

We start by asking questions about whether wealth building is really that easy. First, we struggle with the daily decisions that often lead to the "spending less" part. Coffee today or retirement in thirty years? Our brain isn't designed to clearly make that decision. Even the medium-term decisions like a new car or the big family vacation get hard to evaluate against worries, desires, and the pressure of comparison. Collins doesn't spend a lot of time trying to solve those problems for you. He just says it is important to build savings because it gives you freedom—today to leave a job and in the future to have security.

Most of the book is about how to invest. Collins is a zealot for the "buy and hold" approach with index funds, and this is where the book shines. Collins methodically explains what makes all the other paths less reliable. Timing the market is impossible, contrary to what the financial pundits will tell you. To this Collins writes, "For serious investors…all of this is useless and distracting noise. Worse, if you pay attention to it, it is positively dangerous to your wealth. And your sanity." Stock picking (thinking you can predict a company's prospects years into the future) isn't any safer. The "experts" actively managing funds are no better than us. Sure, you and they might get lucky and time the market right or invest in the right firm, but the alternative just provides more reliable returns over time.

I love this description from Collins about the reliability of stocks with a broad stock index fund: "Stocks are not just little slips of traded paper. When you own a stock you own a piece of a business. These companies are filled with people working endlessly to expand and serve their customer base. They are competing in an unforgiving environment that rewards those who can make it happen and discards those who can't."

Collins believes there are only two funds you need: a total market stock fund and a total market bond fund. He loves Vanguard (as do I) for their low fees, which means better returns over time. Collins admits to taking an aggressive approach with most of his money on the stock side, but he says individuals need to invest in a way that matches their tolerance level and lifestyle goals.

Read the book because you need to be convinced or reminded there is a simple path to building wealth that anyone can be successful with.

COLLINS'S PORTFOLIO ADVICE INCLUDES THE FOLLOWING:
- Vanguard Total Stock Market Index Fund (VTSAX) provides solid financial returns with coverage in over 3,700 US-based companies.
- Vanguard Total Bond Index Fund (VBTLX) invests in over seven thousand bonds, provides income, and balances the risks of holding stocks.
- Cash should be held for what you need for emergencies and comfort. Invest the rest.

CHAPTER 6
PURPOSE

"When you walk with purpose, you collide with destiny."
—Bertice Berry

There are moments in our lives when knowing our life's purpose seems to be the most consequential thing we could possess. In that grasping, purpose remains elusive. None of these books will give you the answer. Finding purpose is doing the deep and often quiet work to uncover our desires. We need to know something about our passions that will drive us and the ways in which we might help others. In this chapter, we have a coach, an educator, a pair of designers, and a poet—each showing us how we might uncover our purpose.

Finding Your Own North Star: Claiming the Life You Were Meant to Live
by Martha Beck

"All of the advice in this book boils down to just one thing: You are designed with the ability to find the life you were meant to live. I can't do it for you. Neither can your mother, your lover, your religious leader, or anyone else."

MARTHA BECK opens her book by asking the reader to think through a series of questions. She asks you to think about times when you are in low-energy states. Who is around you? How do you feel? What kinds of mistakes are you making? These are the kinds of exercises that many often skip when they are reading books. She then shifts the focus and asks about best-case scenarios, the ones that generate happiness and joy. Beck adds that one in twenty clients can't describe the best case, and she warns, "If you find it difficult to do the following exercises, you are almost certainly in the wrong life."

Finding Your Own North Star is a guide to building an internal compass that keeps us headed in the right direction. Beck says there is an inherent tension between two selves, what she calls our "social self" and "our essential self." The social self acts from learned habits and the desire for social harmony. "To find your North Star, you must teach your social self to relax and back off," Beck writes. The essential self arises at the genetic level and, depending on your beliefs, might arrive with you at conception or birth. This identity would arise independently of where you grew up or what kind of upbringing you had. According to Beck, these two selves normally compete for airtime, and if they diverge too far from one another, the essential self shifts from helpful guide to demanding boss.

The work is to develop ways to be more in tune with the essential self. Beck offers some interesting questions to ask yourself in seeking better alignment. What categories of information do you remember better than anything? What people in your life do you feel most comfortable with? What activities are you most likely to lose track of time while doing? If you are on the right track, Beck says, "Many people experience their true path not as something that happens to them but as the simultaneous loss of self and complete connection with the universe."

At this point in my review, I have only covered the first sixty pages of the book. There are two chapters on how we generalize "everybody is against me and my choices" and how that opposition rarely holds up to any scrutiny. Then there are five chapters on feelings and the likelihood that you are disconnected from the signals that can indicate you are headed in the right direction—bodily sensations; emotions like fear and grief; and, if your belief extends this way, deep intuition about the people, places, and things that you next need in your life. With all these new modes of awareness and connections, there are plenty of places to get stuck. Consider this advice from Beck: "Self-love is the single most important tool you will ever use in your search for your own North Star."

What I am describing is not a one-time discovery. Life cycles us through the hero's journey many times in our life, and the final third of the book is Beck's explanation of that process of change. First, it starts with a catalyst that shifts your identity—graduation, job loss, marriage, divorce, addition to the family, death of a loved one. In this new identity, you navigate a clumsy state with more freedom and more loss. That confusion eventually gives way to dreaming, possibility, and planning. Next, you move out into the world and do the work to create a new future. Plans run into reality. You adjust, modify, and pivot. There is never really a final arrival at a destination, but the adjustments become smaller and your confidence grows in the knowledge that you are living your life in alignment with your North Star.

HOW TO USE EMOTION TO MOVE TOWARD YOUR NORTH STAR:

- **Fear:** This might be anger. Truth resolves fear, and "the urge to find the real facts is destructive only to people or systems (friendships, family dynamics, political dynasties) that are based on lies." In the face of fear, follow your desire.
- **Grief:** This might again be anger or even fear, especially in women. "True clinical depression isn't really grief—it's the numb hopelessness that comes from feeling we can't act on anger or fear." Make room for loss.

YOU: PURPOSE

- **Anger:** This might be grief, especially in men. "When you're genuinely angry, it means one of two things: Either something that your essential self needs is absent, or something your essential self can't tolerate is present." Anger will push you toward your North Star.
- **Joy:** True joy doesn't come from a chemical. "People who haven't felt much joy tend to hang onto every shred of happiness like a drowning victim gripping a rescuer by the neck." Rule 1: If it brings you joy, do it. Rule 2: No, really. If it brings you joy, do it.

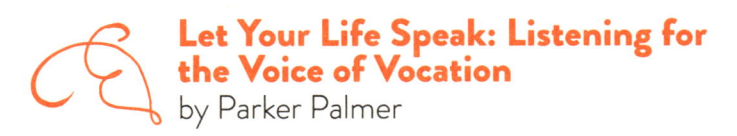

....

Let Your Life Speak: Listening for the Voice of Vocation
by Parker Palmer

"The deepest vocational question is not 'What ought I to do with my life?' It is the more elemental and demanding 'Who am I? What is my nature?'"

IF YOU HAD just finished Beck's book and started into Parker Palmer's *Let Your Life Speak*, you might be struck by the similarities. Palmer writes about the inner journey to find purpose, its deep connection to others, the pursuit of a moral life, and the recurring seasons we pass through in our lifelong search. Those similarities give me comfort. It's helpful to see more clearly those places where we need to spend time in what can feel like a frustrating and elusive search for identity. Palmer's book is also different from Beck's.

Let Your Life Speak is a short one. The exploration is six chapters, just over one hundred pages. He shares only his life story as an example to illustrate the challenges in finding meaning. Palmer offers the word "vocation," which draws its meaning from the Latin word for "voice," to describe that lifelong process. "Vocation does not come from willfulness," he writes. "It comes from listening."

In that listening, he suggests we might do some of the following. We could spend time really understanding our nature—seeing and accepting both our limits and our potential. We could explore who we are in relationship with others. Palmer quotes Quaker teacher

Douglas Steere, who says the question "Who am I?" always leads to "*Whose* am I?" Palmer writes, "We must ask the question of selfhood and answer it honestly as we can, no matter where it takes us. Only as we do so can we discover the community of our lives." Expect that sunlit paths will lead to dark trails and that we'll return to the light anew. If this all sounds airy and ethereal, it's because the process of discovering our lives is mysterious. Palmer embraces the mystery and will help you do the same.

A GUIDING QUOTE FOR YOUR WALL:
"Vocation, at its deepest level, is 'This is something I can't not do, for reasons I'm unable to explain to anyone else and don't fully understand myself but that are nonetheless compelling.'"

Designing Your Life: How to Build a Well-Lived, Joyful Life
by Bill Burnett and Dave Evans

"As you begin to think like a designer, remember one important thing: It's impossible to predict the future. And the corollary to that thought is: Once you design something, it changes the future that is possible."

I CHOSE THE opening quote for two reasons. First, "designing your life" probably sounds like some kind of fancy process. That quote probably reinforces that perception. Bill Burnett and Dave Evans say design thinking is something simpler and works best when "you have a desired outcome, but no clear solution in sight." That sounds like the situation we find ourselves in as we try to navigate life choices. The second reason for the quote is that new possibilities arise from every step we take. That is an equally important quality to design thinking.

Like other books, the authors' life design process starts with assessing your current states of work, play, love, and health. That follows into a deeper dive of examining the coherency between "who you are, what you believe, and what you are doing." We need to check the alignment between the practical work we do, why we do it, and what fulfillment we receive with the more existential questions of why we are here, what's our purpose, and if we connect with something greater than ourselves. The exercises get more practical as the reader is asked to track and assess where they experience energy and engagement in their daily lives.

My favorite rubric in this assessment process is their **AEIOU.** You might look at **A**ctivities you are involved in, what your role was, and how the activities are structured. The **E**nvironments where you spent time have a significant impact on your enjoyment. The **I**nteractions themselves have different qualities—formal versus informal, one versus many, living beings versus machines. There might be **O**bjects involved that enhance or detract from enjoyment and fulfillment. The **U**sers themselves—customers, coworkers, supervisors—all influence our lived experiences on many different levels.

I want to return to the importance of possibility, because the temptation is so strong to move toward the first idea or opportunity that arises. The authors assure readers that "there are many versions of you, and they are all 'right.'" They ask that you sketch out three different plans—the obvious next step, the path if that obvious step was suddenly gone, and the "if money or fame were no object" path.

After getting feedback from trusted sources, you start to explore by prototyping. "[It's] all about asking good questions, outing our hidden biases and assumptions, iterating rapidly, and creating momentum for a path we'd like to try out," the authors write. In life design, conversations are considered valuable prototypes. You have the opportunity to gather likes, dislikes, origin stories, missteps, and hard-worn advice. We want to gather data from the messy process that is life. Most importantly, the data helps you better imagine yourself in the cloud of possibility. One of the authors' students, Bella, took their advice to heart and prototyped her way to three job offers in the field she wanted. That was after she had two hundred prototyping conversations. No, it doesn't require that many to be successful, but more prototypes are going to lead to more possibilities.

As you narrow the possibilities in your life design process, you will have to discern what's best and make a decision. Like the other authors in this chapter, Burnett and Evans recommend looking for ways of knowing in many places. Use cognitive knowing and analyze all the story-based data. Use kinesthetic knowing and trust what your body is telling you about the pending decision. And use the intuitive way of knowing that may come from journaling, prayer, mediation, or other spiritual practices. It all helps you move toward a well-intentioned life.

SIX DESIGN MINDSETS TO BRING TO LIFE DESIGN:
- **Be curious:** What's the most interesting thing going on here? How could I find out?
- **Try stuff:** How can we try this before the day is out? What can I do that will answer that?
- **Reframe problems:** What perspective do I actually have? What other perspectives do others have? Name them all.
- **Know it's a process:** What are all the steps, both behind you and in front of you? What's the worst thing and the best thing that can happen?
- **Ask for help:** Who are all the different groups and constituencies involved in what you're working on? Who else can you ask for help?
- **Tell your story:** The authors added this one in their follow-up book, *Designing Your New Work Life*, good storytelling creates better connections and more curiosity in others.

Crossing the Unknown Sea: Work as a Pilgrimage of Identity
by David Whyte

"One of the keys to any possible happiness in work must be the little self-knowledge it takes to know what we desire in life, how we are made, and how we belong to the rest of the world."

IF WE ARE GOING to search for a life's purpose, we might also bring a poet on the journey with us. The thoughts and feelings that we have are so often confusing, contradicting, and elusive. We need language and sense-making that belongs more to the domain of the arts than the sciences. David Whyte, after starting his career in marine biology, decided to pursue poetry as a profession, and in this book he shares his journey to uncover that path while bringing different words to the challenge of discovering meaningful work.

"There is almost no life a human being can construct for themselves where they are not wrestling with something difficult, something that takes a modicum of work," Whyte writes. "The only possibility seems to be the ability of human beings to choose good work. At its simplest, good work is work that makes sense and that grants sense and meaning to the one who is doing it and to those affected by it."

Poets and philosophers often come to different conclusions to what we collectively want out of life. I notice that Whyte keeps pointing to freedom. He warns that organizational life may look more like modern-day serfdom than we care to admit, what with the demands it puts on our time and space in exchange for promises of riches and power. Work itself, Whyte writes, "if we do not invigorate and reimagine our participation…begins to enclose us and slowly starve our spirit." We need edges to explore. Sense-making for us and others takes place beyond the well-worn paths.

As a poet, Whyte also raises up language and how its usage helps or hinders that sense-making. The Latin root for *desire* is *desiderare*, which comes from *sider* or "of the stars." We might see our desires as beacons, sometimes dim and other times bright, to help with way-finding in this life. In talking about time, he observes that our wishes to *save time*, *steal time*, *need time*, and *make time* are all actions not within our power (and their use adds to our frustrations). These kinds of observations are what we need on a journey that requires more careful discernment than we often bring.

Whyte implores at the book's end that real conversation requires a different kind of language. He writes, "To my mind, that is the language not enshrined in business books or manuals but in our great literary traditions." We might expect that response from a poet, and the sentiment influences me. I hope this attempt to explore other sources might influence great work and a well-lived life.

WHYTE DESCRIBES WHY PURPOSE IS SO IMPORTANT:
"Why are the stakes so high in our work? Why do we work long hours; ignore our children; neglect our spouse; spend enormous amounts of time away from home; and, at our worst, stoop to theft, bribery, threats, and bullying to get things done? Somewhere in the midst of work is a hidden trove of imaginative treasure that we hope can give us self-respect, independence, and the ease we desire. But to grasp any of these qualities is to attempt to touch the essence of freedom, and freedom can rarely be obtained by using methods and bully-boy tactics that imprison us by their very use. The outlaw is the radical, the one close to the roots of existence. The one who refuses to forget their humanity and, in remembering, helps everyone else to remember, too."

SECTION TWO
PROGRESS

STARTING
GOALS
MOTIVATION
HABITS
FOCUS
CREATIVE WORK

CHAPTER 7
STARTING

"The journey of a thousand miles begins with one step."
—Lao Tzu

Starting something new is a big deal. Taking the first step is the most important part of the process. We can also make sure we get started on the right foot. This whole chapter is about those new beginnings. Michael Watkins writes about finding success quickly when you start a new job. Hal Elrod writes about starting each morning right. Noah Kagan proposes that you could start a new business next weekend. Meg Jay writes about the importance of your twenties and how it sets the course for the rest of your life. And Josh Kaufman says skip getting another degree; there are easier ways to get started learning the important aspects of business.

PROGRESS: **STARTING**

90 The First 90 Days: Proven Strategies for Getting Up to Speed Faster and Smarter
by Michael Watkins

"The president of the United States gets 100 days to prove himself; you get 90. The actions you take during your first few months in a new role will largely determine whether you succeed or fail."

A GOOD BUSINESS BOOK will always make the case for why the reader should care. In *The First 90 Days*, Michael Watkins describes the problem better in five pages than almost any book I have ever read. Consider that in a typical year, a quarter of Fortune 500 managers will change jobs. Transitions are important to long-term career prospects and among the most challenging times in our professional careers. Our awareness needs to extend beyond us to the fact that a leadership change impacts on average a dozen people, ranging from peers to bosses to direct reports. Our success may come from helping someone else in their first ninety days. The objective is to provide value as soon as possible. Surveyed leaders say transitions normally take six months. Watkins says, through his research, that you can shorten that time by 40 percent using the techniques in the book.

Watkins says, "Leadership is ultimately about influence and leverage," and both of those are largely situational, making it very important to assess the environment you are entering. Startups and Fortune 500 corporations are organized and managed very differently. Being promoted from within versus being hired from the outside can disguise key differences in cultural knowledge and staff support. Influence and leverage also arise from where we prefer to spend time, so be aware of the types of problems you like to get involved in.

All of these make new leaders suddenly realize how little they actually know. Watkins writes, "When a new leader derails, failure to learn effectively is almost always a factor." Leaders need to take the opportunity to ask questions about the past, present, and potential future. The author writes about a process that GE has used with new managers. With the help of a facilitator, reports are asked questions like "What do we want to know about the new manager?" and "What do we want the new manager to know about us?" Results are shared anonymously and a sharing session is convened to discuss them. Having been through this process several times, I want to punctuate how effective it can be to orient both the leader and new reports.

This book is full of valuable advice, and I am going to run out of room trying to share it all. Let me end with this: Secure early wins. A new hire proves themselves with accomplishments. Stay focused on a few promising opportunities. Keep close to the wins that matter to your manager. Get those wins without sacrificing your reputation. "Your actions during your first few weeks inevitably will have a disproportionate impact, because they are as much about symbolism, as about substance."

The advice in *The First 90 Days* can be applied to other parts of your life. If you take a new board position at a community nonprofit, think about building alliances. With a slight modification of language, the chapter on achieving alignment provides good advice for personal relationships, too. The self-reflection exercises in "Managing Yourself" are useful in any time of change. The most important insight from the book is realizing the opportunities and complexities in every major life transition.

TRAPS TO AVOID WHEN STARTING A NEW JOB:
1. Coming in with "the" answer and reaching conclusions too quickly.
2. Setting unrealistic expectations and failing to establish achievable objectives.
3. Falling prey to the "action imperative" and making poor decisions.
4. Failing to learn about the cultural and political dimension of your new role.
5. Attempting to do too much and never reaching critical mass on key initiatives.

The Personal MBA
by Josh Kaufman

"Most business books—and business schools—assume that the student already knows what businesses are, what they do, and how they work—as if it were the most obvious thing in the world. It's not. Business is one of the most complex and multidisciplinary areas of human experience, and trying to understand how businesses work can be difficult, even though they surround us every day."

THE ARGUMENT that Josh Kaufman makes in *The Personal MBA* is that the educational degree that so many pursue is not worth the time lost or money spent to earn it. He claims that business school is not needed to learn the fundamentals of business. As a holder of said degree, you won't hear me strongly dispute that conclusion.

Now, I have watched (and helped a little with) this project over the years, and there was no question for me that *The Personal MBA* was going to be included in this collection, but it was harder to figure out the best place to put it. Josh's synthesis of the seven core categories with 271 different concepts covers an enormous array of material that intersects with chapters throughout this book. I might have even wondered a little, "Should everyone just read *The Personal MBA* instead of *100 Best Books*?" And that's when I realized that this is a perfect book for this chapter on starting— starting out in the business world, starting a new job, starting a new project. Kaufman's concepts are presented in short entries. Concepts that are used elsewhere in the book are bolded, which adds wonderful context and connection for those starting out. And he often cites sources or suggests other books to let the reader dive deeper on a topic.

CONCEPTS THAT CAUGHT MY ATTENTION:

- **Force Multipliers:** "Investing in Force Multipliers makes sense because you can get more done with the same amount of effort. ... As a general rule, the only good use of debt or outside capital in setting up a system is to give you access to Force Multipliers you would not be able to access any other way. ... By investing in Force Multipliers, you free up your time, energy, and attention to focus on *building* your business instead of operating it."
- **Reference Levels via conservation of energy:** "Sources of information that change your Reference Levels are valuable at prompting action. ... Good books, magazines, blogs, documentaries, and even competitors are valuable if they violate your expectations about what's possible. When you discover that other people are doing something you once considered unrealistic or impossible, it changes your Reference Levels in a very useful way."
- **Status Signals:** "Every minute of every day, a nontrivial part of your brain has been devoted to keeping track of how you measure up against the rest of the world. ... That's why humans have direct incentives to explore, create, and build skills in millions upon millions of different areas: Being "the best" in something is a straightforward way to increase Social Status. ... Rare or expensive items, awards, honors, victory in recognized competition, and verifiable public acclaim are all examples of Status Signals."
- **Modal Bias:** "...is the automatic assumption that our idea or approach is best. ... There is always more than one way to get something done, and good ideas can come from anywhere. ... The best way to avoid Modal Bias in your own decision-making is to use inhibition to temporarily suspend judgment. Part of the value of understanding cognitive biases is the knowledge that you are not immune to them, and knowing they exist doesn't make them any less influential."

The Defining Decade: Why Your Twenties Matter—and How to Make the Most of Them Now
by Meg Jay

"Knowing you want to do something isn't the same as knowing how to do it. And even knowing how to do something isn't the same as actually doing it well."

I AM RAISING CHILDREN in their late teens. Two are in college and the third will be graduating high school soon. So I have a high interest and an obvious bias in saying that *The Defining Decade* belongs in this collection. The topics that psychotherapist Meg Jay addresses speak to twenty-somethings in the twenty-first century. Young adults were sold the dream—that their twenties would be the best decade of their lives…except that the average college graduate now owes $30,000 in school debt, and their first job in the workforce will likely be less than full-time or in an area outside the major they studied. And this isn't a small problem—there are over fifty million twenty-somethings in the United States alone. Jay writes, "Too many twenty-somethings have been caught in a whirl of hype and misinformation, much of which has trivialized what is actually the most defining decade—and, in many ways, the *most difficult* decade—they will ever know."

The first section of the book is about work. The primary message is clear: find a way to get started, because a wasted decade comes at a high cost. The first ten years of your career play a crucial role in shaping your lifetime earning potential. Twenty-somethings who are unemployed in long stretches report heavy drinking and depression well into middle age. The trouble is, most twenty-somethings find themselves overwhelmed with the possibilities. Narrow the scope of your choices. The available options are not actually limitless. Focus on five or six potentials. Make a list of ways that you show up in the world, whether degrees, past jobs, or hobbies. Let those help you determine your preferences. Make bolder bets by working for a startup or moving cross-country. And, just as important as the work itself, consider *where* you will be and *who* you will be with. To paraphrase Jay here, *an interesting life doesn't come from resisting choices, it comes from making choices.*

Love is another important choice you'll make in your twenties. The vast majority of twenty-somethings will be "married or partnered or dating or living with their future partner in the next ten years." Jay quotes *New York Times* columnist David Brooks asking, "Have you ever taken a class in marriage?" Jay adds, "Money, work, lifestyle, family, health, leisure, sex, retirement, and even death becomes a three-legged race." If we are going to live in some tandem with someone else, we need to understand what we need in a partner. Jay spends four chapters conveying how the dynamics of casual dating can undermine you finding your way to healthy committed relationships. There is no perfect list of qualities to look for in a partner. "We know that people who are emotionally stable or agreeable or conscientious tend to make better partners. So do people who are open and curious, too." Picking a partner brings with it an expansion of your family. Pay attention to the clues available from those early interactions. If you are thinking of having a family, finding a good partner needs to be a priority in this decade of your life.

The last section explores the brain science of twenty-somethings. Research shows that their brains remain highly adaptable, maintaining the rapid flexibility that began during puberty. All these new life experiences give rise to worry and fear. This creates a cocktail of negative emotions about yourself and around the anxiety-ridden situation. Jay describes this wonderfully in how twenty-somethings need better information, and that they need to take that information to learn to master the hard things. As Jay says, "Never again will we be so quick to learn new things. Never again will it be so easy to become the people we hope to be."

JAY'S SUGGESTED QUESTIONS FOR A ROMANTIC PARTNER:
- Do I make you a better person?
- How are we going to manage our money?
- What do you think of our sex life?
- What do you want your career to look like?
- Do you want to have kids?
- How do we handle problems?
- Why do you like me?

PROGRESS: **STARTING**

Million Dollar Weekend: The Surprisingly Simple Way to Launch a 7-Figure Business in 48 Hours
by Noah Kagan with Tahl Raz

"From now on, everything you do in this book, and after, should be viewed as an experiment. This has been a profound shift for people who worry that 'starting a business' is this big daunting thing. Experiments are supposed to fail. And should they fail, you just take what you've learned and try again a little bit differently."

HERE ARE THREE THINGS THAT ARE TRUE:

1. You can start a business in two days.
2. Money is not a barrier.
3. Overcoming the word "no" will be your biggest problem.

I love entrepreneurship, and it's taken a long time to find a book that doesn't lead with the fine details of legal paperwork, accounting software, and office space. Yes, you will need those, but it's not where the important work is when you are starting a new business.

Noah Kagan makes it simple. You only need two things: something people want and the people who want it. I know. It seems too easy. Products and customers. Supply and demand. Obvious. Why do I need the book? Well, like so many other books in *100 Best Books* say, you are going to get in your own way. You'll avoid the pain of the rejection that tells you if you are on the wrong path. You'll make something you want (which is an awesome starting point) but miss that customers need to want it too. You'll ask for their opinion of the idea rather than their money to preorder the product.

Of course, you do need an idea. Start by focusing on the most painful problems the people around you. That is the same advice I give authors at Bard Press when we are developing their books. Find the problem that intersects with your passion and experience. Then, choose a large niche that you're a part of—something you understand from the inside. Narrowing your search with these questions means you already know the problems, the people, and the possibilities.

The harder part is getting customers. The goal is to start talking to them as soon as possible. Get their help validating your business. "There's a big difference between what people say and what people do," Kagan writes. "Everyone's interested until they have to pay." Use the *rejections* for important follow-up questions like "Why not?" "Who is the one person you know who would really like this?" and "What *would* make this a no-brainer for you?" That last question can lead you off in a completely different but more viable direction than where you were headed.

Those first two steps will get you those first ten or twenty orders and prove you have found a vein of value for folks. You also need a plan for growth. How are you going to reach more customers? By running more experiments. There are probably more people in your network you could reach out to. You could pay for ads. Influencers could lead you to new prospects. Publicity, search engagement optimization, content marketing, contests, and collaborations are all potential paths to get your next orders for your million-dollar business.

FIVE FOCUSING QUESTIONS FOR YOUR MARKETING PLAN:
1. What is your one goal for this year?
2. Who exactly is your customer and where can you find them?
3. What is one marketing activity you can double down on?
4. How can you delight your first one hundred customers?
5. If you *had* to double your business with no money in thirty days, what would you do?

PROGRESS: **STARTING**

The Miracle Morning: The Not-So-Obvious Secret Guaranteed to Transform Your Life (Before 8 AM)
by Hal Elrod

"Arguably the most significant obstacle standing between us and creating the lives we want [is] getting yourself to do what you need to do, when you need to do it, whether you feel like it or not."

YOU COULD FIND some version of that opening quote in almost any self-help book worth its weight in pulp. This is the kind of high-octane motivation Hal Elrod supplies in *The Miracle Morning*. What makes it different from other books (and why it made my list) is the focus he puts on *when* you should focus on those motivational practices. That *timing* changes everything.

When we know the point where motivation belongs in our day, we see better where it will have the greatest impact. With *The Miracle Morning*, Elrod shows the benefits to starting our morning with activities that create the right physiological state to support what we want to accomplish in the rest of our day.

Elrod draws inspiration from the greatest hits of motivation—silence, affirmation, visualization, exercise, reading, and scribing (S.A.V.E.R.S.)—and gives readers plenty of room to explore how to practice them. He reports that "roughly 70 percent of Miracle Morning practitioners schedule 60 minutes to complete their S.A.V.E.R.S., about 20 percent schedule 30 minutes, and the remaining 10 percent spend more or less time on their routine." Elrod also provides a template for a six-minute Miracle Morning for those with less time. With sixty seconds spent on each practice, he says he can still get 60 to 70 percent of the benefit.

What makes *The Miracle Morning* even more effective is how Elrod anticipates your objections. If you are not a morning person, he has an answer. If the morning is not the start of your day, he has an answer. Afraid you'll not stick with the Miracle Morning? Well, you'll find a chapter on habit-building to help. You'll even find a new chapter in the updated edition titled "Miracle Evening" to help create a better nighttime transition and get better sleep.

The Miracle Morning is a great manual for starting a morning ritual or improving the one you already have.

TIPS FOR BEING MORE EFFECTIVE ON S.A.V.E.R.S. ACTIVITIES:

- **Silence:** Meditation, breathwork, or prayer all work. Focus on the mental state you want to experience more.
- **Affirmations:** "I commit to…" is the best start. Add a reason it is important with "because…" then end with when and where you will take action.
- **Visualization:** Now visualize both the outcome you want and the actions you took to get there.
- **Exercise:** Even a short exercise session will boost your circulation and increase your energy!
- **Reading:** Ten pages each day turns into eighteen books read each year.
- **Scribing:** Journaling can document progress, elevate gratitude, and increase commitment to the next day's goals.

CHAPTER 8
GOALS

> "It is good to have an end to journey toward, but it is the journey that really matters in the end."
> —Ursula K. Le Guin

Goals come by many names—objectives, intentions, aspirations, dreams. Regardless of the word you like, they are powerful motivators for creating action and progress in life. The research is clear that setting goals improves the chances of completing the journey. Keith Ellis says we should call them "wishes" and watch how our world aligns to help us accomplish them. Danielle LaPorte says we should hold lightly the days when we don't make the steps we would like. John Doerr looks at goals through the lens of setting them for organizations. But we'll start with Caroline Adams Miller and Michael B. Frisch, as they provide a wide view to setting goals that work for you.

PROGRESS: **GOALS**

Creating Your Best Life: The Ultimate Life List Guide
by Caroline Adams Miller and Michael B. Frisch

"Just as religious commentators say that there are many paths to God, so there are many ways to create a life list. All of them work, and the only key variable is whether or not the method speaks to you and allows you to successfully follow the necessary steps to completion."

WHEN I FIRST picked up *Creating Your Best Life*, I expected a solid self-help approach to goal-setting. The orange-yellow cover and the continued hype in the subtitle further sold that framing. And then the reader gets a foreword from Gary Latham, one of the first to establish a research-based approach to goal-setting. Next, we find out that Miller studied under Martin Seligman (the godfather of the positive psychology movement) and joined the inaugural class at University of Pennsylvania to be awarded a master's degree in applied positive psychology. The book revolves around this research-informed perspective into the wide array of factors that impact successful goal-setting and the accomplishment of those goals.

Creating Your Best Life takes the tell-you-everything approach to goal-setting and covers every aspect of the topic that you might know, might imagine, and hadn't thought of yet. The first chapter covers goal-setting historically (Leonardo da Vinci was a big goal-setter), in pop culture (through movies like *Last Holiday* and *The Bucket List*), and poignantly (sharing the story of Randy Pausch's last lecture). The authors set the scene for the wide interest in goal-setting by stating, "Just as we are all distinct individuals with different chromosomes, backgrounds, and family situations, we all have our own passions, longings, strengths to tap, and goals that reflect where we want to go and what we wish to leave behind as our legacy."

Discerning our goals can be hard. The authors suggest writing down five goals you have already accomplished and love to tell others about. They talk about the power of risk-taking and the toxicity of living with regrets. They recommend everything from scrapbooking to vision boards, mind maps to time capsules. There is a values-sorting exercise that they call the Happiness House. The reader is encouraged to build floors in their "house," with the most important ones serving as the foundation and less important values on the upper floors.

The rooms in the Happiness House match up to the Wheel of Life charts you might have seen in other frameworks. Health, Spiritual Life, Work, and Money are included. Key relationships are divided among Love, Children, Friends, and Relatives. They include location-based interests in areas like Home, Neighborhood, and Community. The final components often appear in longer values-sorting exercises—Self-Esteem, Goals and Values, Play, Learning, Creativity, and Helping. I mention these "rooms" because Part Three of the book digs into each of them in more detail.

That detail is the value of *Creating Your Best Life*. There are thirty pages of worksheets that are referenced throughout the book to get you engaged and thinking more about your goals. Miller and Frisch move quickly, but each point is another angle to consider as you set your goals and run into the inevitable roadblocks that keep you from achieving them.

GARY LATHAM'S SUMMARY OF THE GOAL-SETTING THEORY:

1. A specific high goal leads to higher performance than no goal-setting or simply urging people to do their best.
2. If there is a goal, higher goals lead to higher performance than easy goals.
3. Praise, money, and participation lead to an increase in performance only if they lead you to set and commit to specific high goals.

The Desire Map: A Guide to Creating Goals with Soul
by Danielle LaPorte

"What we strive for in perfection is not what turns us into the lit angel we desire, what disturbs and then nourishes has everything we need."

GOALS THAT ALIGN with who we truly are bring fulfillment and happiness. Most book-bound advice doesn't dig deep enough. They often exclaim, "Build goals around what you want in your life!" and then they wrap those goals in hustle, hype, and external validation. Goals become tied to the achievement of crossing things off a bucket list. I wanted one book in this chapter that put the emphasis in a different place.

Danielle LaPorte says our starting point should be desire. "Something phenomenal happens when you start to examine your desires," she writes. "You get closer to your reality—all that you can appreciate and everything you want to change." LaPorte picks a deliberately feminine word. The whole book is laced with spirituality, self-help, and radical honesty towards the pursuit of goals.

"Maybe you don't need to make six figures a year. Or be married by the time you are thirty. Or be team captain. Or sit in an ashram watching your in breath and out breath. Or have a pension. ... Or maybe those are exactly the things that you need." The whole point of goal-setting should be to create goals you connect with. I was at a conference recently and a woman stood up and said, "I bought a cabin last year. It only takes fifty-five minutes to get there from my house. It is decorated for Christmas year-around. And I love it." I loved hearing it too. LaPorte's whole point is to identify and lean into our core desired feelings.

The big/bigger/biggest life crowd will probably not like this wishy-washiness. "Feelings can deceive us," they say. Or, "You need to ignore how you feel and just do it anyway." LaPorte invokes the hungry ghost from Buddhist mythology, saying we need to be careful not to engage "the over-needful, ravenous part of our psyche that demands to be fed. ... It's scared, it's always empty, and it will never be pleased." It's OK to admit the way we want to feel and do things that generate those feelings. That work also requires feeling the unwanted and negative feelings, too, if we want to know we are going in the right direction.

Halfway through the book, LaPorte shares three pages of commentary from people and how they feel about goals. The feelings run the gambit from "goal-setting sucks" to "I like being in the 3 percent of the population who does it and works toward them." Failure, course correction, and success beyond your wildest dreams are all a part of living our goals. Maybe this Bruce Lee quote is helpful here: "A goal is not always meant to be reached; it often serves simply as something to aim at."

Or as we connect our desires to our goals, we could invoke Pema Chödrön when she wrote, "When resistance is gone, so are the demons." Wanting more is not a problem. Letting go of what doesn't serve us is OK too. And "be suspicious of what you want," as Rumi says. "Fierce but flexible," LaPorte writes. The vastness of the universe *and* the specificity of this moment have the power together to inform the direction we choose to walk. Swim in all of it and see what you find.

LAPORTE QUOTES GARY LATHAM AND EDWIN LOCKE'S RESEARCH:

1. "Goals direct attention and effort toward goal-relevant activities and away from goal-irrelevant activities."
2. "Goals have an energizing function. Goals create effort."
3. "Goals affect persistence. Goals prolong effort."
4. "Goals rally us to bring task-relevant knowledge and strategies to the problems at hand."

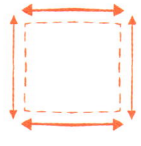

Measure What Matters: How Google, Bono, and the Gates Foundation Rock the World with OKRs
by John Doerr

"Measuring what matters begins with the questions: What is the most important for the next three (or six, or twelve) months? Successful organizations focus on the handful of initiatives that can make a real difference, deferring less urgent ones."

MEASURE WHAT MATTERS addresses goal-setting from the perspective of an organization. Many of the tenets that make goals valuable for individuals are the same for groups. Groups of groups need to focus and maintain priorities. They need ways to create accountability. Organizations need goals that expand what is possible. A book like this shows what else goals provide and adds a needed context for this different application of goal-setting.

John Doerr, a highly successful Silicon Valley venture capitalist, opens the book with his lineage of organization goal-setting that starts with Peter Drucker. The consultant-philosopher's "management by objectives" (MBOs) captured corporate America in the 1950s and 1960s, saying that they "give common direction of vision and effort, establish teamwork, and harmonize the goals of the individual with the common weal." Doerr cites a meta-analysis that found high commitment to MBOs produced productivity gains of 56 percent, versus just 6 percent where commitment was low. As a first iteration, MBOs helped but also suffered from their sole sourcing from upper management, their unhealthy tie to compensation, and a lack of frequency of their updating.

Doerr's more immediate teacher was Andy Grove, the storied CEO of Intel. Grove adopted MBOs but added several components to their application. Doerr writes, "In nearly every respect, the new method negated the old." Grove made goals through Intel both public and transparent. iMBOs, as they were called (with an *i* for Intel), were revisited on a monthly or quarterly basis. Objectives were dialed up to be both aggressive and aspirational. The most important component, though, is highlighted in the naming itself that Doerr adopted and brought forward into the organizations that he invested in and worked with over the last twenty years.

Objectives and key results (OKRs) address goals in two important dimensions. Doerr credits Bill Davidson, the head of Intel's microcomputer systems division, with this distinction: "We will achieve a certain OBJECTIVE as measured by the following KEY RESULTS…" This linkage of *as measured by* connects the all-important *what* with the equally important *how*. Grove also suggested pairing quantity alongside quality when developing key results as a way to balance "the effect and the counter-effect." For instance, a warehouse might measure shipments made and track the number of shipments with errors to achieve that balance.

So you could read Drucker's *Practice of Management* and Grove's *High Output Management*, but Doerr's work is a worthy successor for several reasons. In Doerr's role as a venture capitalist, he has had the opportunity to teach this OKR framework to numerous organizations and benefit from that as an investor. That mutual success has made the concept of OKRs better.

Doerr also does something remarkable and invites the leaders of those organizations to share their experiences. In the book, you hear from Davidson about Intel's devotion to these metrics. You hear from Bill Gates and Patty Stonesifer about their application at the Gates Foundation. Google CEO Sundar Pichai writes about the development and rollout of the Chrome browser. The late Susan Wojcicki, the former CEO of YouTube, details their early goal of reaching a billion watched hours. This approach almost gives *Measure What Matters* the format of a timely, guest-driven podcast that still works in the format of a book. Those perspectives give real depth to goal-setting at the organizational level.

ADVICE FROM THE BOOK'S GREAT RESOURCES SECTION:
- OKRs are often written based on what the team believes it can achieve without changing anything they are currently doing, as opposed to what the team or its customers really want.
- A team's committed OKRs should credibly consume most but not all of their available resources.
- If your objective doesn't fit on one line, it probably isn't crisp enough.
- Make sure the metrics are unambiguous.
- Use real dates. If every key result happens on the last day of the quarter, you likely don't have a real plan.

The Magic Lamp: Goal Setting for People Who Hate Setting Goals
by Keith Ellis

"Wishing really works, if you do."

THE MAGIC LAMP appeals to me. I am competitive. I love big goals. I love winning. I also know that some people are going to hate the book, from the very first page, for all the same reasons—how it ignores systemic barriers that impede people, how it provides yet another set of talking points for hustle culture. That's probably enough to know if this book is for you or not. For myself, I sometimes need a strong dose of "can do."

Keith Ellis says we should start thinking of goals as wishes. He says the change in word choice adds energy to that which we pursue. If the naysayers are still reading, I can see you shaking your heads. My guess is that you don't think wishes can come true. Like goals, Ellis writes, "Before you can make wishes come true, you must first decide what to wish for. Once you decide what you really want, the rest falls in place. You awaken each morning with a reason to get out of bed. Your days are filled with meaning. You are able to take advantage of your talents, your time, and your opportunities because you have a purpose." If you are lacking inspiration, Ellis says to get out a piece of paper, clear your mind of judgment, and keep your pen moving as you answer the question: "What would I really want from life if I were absolutely, positively certain I would get it?" Pause for a moment, turn the paper over, and do the same work with a slightly different question: "What would I really want to accomplish in life if I were absolutely, positively certain I would do it?"

Another route might be to ask, "What do I enjoy doing?" because the doing is what will create the accomplishments and get you what you want. The doing is the price you pay to make your wish come true. Make sure you are really aligned with the necessary work.

I don't have enough room to summarize his whole process. He talks about habits and inertia, plans and time, help and focus and persistence—each as a five- or six-page chapter that's sorted to give you just the right next thing to think about.

Ellis also distinguishes himself by ending the book with two sections that every advice book should contain. First, there is a twenty-five-page set of FAQs that attempt to answer the queries you still might have after finishing the book. The FAQs both summarize and deepen the material presented. The second is an annotated section with almost fifty resources on everything from leadership to public speaking to getting published. Giving the reader a gift like that is similar to showing your work in a homework assignment—you get to better understand where the writer is coming from and benefit from seeing the research firsthand.

HOW ELLIS TEACHES READERS TO MAKE WISHES:
1. Write it.
2. Be specific.
3. Set a deadline.
4. Make it something you can measure.
5. Wish only for what you can control.
6. Wish for what you want, not what you don't want.
7. Begin your wish with "I choose."
8. Make it emotional.
9. Be brief.
10. Believe in it.
11. Take immediate action.

CHAPTER 9
MOTIVATION

"People often say that motivation doesn't last. Well, neither does bathing—that's why we recommend it daily."
—Zig Ziglar

Motivation is an interesting and somewhat strange subject. Try to go look for the place where your desire to act comes from. It's hard. Edward Deci, who did important early research on self-motivation, said that our intrinsic desire could be easily dampened or shifted by common influences around us. Researcher B. J. Fogg confirms that, telling us that motivation is the least reliable way to change behavior (see Chapter 10, "Habits"). And yet we know there are points in our life when something is driving us forward. It seems worthwhile to explore that and better understand what motivates us.

Drive: The Surprising Truth about What Motivates Us
by Daniel Pink

"Human beings have an inherent tendency to seek out novelty and challenges, to extend and exercise their capacities, to explore, and to learn."

DANIEL PINK opens *Drive* with a summary of Edward Deci's work on intrinsic motivation. Using seven-piece interlocking block puzzles, Deci asked two groups to solve a set of problems with the puzzles across three consecutive daily sessions. Both groups were given the same problems and additional free time. Deci was interested in how the groups spent that extra time. He tracked how much time the two groups spent working with the puzzles during that time. The key variable was his choice to pay one group for the number of problems they solved. He did this during the second session, and that group's free time spent puzzling increased by 50 percent. When he invited both groups back for the third day, he told the group paid the day prior that no money was left. When he tracked the paid group that day, their free time spent with the puzzles plummeted to levels below the first day in the lab when neither group was offered money. There are now hundreds of studies that confirm tangible rewards have a negative impact on intrinsic motivation.

Now, in Deci's experiments, he was asking people to engage in creative work, and in the world we live in today, more and more of our work encompasses exactly those kinds of creative tasks. Research by Teresa Amabile of Harvard Business School confirms that creativity and intrinsic motivation are negatively impacted by both rewards and punishments. Interestingly, the same research found that routine and "algorithm" tasks do benefit from a carrots-and-sticks approach because intrinsic motivation contributes less to those.

It's also good to point out that rewarding an activity you want more of can often get us more of what we *don't* want. A set of scholars at leading business schools caution against goal-setting, saying "substantive evidence demonstrates that in addition to motivating constructive effort, goal-setting can induce unethical behavior."

Examples abound: Jeff Skilling of Enron, Elizabeth Holmes of Theranos, et cetera, et cetera. Paradoxically, punishments can also get us more of what we don't want. A day care center in Israel wanted to encourage parents to pick up their children on time and instituted a small fine for parents who showed up late. The number of parents showing up late doubled!

In his typical fashion, Pink presents a great survey of the topic of motivation—both the unexpected problems and a highly tactical approach to better engage motivation within yourself and others. In the second half of the book, he describes how autonomy, mastery, and purpose (or in Deci's words of self-determination theory: autonomy, competence, and relatedness) each help with motivation. With autonomy, people want to feel ownership over their behavior, as can be seen in letting workers control their working hours and location or even allocating work hours toward projects of personal interest. People also want to be good at the things they do; they want to get better at them, and through that effort, mastery creates a deeper sense of engagement. Purpose is merely the belief that our work matters, or as Mihaly Csikszentmihalyi says, "One cannot live a life that is truly excellent without feeling that one belongs to something greater and more permanent than oneself."

PINK QUOTES ANDERS ERICSSON'S FIVE FACTORS FOR MASTERY:
1. Engage in deliberate practice with the purpose of improving performance.
2. Repeat, repeat, repeat. Repetition matters.
3. Seek constant critical feedback.
4. "Those who get better work on their weaknesses."
5. Prepare to be physically and mentally exhausted.

PROGRESS: **MOTIVATION**

Grit: The Power of Passion and Perseverance
by Angela Duckworth

> "In sum, no matter what domain, the highly successful has a kind of ferocious determination that played out in two ways. First, these exemplars were unusually resilient and hardworking. Second, they knew in a very, very deep way what it was they wanted. They not only had determination, they had direction."

ANGELA DUCKWORTH starts *Grit* with the question: Which do you value more, talent or effort? If your answer follows the research, you'd be very likely to say hard work matters more than natural ability. Now, if I presented you with two resumes for an open job position, the research shows that our bias shifts to the candidate with early success and natural talent. In short, we say one thing and believe another.

Duckworth's research is remarkable because for the first time she was able to predict success in a variety of settings. She could assess which cadets at West Point would make it through the first year at the academy. Her work showed which students were most likely to win the National Spelling Bee. When she joined forces with Teach for America, her research on grit could predict student outcomes based on the attitudes of the teachers that worked with them. Longevity in sales positions and the likelihood of students pursuing graduate degrees also connect to the amount of grit people have.

Duckworth believes grit is a combination of passion and perseverance. The latter is the quality we most often connect with grit. In Duckworth's research, people tend to score higher on perseverance, but passion matters just as much. In common Western usage, passion means the intensity one feels for something. Duckworth invokes a particular usage that better aligns with grit, saying that passion is "a little bit of *discovery,* followed by a lot of development, and then a lifetime of *deepening.*" Passion is the thoughts we have and encourage; perseverance is the actions we take.

After hearing more about the strong benefits of grit, everyone asks Duckworth if grit can be developed and cultivated. The answer is yes,

PROGRESS: **MOTIVATION**

and most of the book focuses on that question in a variety of professional and personal domains. The development of grit is a process that alternates between passion and perseverance, starting with interest. Research shows interest in one's job predicts both job performance and satisfaction. We already know the difficulty here given the dissatisfaction many people have with their jobs (two-thirds of employees are dissatisfied, according to Gallup). Duckworth advises, "Before hard work comes play." Try lots of things with the freedom and autonomy to pursue different paths (see *Drive*).

After interest develops, the effort of practice is needed to develop proficiency. Here Duckworth's research intersects with Anders Ericsson's research on expertise. Practice is important, but both researchers found a particular kind of practice improves grit. Individuals focus on a particular skill that needs to be developed. They set a goal that is difficult to achieve. And they pursue getting immediate feedback that focuses on what's wrong, rather than what's right. Ben Franklin, someone we know for his wise and memorable quotes, practiced this by reading his favorite essays, putting them in a drawer, and then rewriting them—in each case attempting to capture the arguments as successfully as the originals.

Grit continues to develop through passion and practice. Paragons of grit deeply value how their work connects with others. Duckworth, for example, identifies her purpose as "[using] psychological science to help children thrive." The further development of perseverance comes through the belief that things can get better. This is where Duckworth's work dovetails with Carol Dweck's growth mindset findings (see *Mindset*). Gritty individuals possess hope, use optimistic self-talk, and believe they can overcome adversity. It's the same approach Duckworth uses throughout the book as she shares her own challenges as a researcher, a psychologist, and a parent.

FOUR TRAITS FROM STANFORD PSYCHOLOGIST CATHERINE COX'S 1926 STUDY OF CREATIVE AND SCIENTIFIC FIGURES:

1. Degree to which they work with distant objects in view (as opposed to living from hand to mouth). Active preparation for later life. Working toward a definite goal.
2. Tendency not to abandon tasks from mere changeability.

Not seeking something fresh because of novelty. Not "looking for a change."
3. Degree of strength of will or perseverance. Quiet determination to stick to a course once decided upon.
4. Tendency not to abandon tasks in the face of obstacles. Perseverance, tenacity, doggedness.

The Progress Principle: Using Small Wins to Ignite Joy, Engagement, and Creativity at Work
by Teresa Amabile and Steven Kramer

"Far too many managers are unaware of the importance of progress and therefore neither worry about it nor act to support it. As crucial as progress is to inner work life, and as obvious as it might seem, we are convinced that most managers simply don't think about it, systematically, every day."

MOTIVATION is desire or willingness to want to do something. We can be encouraged from the outside. A need to act can arise from within. We might also be motivated by helping others. The research of Teresa Amabile and Steven Kramer says there is another factor that we should not leave off that list. As a matter of fact, it contributes more than extrinsic, intrinsic, or altruistic motivation.

If we start with the end in mind, there are certain qualities we want our work life to have. We want to be creative in our work. We want to be productive. We want to stay committed to the effort. And we want to have good relationships with those we interact with. Each of those qualities is highly influenced by what the authors call the "inner work life."

As you might expect, the inner work life consists of the thoughts and feelings that others around us can't see. We react to the events of the day and experience corresponding emotions. We then build a larger story around how we perceive our manager, our coworkers, and our employers. Those both connect to the motivation we feel for what we do next, when we'll do it, how we'll do it, and sometimes whether we'll do it all.

Managers and executives still carry a bias that treats workers as rational and logical agents from a nineteenth-century economics textbook. Never accurate and now wholly turned on its head, we know that emotions are essential for decision-making and that our emotional state impacts the quality of our work. For those who need further proof, the authors quote Gallup's James Harter and his study of two thousand companies and their 142,000 employees' job satisfaction and perception of their work environments at several points over time. Harter found that you could predict sales, profitability, customer loyalty, and employee retention all by looking at employee satisfaction with their organization, their managers, their coworkers, and the work itself.

The landmark research of Amabile and Kramer collected the inner lives of 238 individuals. Each day, the researchers asked, "Briefly describe one event from today that stands out in your mind." They collected over twelve thousand responses and concluded, "From the highest-level executive office and meeting rooms to the lowest-level cubicles and research labs of every company, events play out every day that shape inner work life, steer performance, and set the course of the organization."

In examining the data, the researchers looked at both positive and negative events and their emotional impact. To their surprise, the events that had the largest emotional impact were connected with the kind of progress made on meaningful work. Of the best days, 76 percent involved reports of forward progress, and of the worst days, 67 percent involved the detailing of setbacks. Amabile and Kramer believe this connects with self-efficacy, a basic human drive for people to believe they can plan and execute strategies to achieve their desired goals. Progress motivates people to accept more difficult challenges and to persist longer, while setbacks increase negative emotions and further inhibit motivation. The authors also identified two other important factors: catalysts that directly facilitate the timely, creative, high-quality completion of work and nourishers that foster more human connection, both further helping improve inner work life.

The authors tell multiple stories of asking managers about the role of progress in motivating employees, and in each case, its role is discounted or dismissed completely. Like these managers, ignore the authors' insightful research at your own risk.

AMABILE AND KRAMER FOUND SEVEN MAJOR CATALYSTS THAT HELP CREATE PROGRESS:

1. **Setting clear goals:** People have better inner work lives when they know where their work is headed and why it matters.
2. **Allowing autonomy:** Let people have freedom in how they do their work and know those choices will be honored.
3. **Providing resources:** Provide the necessary funds signaling the value the work has to the organization.
4. **Giving enough time:** Beware of extreme time pressure over long periods, but low to moderate pressure seems to encourage positive inner work life.
5. **Helping with the work:** Information, collaboration, or brainstorming can help a colleague make progress.
6. **Learning from problems and successes:** Analyze problems and create plans to resolve issues while also analyzing successes and celebrating knowledge gained.
7. **Allowing ideas to flow:** Encourage debate and respect critical feedback to reach the best ideas.

The Happiness Advantage: How a Positive Brain Fuels Success in Work and Life
by Shawn Achor

"Happiness is not the belief that we don't need to change; it is the realization that we can."

I WANT TO open this review with the primary finding from a meta-analysis of over two hundred studies with a combined 275,000 participants: "Study after study shows that happiness *precedes* important outcomes and indicators of thriving." Happiness arises before success, not as a result of the outcomes we work or wish for. A study of college freshmen showed one's level of happiness that first year in university predicted their income level *nineteen* years later. US Navy squadrons with commanding officers who are openly encouraging far more frequently win commendation for efficiency and preparedness. Shawn Achor restates it this way: "Happiness is the joy we feel striving after our potential."

Another aspect that is often masked when we talk about happiness is the broader range of emotions that positive psychology is studying. The ten most common positive emotions according to Barbara Fredrickson at University of North Carolina are joy, gratitude, serenity, interest, hope, pride, amusement, inspiration, awe, and love. So, yes, let's orient toward joy, and all the other wholehearted emotions that can arise alongside it.

In *The Happiness Advantage,* you will find topics like habits, focus, and relationships that are covered in other chapters of this book. However, the framing is different. Achor presents copious examples from the research on happiness to show how those topics don't just lead to success. They also lead to awe, gratitude, and love. And as it relates to research, Achor presents the material with a framing toward the world of work, which makes it more useful in a collection like *100 Best Books.*

ACHOR'S SEVEN PRINCIPLES WITH AN EMPHASIS ON WORK:

1. **The happiness advantage:** Positive emotional states literally broaden our visual field of view, lengthen lifespan, and speed up diagnostic decision-making. Marcial Losada's workplace research shows that the ratio of positive to negative interactions needed for creating successful teams is 2.9013, and a ratio of six to one is where teams do their best work.
2. **The fulcrum and the lever:** We can change how our brains process the world and our experience in it. A study of 112 entry-level accountants found that those who believed they could accomplish what they set out to do had the highest job performance reviews ten months later. Their belief was a better predictor of outcome than their skill level or the training they received.

3. **The Tetris effect:** Our natural state is to scan our environment for threats, but if we shift those scans to searching for the positive, we invoke happiness, gratitude, and optimism. Make a daily practice of writing down three good things that happened, to enhance the positive that is always there.
4. **Falling up:** "The people who can most successfully get themselves up off the mat are those who define themselves not by what has happened to them, but by what they can make out of what has happened. These are the people who actually use adversity to find the path forward." MetLife found that agents who deal well with adversity and are highly optimistic sold 88 percent more than pessimists and were 50 percent less likely to quit.
5. **The Zorro circle:** Studies show that the belief that we have control over our outcomes creates higher academic achievement, greater career achievement, and more happiness at work. And that belief in our own control leads to greater satisfaction in nearly every other aspect of life.
6. **The twenty-second rule:** Build habits through repetition. Don't use the weaker mental force called willpower and suffer from disappointment when a new routine fails to take hold. See Chapter 10, "Habits"!
7. **Social investment:** As confirmed in many other sources, Achor's own study of 1,600 Harvard undergraduates showed that social support was a far greater predictor of happiness than any other factor, scoring 0.7 on correlation. I'll end with one of my favorite quotes from the book: "The only way to save ourselves is to hold on tight to the people around us and not let go."

CHAPTER 10
HABITS

"We are what we repeatedly do. Excellence, therefore, is not an act, but a habit."
—Aristotle

Forty-three percent of the actions you take today will be nearly automatic. Each one will start with a cue that kicks off a well-rehearsed routine. Upon completion, you'll be rewarded with the shot of dopamine that creates a satisfying sense of fulfillment.

We call these action sequences habits, and they have been getting a lot of attention. New advances in neurological and behavioral research over the last thirty years have led to the publication of many books that attempt to translate those findings into important insights we can use.

As Charles Duhigg writes in *The Power of Habit:* "Habits are powerful, but delicate. They can emerge outside our consciousness, or can be deliberately designed. They often occur without our permission, but can be reshaped by fiddling with their parts.

They shape our lives far more than we realize—they are so strong, in fact, that they cause our brains to cling to them at the exclusion of all else, including common sense."

Therein lies the promise, the problem, and the reason we need to better understand our habits.

Good Habits, Bad Habits: The Science of Making Positive Changes That Stick
by Wendy Wood

"We can do something once and it's a decision, but if we do it many times in the same way, it becomes something totally different."

THAT "SOMETHING TOTALLY DIFFERENT" is what has taken several decades to understand. Competing areas of psychology fought for years about what was a habit, what created habits, and whether habits really mattered. At a low point in the 1980s, goals and evaluations gained favor in psychology circles, and research moved away from looking more deeply at the complexity of habits. Wendy Wood was one of the researchers who stuck with habits, and as a reader, you get a front row seat in watching how our understanding of habits has evolved. The way she describes habits gives them greater context.

A set of steps repeated over and over get stored in procedural memory, a part of the brain that operates separately from other neurological systems. This separation means we can't think our way into new habits when the encoding process that governs them is structurally hidden from our consciousness. This gives our habits the benefit of long retention not easily overwritten and gives us the opportunity to use our mental energies on more challenging problems. This insight informs other findings around research that we wouldn't traditionally connect with habits.

We have a perception that self-control is an active practice of determination. We envision someone biting their lip or grabbing their chair, white-knuckled, resisting the urge to reach for a sugary treat. The common wisdom defines self-control by the resistance that one experiences. The research indicates something different with people who exhibit high levels of self-control—they seldom report resisting, because there is less often a mismatch between a goal and a desire. Further research has shown that individuals with high self-control perform better on habitual, automatic tasks. Wood quotes those who did the study, saying "self-control may in general operate more by forming and breaking habits."

The best part of *Good Habits, Bad Habits* is Wood's skillful intertwining of how habit-based thinking intersects with all parts of our life. Wood highlights Gary Klein's work with firefighters and how important intuition (or habitual decision-making) is in all lines of work. She discusses the benefits of combining intrinsic, extrinsic, and even uncertain rewards working to change behavior. She even brings out how habits can take away certain things, saying that "repetition strengthens our tendency to act, but it also weakens our sensation of that act."

If there is anything we can learn from researchers like Wood, it's how reliably habits can form given the natural circuitry seated deep inside the brain. We also now know that our habits are easily overlooked by our conscious selves. I am both reassured and a little disappointed by those findings. Habits are not about motivation or willpower. Those two both require repeated prefrontal cortex decision-making, and we only have a limited supply of that brain function in a given day. By leaning into our routine-friendly subsystems, we can be much more effective in creating new habits.

THREE MORE PIECES OF ADVICE FROM WOOD:

1. Consider your environment. For every four additional liquor stores per square mile, men drink 32 percent more beer and women drink 16 percent more wine.
2. Multistep rituals (in Brazil called *simpatias*) reduce anxiety, lower heart rate, and give people a sense of control in times of high uncertainty.
3. Given stress, tiredness, distraction, or lack of ability, our balance tips back toward the habits we have. Make sure you have good ones.

Tiny Habits: The Small Changes That Change Everything
by B. J. Fogg

"I've found that there are only three things we can do that will create lasting change: Have an epiphany, change our environment, or change our habits."

B. J. FOGG picks up at the next logical point on habits: how you effectively and efficiently program yourself for new habits. And I use the word "program" here deliberately.

His research and his writings isolate the particular components of what make up habits and show people how to best utilize each to create new habits. Think of Fogg like a trainer you might hire if you really wanted better habits. He makes it simple to learn. He discerns the particular techniques that work best. And he's also creative in his suggestions on how to engage them.

Only a few pages into the book, Fogg starts talking about a universal model for behavior. He says the model applies to everything, good and bad. Every behavior has three components: motivation, ability, and prompt. Simple, right? When you are trying to change a behavior, start with the prompt and ask if there was a reliable trigger for the behavior. Next, ask how able you were to do the new behavior? Ability affects everything from having necessary resources to knowing what steps need to be taken to perform the new behavior. The final factor to check is motivation. High motivation makes creating a new behavior easy, but motivation fluctuates and can interact with other competing motivations.

Notice I changed the sequence a little from Fogg's original order above. Fogg specifically recommended the altered order for diagnosing behavior change and getting the change you desire. It's another example of the level of process and utility built into the book. You are really getting a three-hundred-page workshop when you read *Tiny Habits*.

Now, imagine you wanted to start a thirty-minute daily meditation practice. Fogg would say take that behavior and make it as small as you can. What if you started with three long breaths seated on the floor in front of your couch? This is where making a habit tiny is a powerful way to work with the ability component. Wendy Wood also stresses this factor with a slightly different term, saying, "If you leave [my] book with one word and one idea, I hope it's friction." Make it easy. Or if you are trying to break a habit, make the behavior hard to do.

There is in fact a whole chapter on how to break habits. And a chapter on working with others on habits. And appendices with scripts, flowcharts, and lists to help you brainstorm habits for common challenges. As I keep saying, this book is packed with tips and lessons to learn how to change your behavior and teach others to do the same.

THE ANATOMY OF TINY HABITS:
1. **Anchor moment:** An existing routine or event that reminds you to do the new tiny behavior.
2. **New tiny behavior:** A simple version of the new habit you want, performed right after the anchor moment.
3. **Instant celebration:** Do something to create positive emotions immediately after the new tiny behavior.

After I [the trigger], I will [your action], and then [your celebration].

Atomic Habits: An Easy and Proven Way to Build Good Habits and Break Bad Ones
by James Clear

"You do not rise to the level of your goals. You fall to the level of your systems."

THAT QUOTE sums up James Clear's approach to habits. We can't depend on the normal triage of to-do lists, willpower, and hope to accomplish what we want to get done. It just takes too much energy. Big projects require consistent efforts over time. Let me speak from personal experience. This book you are reading took over four years to write. The first eighteen months were marked by bursts of activity followed by long stretches of dead time. Things didn't change until I built a system.

Clear's first advice is to make your desired habit obvious. We need a cue to kick off the automated routine. You could put your running shoes next to your bed or put your vitamins at the place where you eat. My cue for writing was finishing breakfast at eight in the morning, walking to my desk, and opening my computer to the already open document that I placed there at the end of the day before. This is what researchers call habit stacking: taking an already existing habit and using that routine to help build the next habit.

Clear's second tenet is to make the new habit attractive. Desire plays a crucial role in activating the neural circuitry for action. We want to use the same mechanism that creates our wanting of chocolate cake and reality television. As we look to form good habits and break bad habits, it's useful to look at the motivations that we naturally possess. "At a deep level, you simply want to reduce uncertainty and relieve anxiety, to win social acceptance and approval, or to achieve status," Clear says. We might also associate the habit with invoking its benefits rather than focusing on the action itself. Wanting to go running is good, but building endurance and speed might connect better with those deeper cravings.

Make it easy is the third piece of Clear's advice. This is where repetition appears. Effortful practice (see Ericsson and Pool's book *Peak*) connects neurons and creates pathways that make actions more and more automatic. "Habits form based on frequency, not time." We could recall Fogg's insight that everything pivots around friction. Placing your shoes next to the bed is a cue that also reduces friction. You can also start small. Don't worry about the run—just put your shoes on and get them tied.

Finally, if we don't create a reward, it will be hard to return back to the habit. In other words, "What is *immediately* rewarded is repeated. What is *immediately* punished is avoided." As I worked on *100 Best Books*, I tracked pages read and words written. Tracking both activities gave me a daily reward and indicated progress on a long-term project. Having an accountability partner is another way to improve the chance you will return to a newly forming habit. Clear ends the book by saying, "The secret to getting results that last is to never stop making improvements. It's remarkable what you can do if you just don't stop."

FINAL QUOTE FROM CLEAR ON FORMING HABITS:
"If a behavior is insufficient in any of the four stages, it will not become a habit. Eliminate the cue and your habit will never start. Reduce the craving and you won't experience enough motivation to act. Make the behavior difficult and you won't be able to do it. And if the reward fails to satisfy your desire, then you'll have no reason to do it again in the future. Without the first three steps a behavior will not occur. Without all four, a behavior will not be repeated."

....

7. The 7 Habits of Highly Effective People: Powerful Lessons in Personal Change
by Stephen R. Covey

"Habits are powerful factors in our lives. Because they are consistent, often unconscious patterns, they constantly, daily express our character and produce our effectiveness... or ineffectiveness."

AFTER TALKING ABOUT the science of habits and a direct model for behavior design, it feels like we might want to look at some kinds of habits worthy of adoption. That's what Stephen Covey did when he studied two hundred years of personal development literature for his doctoral research. In examining self-help, popular psychology, and self-improvement writings, Covey identified two distinct philosophies of self-improvement. The first philosophy is consistent with the principles found in the works of early American visionaries like Benjamin Franklin, who expressed integrity, industry, humility, and simplicity as important. Covey calls this the "Character Ethic," and this was the dominant philosophy in American success literature until the early twentieth century.

Covey found the literature changed significantly after World War I, with a shift in emphasis from quality of character to improvement of personality, behavior, and attitude, or what he called the "Personality Ethic." He takes aim at books, though not by name, like *How to Win Friends and Influence People, Think and Grow Rich,* and *The Power of*

Positive Thinking, saying that at best these books focus on secondary traits, and as Covey writes, "What we are communicates far more eloquently than anything we say or do."

As for the seven habits, Covey divides the first six equally between habits of private victory and habits of public victory. The first private habit, "Be Proactive," can take many different forms. We might examine the circle of influence we have in our life and compare it to our broader circle of concern. His second habit, "Begin with the End in Mind," encourages the use of imagination to envision a set of creative choices about the future. Covey advocates the development of personal mission statements to codify the varying roles and responsibilities of home, work, and community.

"Put First Things First" takes that newly defined identity derived from the mission statements and matches up tasks and priorities to ensure alignment. When Covey asked readers which habit was the most difficult to adopt, this management process ranked number one, and he wrote another book, *First Things First,* to further explore its challenges.

"Self-mastery and self-discipline are the foundation of good relationships with others," Covey writes, and he then moves forward with his three public habits: "Think Win-Win," "Seek First to Understand...Then to Be Understood," and "Synergize." All are based on relationships. "Think Win-Win" is about interpersonal leadership that creates mutual benefits for all parties. The classic negotiation book *Getting to Yes* uses the same philosophy, calling for individuals to use an abundance mentality in their interactions and look past the confining paradigm of the zero-sum game.

Being a good listener is a skill that is helpful in any relationship and sits at the core of "Seek First to Understand, Then to Be Understood." When someone is speaking to us, our natural response is to listen autobiographically: agreeing or disagreeing, asking questions from our point of view, giving advice based on our own experiences, trying to figure out what is making someone feel the way they do based on how we would react. Covey spends much of the chapter on an extended example of a conversation between a disillusioned son and a well-intentioned father. Covey replays the conversation a number of times showing how ineffective listening with our biases can be. When listening, the author writes, "Rephrase the content and reflect the feeling." Then he shows how the conversation completely changes. The second half of the discussion of this habit is about presenting ideas, and Covey returns to Aristotle's rhetorical philosophy of ethos (character), pathos (emotion), and logos (logic).

"Synergize" encapsulates the entire Seven Habits process. When people join together, the whole is greater than the sum of the parts, and greater insights and previously unseen results are achieved. Covey suggests synergy is the third alternative to "My way or the wrong way." All relationships grow when trust and cooperation grow.

The seventh habit, "Sharpen the Saw," returns to the individual but "will renew the first six and will make you truly independent and capable of effective interdependence." Covey believes we all have four dimensions that need continual renewal: the physical, the mental, the spiritual, and the social/emotional. He suggests spending an hour working on the first three every day. Find time for a cardiovascular workout. Read the classics. Keep a journal. Meditate or pray. It is only through recharging that we have the energies to succeed in the other aspects of our lives.

SEAN COVEY'S INSIGHTS FROM THE NEW EDITION OF *THE 7 HABITS*:

1. **Be Proactive:** Positive energy expands the things you can control.
2. **Begin With the End in Mind:** Everyone has a unique contribution to make. Write yours down.
3. **Put First Things First:** Set aside thirty minutes every week and plan your week. Watch it change your life.
4. **Think Win-Win:** Cooperation outperforms competition every time.
5. **Seek First to Understand, Then to Be Understood:** This is the route or technique to better relationships.
6. **Synergize:** There is always a third alternative.
7. **Sharpen the Saw:** Don't ever feel guilty for taking time for yourself.

CHAPTER 11
FOCUS

"If you chase two rabbits, you will not catch either one."
—Russian Proverb

We all identify with the challenge of getting things done. Our livelihood and our legacy are ultimately judged by the work we do in the world.

Part of what makes the topic difficult is the disagreement about what precisely the cause is of not getting things done. The problem looks different for different people. For some they see all the possibilities and overanalyze the options to the point of decision paralysis. Others plow into their to-do list with vigor but often without connection to a broader vision. Folks like myself are easily tempted by a new idea, followed by another, and then another. Each of these reflects a natural tendency toward the work we each like doing but also shows the potential downsides of those inclinations.

Time commonly gets blamed. We often say things like "I don't have enough time" or "I need to manage my time better." We can't control time or accumulate more of it. And we certainly can't manage time.

The choice we have available is what we do with our attention. Attention is the precious resource we need to manage and direct toward the work we want to accomplish. The skill we want to build is *focus*. We benefit enormously from strengthening our ability to concentrate on a task. That sustained focus is what changes the world, one task at a time. The four books in this chapter each approach the topic differently and offer a variety of perspectives on how focus is the core competency of success.

The Effective Executive: The Definitive Guide to Getting the Right Things Done
by Peter Drucker

"To ask, 'What can I contribute?' is to look for the unused potential in the job. And what is considered excellent performance in a good many positions is often but a pale shadow of the job's full potential of contribution."

PETER DRUCKER starts *The Effective Executive* by asking: If the ultimate measurement of manual labor is efficiency, what is the corollary measure for knowledge workers? The main thesis of his book is that rather than doing things right, knowledge workers must strive for effectiveness by doing the right things. "Nothing else, perhaps, distinguishes effective executives as much as their tender loving care of time," Drucker says.

In his classic style of driving to the heart of the issue, he quotes studies that show how humans have a poor perception of time and are worse at remembering how they spend their time. Drucker suggests keeping a diary to track one's activities. If more than half of your time is dictated by others, control needs to be gained back. Three common time sponges that need special attention include doing things that don't need to be done, doing things that could be better done by others, and doing things that require others to do unnecessary things.

Drucker dedicates a whole chapter to contribution, asserting that this type of measurement provides focus. At the organizational level, an eye on contribution shifts the attention upward and outward toward clients, customers, and constituents. He believes that communication, teamwork, self-improvement, and development of others all become natural extensions of contribution.

Contribution itself comes only with concentration. Drucker felt this was the one true secret to effectiveness, and his statement, "Effective executives do first things first and they do one thing at a time," foreshadows both Stephen Covey's *The 7 Habits of Highly Effective People* and David Allen's *Getting Things Done*. With a focus on one activity, executives ask important questions about abandoning weak initiatives, especially ones that have never met expectations. Leaving the past is central to progress. The very nature of the job of the executive is to make decisions about committing resources to the possibilities of tomorrow.

Decision-making is Drucker's final practice of effectiveness. Being effective is solving the problem once. Effective executives look at problems as generic to start with and try to solve them with rules that will be simple and easy to follow for everyone, not just those involved in the current issue. Solutions that everyone in the organization can understand improve the likelihood of their adoption. The decision is not complete until it is put into action. Drucker again preceded recent authors like Larry Bossidy and Ram Charan in *Execution,* when he emphasized the idea that a decision is merely intent if it is not a part of someone's responsibilities.

Time. Contribution. Concentration. Decision-making. Each of these subjects has been covered in a myriad of works since *The Effective Executive.* Drucker stands apart in his writing directed to the executive and covering the topics at just the right level of detail and from just the right perspective to enable action.

DRUCKER ON DOING FIRST THINGS FIRST:
- Effective executives do the first things first, and they do one thing at a time.
- No matter how well an executive manages their time, the greater part of it will still not be their own.
- To get really productive time requires self-discipline and an iron determination to say no.
- Concentration is necessary precisely because the executive faces so many tasks clamoring to be done.
- The only question around priority is which will make the decision—the executive or the pressures.

Get Everything Done: And Still Have Time to Play
by Mark Forster

"Regular focused attention is the key to virtually every problem and challenge in life, and the more we learn how to direct and focus our attention, the more skilled we will be at life."

IN THE INTRODUCTION to *Get Everything Done,* Mark Forster offers a challenge to the reader. He asks readers to think about one thing they want to accomplish tomorrow, and when tomorrow arrives, do it. If you are successful, Forster says pick another item for the next day, but choose a task that is slightly more difficult to complete. If that ends up being too easy, commit to completing two things the following day. Some find the exercise easy, while others struggle with the shifting priorities and commitments. Repeat this daily ritual until you feel confidence in your ability to finish what you say you are going to start. Create a habit of focused attention.

    I appreciate there might be some risk in choosing an author and work that you may not know for this collection, but Forster has written five books, addressing the problems with traditional time management, creating goals that create real change, and explaining the nuances of different techniques to get more done. The conclusions all come from his work as a coach, and I think we too often forget that we read books to learn things. That means we need authors who are good teachers.

    As a coach, Forester says that time management is the number one requested item for help. You might recognize some of the symptoms of his new clients: always behind on work, becoming distracted by all the other things to do, feeling stretched by more and more things to be done. The primary technique of time management that Forster begins with is saying no. Start by reducing the amount of work you have or by slowing down the rate by which you take it on. Forster suggests that we take on too much by saying yes too often to those around us. We have to literally learn how to say no to loved ones and those we value in our lives. Be prepared to say no more than once.

After we reduce the number of things we need to do, we allow more focus and improve our ability to get those fewer things done. I could talk about how Forster says we need checklists rather than to-do lists or his highly adaptive version of working intervals (you might recognize it as the Pomodoro technique). Those tactics all drive at the core problem: overcoming resistance. Resistance to getting work done may not look like resistance at first—procrastination, unfocused anxiety, and (my personal crutch) spending time on trivial work. Antidotes like breaking large tasks into smaller ones and building routines through strong habits reduces the ways we waste our precious attention and, as Forster says, helps us avoid sabotaging "all of our goals and plans and hopes and dreams." *Get Everything Done* is the perfect starting point for making sure your action system addresses the big problems that keep you from getting work done.

THOSE WHO ARE SUCCESSFUL AT MANAGING THEIR LIVES ARE VERY DIFFERENT FROM THOSE WHO ARE NOT:

- Good time managers are decisive; poor time managers are impulsive.
- Good time managers work from the big picture; poor time managers get bogged down in trivia.
- Good time managers have good systems; poor time managers have poor systems or none at all.
- Good time managers keep work and play in balance; poor time managers have work and play unbalanced—so both aspects suffer.
- Good time managers' response to fear is action; poor time managers' response to fear is avoidance.

GTD Getting Things Done: The Art of Stress-Free Productivity
by David Allen

"A significant part of your psyche cannot help but keep track of your open loops, and not as an intelligent, positive motivator, but as a detractor from anything else you need or want to think about, diminishing your capacity to perform."

GETTING THINGS DONE is one of the best titled books of all time. It's exactly what we all want and what we wish we could do more. David Allen believes the problem starts with all the things we are trying to do. The first problem is almost all of us have no idea how many things there are on our to-do lists. Through thirty years of working with clients, Allen estimates most people have between fifty and 150 things that they are trying to get done at any given time. The question that Allen asks for the rest of the book is "OK, great, so what are those things?"

We quickly discover that we don't know. We think we can store all the things in our brain, on some sticky notes, in email, on our calendars, through unopened letters and the pile of books sitting next to our bed. With no universal list, our brain keeps looking at all of these piles of things to do, nervously wondering if there is something hidden in the stacks that needs our immediate attention.

Once we have collected all the things to be done, a different problem appears: What's next? Some things, like bills, have a clear next action attached. Other tasks, like our stack of unread books, carry intentions that may shift over time with changing interests. That ambiguity exists alongside many things on our lists. Progress requires clarity, or those things will continue to consume valuable attention. My biggest learning from Allen to this day is his advice to start every item on our list with a verb—read new book, pay electric bill, buy plane ticket. Knowing what the next action is clarifies our relationship to the task and closes the open loops.

To keep organized, Allen says we need buckets—a projects list, support materials for projects, a calendar, a next actions list, a waiting-for list, reference materials, and a someday list. There is a lot there. It's the longest chapter in the book. With everything in its bucket, you build a regular cadence to reflect on everything. The "weekly review" acts as a cornerstone activity of *Getting Things Done*, providing an opportunity to update everything with inputs and intuitions about where your projects are headed. Finally, we engage with the work balancing context, available time, available energy, and priority.

"I'm in the focus business," Allen says in the final part of *Getting Things Done,* as he walks us through the thinking that gets us into trouble with the work we want to do. He says that intelligent and creative people are the most likely to procrastinate because they have the imagination to envision the nightmare scenarios of all that could go wrong. The solution is to figure out the next action. Allen says our lives are equal parts making it up as we go along and making it happen. When we leave our work ambiguously defined, we fail on both counts. Defining the next action, Allen says, "forces clarity, accountability, productivity, and empowerment." That focus benefits you and, if instilled in a culture, can bring the same benefits to teams and organizations. Remember this is all in service of using your valuable attention to focus *on* the work, not think about the work.

BASIC REQUIREMENTS FOR MANAGING COMMITMENTS:
1. Anything you consider unfinished in any way must be captured in a trusted system outside your mind, or what I call a collection tool, that you know you'll come back to regularly and sort through.
2. You must clarify exactly what your commitment is and decide what you have to do, if anything, to make progress toward fulfilling it.
3. Once you've decided on all the actions you need to take, you must keep reminders of them organized in a system you review regularly.

The ONE Thing: The Surprisingly Simple Truth about Extraordinary Results
by Gary Keller and Jay Papasan

> "'Going small' is ignoring all the things you could do and doing what you should do. ... It's realizing that extraordinary results are directly determined by how narrow you can make your focus."

EARLY IN *The ONE Thing*, Gary Keller tells a story of coaching sessions he was holding with a set of newly hired executives. He quickly noticed that work was getting done, but not the most important work. So he shortened the list to three things for each week, but his team still left their biggest tasks incomplete. He narrowed it down to two items with no better results. Finally he said, "What's the ONE thing you can do such that by doing it everything else would be easier or unnecessary?"

While the first three books in this chapter might not seem like they are about focus, there is no question what *The ONE Thing* is about, and several opening chapters dispel commonly held beliefs about attention and focus: Extraordinary results come from a small number of things, not by treating everything equally. If we know multitasking is dangerous (for instance, texting while driving), why would we ever tolerate it when doing our most important work? Discipline helps but habits activate important actions more consistently. Do your most important work early in the day; don't depend on willpower.

Those myths are further resolved through a three-part mindset. The first is the focusing question that Keller asked his executives—"What's the ONE thing...?" The question can be used in a big-picture sense to create vision, strategy, or direction. It can also be used in a smaller sense to start a day or return to the activity that is going to generate the most leverage.

The second mindset is making "the ONE thing" question a habit and because, as they quote Ross Garber, "Many things may be important, but only one can be the most important." You might build the habit by saying, "Until my ONE thing is done, everything else is a distraction." The authors say the back of their book—composed of a large question mark above a small block of text saying "What's Your One Thing?"—was designed to be used as a visual reminder.

Finally, when you have the answer, you need to block out time on your calendar every day to work on your ONE thing. To paraphrase their work, you go small on the task and then you go big on the time devoted to it. The authors call this time-blocking, and they recommend four hours a day. Yes, four hours. Stephen King does it with his writing. Top real estate agents do it with lead generation. The toughest part of time-blocking is protecting that time from other incursions like phone calls, coworker drop-ins, and new ideas that bubble up but are outside the scope of your ONE thing.

The authors sum up their book by saying, "At any moment in time there can only be ONE thing, and when that ONE thing is in line with your purpose and sits atop your priorities, it will be the most productive thing you can do to launch you toward the best you can be."

FOUR PROVEN WAYS TO TIME BLOCK AND BATTLE DISTRACTIONS:
1. **Build a bunker:** Find somewhere to work that takes you out of the path of disruption and interruption.
2. **Store provisions:** Have any supplies, material, snacks, or beverages you may need so you can avoid leaving your bunker.
3. **Sweep for mines:** Turn off your phone, shut down your email, and exit your internet browser.
4. **Enlist support:** Tell those most likely to seek you out what you're doing and when you'll be available.

CHAPTER 12
CREATIVE WORK

"There are two kinds of people, those who do the work and those who take the credit. Try to be in the first group; there is less competition there."
—Indira Gandhi

In a book about work and life, I thought we needed a chapter specifically for work. Much of what is covered here is the application of the other concepts in *100 Best Books*. I want more people to be inspired by the work they do. That requires bringing energy, imagination, and possibility to those efforts no matter what field you work in. We need examples, anecdotes, stories, and quotes from the people making creative ways to work. Let's start with Tom Peters being specific and inspiring.

50 The Project 50: Reinventing Work
by Tom Peters

"The high impact project is the gem...the nugget...the fundamental atomic particle from which the new white collar world will be constructed and/or reconstructed. ... I aim to focus in these pages on what I call 'the missing 98 percent'...the 'stuff' of creating...and selling...and implementing...projects you'll still be bragging and chortling about...**10**(!) years from now."

I AGREE! The fundamental particle of work is the project, and the project is made up of smaller components. Those components are governed by other forces that are talked about at length in the reviews throughout this book. But the project itself needs more attention. The coming together of people, effort, circumstances, standards, need, and purpose creates the possibility for solutions that are generous, considered, noteworthy, and deeply rewarding. Is that not the kind of work we all want to be doing?

I am channeling a bit of Tom Peters here. There is an exuberance and determination to his writing, with a touch of discontent. He constantly sees the possibility of everything being better and how that positively impacts everyone and everything involved in a project. I think business and even work itself has gotten a bad reputation. When I read a book like *The Project 50*, I am revitalized. It makes clear all the ways that "better" is possible on every project. Take this, for example:

"Consider carrying around a little card that reads:

WOW!
BEAUTIFUL!
REVOLUTIONARY!
IMPACT!
RAVING FANS!"

The physical book is out of print and hard to find, but you can still find it as an ebook. I included *The Project 50* because the inspiration is directed squarely at work, and we need more inspiration at work.

Peters loves lists; he includes them in every one of his books. He says they are critical. In fact, #39 in his *The Project 50* list is "Listmania. Ye Shall Make Lists…and the Lists Shall Make Ye Omniscient. (No Joke)."

IN AN ODE TO LIST MAKING, HERE'S MY TOP TEN LIST FROM *THE PROJECT 50*:

1. Bugs in the invoicing system. The yearly storeroom cleanup. What could these become? Always look for the wider, weirder, or deeper source for your projects.
2. "On time. On budget. Who cares?" Projects should stir our souls.
3. Concoct a real test of some part of "it" in the next seventy-two hours. Quick prototyping. Now. Now. Now.
4. Read great books on great projects, like the Pulitzer Prize-winning *Making of the Atomic Bomb* by Richard Rhodes, *The Last Place on Earth: Scott and Amundsen's Race to the South Pole* by Roland Huntford, or *747: Creating the World's First Jumbo Jet and Other Adventures from a Life in Aviation* by chief engineer Joe Sutter. *Apollo 13* is my all-time favorite "projects" movie for the high-stakes, life-and-death timeline, and its deep humanity.
5. Who ever put "project management" and "sales" in the same sentence? They should! Sales is the hefty part of the battle. It forces clarity, focus, drive, and faith.
6. Build a binder! Every article. Every pitch deck. All the analytics. It will be more diary than planner. Include the frivolous and foolhardy…and the serious and sober.
7. Humor is the secret weapon. Find the especially zany, zestful, or funny colleague and ask them to get involved immediately.
8. As David Kelley of IDEO, says, "Reward success and failure equally. Punish inactivity."
9. I-M-P-A-C-T! Henry James asked this as his ultimate question of one's work: "Was it worth doing?"
10. Stay with the project to the end. The "last two percent fanaticism" is what often separates a "pretty good job" from a "WOW."

Orbiting the Giant Hairball: A Corporate Fool's Guide to Surviving with Grace
by Gordon MacKenzie

"Orville Wright did not have a pilot's license."

GORDON MACKENZIE, an artist and teacher, wrote *Orbiting The Giant Hairball* about his thirty years spent working at Hallmark. One of his early managers referred to the company's Creative division, in which they both worked, as "a giant hairball." MacKenzie was bothered by that description until he pondered the question, "Where do hairballs come from?" He decides, "Well, two hairs unite. Then they're joined by another, and another. Before long, where there was once nothing, this tangled, impenetrable mass has begun to form." The growing organizational physics of normalcy and conformity pull everyone and everything toward its hairy core.

Now, the mass and scale of the giant hairball is precisely what allows organizations to be successful *and*, at the same time, keeps the people (and the organization itself) from ever reaching its full potential. MacKenzie doesn't think the work is in untangling the hairball. He writes about the *and*—the ways to draw power and strength from the organization *and* stay in a creative orbit.

MacKenzie offers a map to the creativity roadblocks inherent in organizations. Take his boss, Robert McCloskey, in the Contemporary Design division. MacKenzie marvels at the creative chaos his manager managed to keep viable—both in terms of financial viability and cultural viability. "[McCloskey] spent countless hours lobbying [Hallmark founder J. C.] Hall and his courtiers on the value and the values of Contemporary's then-renegade product line," MacKenzie writes. There is a particular kind of work needed to stay in orbit.

That doesn't mean that MacKenzie doesn't run afoul of the hairball. In another story, MacKenzie enlists the facilities manager to help him acquire antique furnishings for his newly orbiting Humor Workshop division. On one trip, he finds a dozen antique milk cans that he believes will serve as perfect wastebaskets. By the next Monday, he and the facilities manager are called into a meeting with the Purchasing department. Policies have been violated.

Roll-top desks and the stained-glass windows they plan to use as cubicle dividers are on the approved furnishings list. Milk cans are not. Accused of procuring unapproved office supplies, MacKenzie becomes furious. His clear-headed partner, much more familiar with the inner workings of purchasing, quickly suggests the items be donated to the corporate art collection and loaned back to MacKenzie's new department. "What a great idea," says the purchasing manager. Case closed.

The story in the book that is worth the entirety of your money and time is when MacKenzie takes a new role, his final position at Hallmark before retiring. He argued with his boss about what his title would be. MacKenzie proposed "Paradox." His manager added "The." And for the next three years, he served as "The Paradox." I choose not to say anything more, but I promise you, hearing the whole story is worth it.

Let me share one more story about orbits and hairballs. This book was originally self-published. I own a copy and it is beautiful—bare book boards, the spine wrapped in black leather, stamped with the title and the author's name. One of the first pages in the book is a translucent sheet, covered in the words "blah blah blah" except for an occasional alternative like "empowerment" or "intrapreneurial" or "restructuring." This amalgamated creation of paper and cloth would never have been approved by one of the giant publishing hairballs. A hairball did acquire the book a couple years later and produced a lesser-quality, more easily producible version (no "blah blah blah" sheet). Still, I am glad the book is available to a much wider audience. All of MacKenzie's words and illustrations are there. It is equally exquisite that the book's publishing journey communicates just as much tension to me as the contents of the book itself.

MACKENZIE WRITES:

"Only the Renegades in Orbit, removed from the Hairball's obsession with quantifying everything, are free to reap the unpredictable bounty of the inscrutable creative process. If an organization wishes to benefit from its own creative potential, it must be prepared to value the vagaries of the unmeasurable as well as the certainties of the measurable."

PROGRESS: **CREATIVE WORK**

Keep Going: 10 Ways to Stay Creative in Good Times and Bad
by Austin Kleon

"Part of the artist's job is to help tidy up the place, to make order out of chaos, to turn trash into treasure, to show us beauty where we can't see it."

AUSTIN KLEON is a student of the process. If you have read *Steal Like An Artist*, you've seen all the ways that he collects the permissions of other artists to draw the conclusion that "NOTHING IS ORIGINAL." If you have read *Show Your Work!*, the second chapter is titled "Think Process, Not Product" and advocates using your notes, prototypes, and research as ways to always be sharing your work with the world. *Keep Going* is all process, from procrastination to procedure to production. And I put the book in this chapter because he says, "I think the principles apply to anyone trying to sustain a meaningful and productive creative life, including entrepreneurs, teachers, students, retirees, and activists."

Kleon starts the book with "Every day is Groundhog's Day." He is of course referring to the famous Bill Murray movie, where weatherman Phil Connors gets stuck repeating the same day. Kleon's warning is that the work of an artist is returning back to the same empty page or blank canvas each day. Establish a daily routine, he says. This has been a hard lesson for me to learn. Several years ago, I signed on for a big client project. I'd never taken on a similar endeavor—the magnitude of it, my lack of skill, the definitive timeline. There was nothing but struggle...until I built a daily routine and put down my expectations. Size, speed, and skills all got solved by having that daily practice. This book you are reading now is a result of that same deliberate process of reading books and writing one review after another, every morning, day after day for three years.

In Chapter 5 of *Keep Going*, there is a section titled "Pay Attention to What You Pay Attention to." As my kids move out into the world, I say exactly that. "Reread your diary. Flip back through your sketchbook," Kleon says. I have an electronic document for each year going back to 2009 where I capture all sorts of notes. I keep quotes I liked.

There are plans for trips, listing the people I plan to meet with. There are important first draft emails where I was working out the right tone and wording. I am always fascinated by both the things I don't remember and the themes that I return to over and over again. Kleon writes, "When you have a system for going back through your work, you can better see the bigger picture of what you've been up to, and what you should do next."

To do the work that this world needs, we need to be open to change. It is a theme in Kleon's book. It is the whole point of creating this collection of a hundred books: to provide as many touchpoints as we can to all the potential ways we can shift and adjust our views and attitudes. Kleon says we should read old books so we can see the similarity of struggle throughout time. Everything we do is in response to something or someone else, so we should also find "like-hearted" people in the here and now, people who Alan Jacobs says are "temperamentally disposed to openness and have habits of listening." Because as Kleon says, "The only way to keep going and the only way to keep making art [is] to be open to the possibility and allow yourself to be changed."

MY FAVORITE LINES THAT KLEON QUOTES:
- "I paint with my back to the world." —Agnes Martin
- "It's as true today as it ever was: He who seeks beauty will find it." —Bill Cunningham
- "I can never find what I want, but the benefit is that I always find something else." —Irvine Welsh
- "Imitate the trees. Learn to lose in order to recover, and remember that nothing stays the same for long." —May Sarton

PROGRESS: **CREATIVE WORK**

The Practice: Shipping Creative Work
by Seth Godin

"Better is possible. But not if we continue to settle, continue to hide, and continue to scurry along the same paths."

I AM HOPING that you won't skip this book because you think it isn't for you. You might think your work is not creative work if you take tech-support calls from your home office. Or write marketing copy in a coffee shop. Or work for a coffee shop. It is all work. And you can choose for it to be creative work. The way Seth Godin talks about work is through the lens of process, because our best, most creative work is going to come from our processes.

Trusting and maintaining your practice is the primary theme of the book. Trying to go deeper than that in a short review is harder because of Godin's approach to writing books. His chapters are just a page or two in length. Some feel familiar. Others stop you cold. The ideas are loosely connected and loosely organized. Over the course of your reading, the 220 different ideas start to reveal a larger mosaic.

Godin wants you to take the "magical thinking" out of your thinking. "Creativity is a choice," he writes. "It's not a bolt of lightning from somewhere else." Ignore the people who tell you that there is a muse and your job is to be there when it calls. That thinking leads us to believe in an illusion like writer's block. Or a myth like "I just lack talent." That pessimism doesn't serve the process, it just gives us a place to hide. That mental trash makes it easy to miss what the real work is.

"The commitment then is to sign up for days, weeks, or years of serial incompetence and occasional frustration," he writes. There is the realization that we have to sell that work to an audience if we are going to be professionals. We are going to have to live in the tension-filled space of waiting to see if what we have made will serve others. It might mean finding better clients. That is a scary place for an artist. Looking at a blank page of possibility every day is scary; the real magical part is becoming the person who does.

It's easier when you focus your art on your audience. "This is not for me. It is for them." This creates abundance. In most cases, more is what is needed. More courage, more practice, more reps, more learning, more sharing. "'Here, I made this.' These four words carry with them generosity, intent, risk, and intimacy."

So, "Chop wood, carry water," Layman Pang says. Just do the work. "If the problem can be solved, why worry? And if the problem can't be solved, then worrying will do you no good," says Shantideva. So just do the work. Godin rephrases Nike's famous slogan as "Merely do it." Add nothing extra and do the work. "Ultimately, the goal is to become the best in the world at being you." And the only way is to—you guessed it—do the work.

THIS IS THE NARRATIVE THAT GODIN SUGGESTS WE RETURN TO AGAIN AND AGAIN:
1. This is a practice.
2. It has a purpose.
3. I desire to create change.
4. The change is for someone specific.
5. How can I do it better?
6. Can I persist long enough to do it again?
7. Repeat.

SECTION THREE
GROWTH

**CUSTOMERS
INFLUENCE
MARKETING
SALES**

CHAPTER 13
CUSTOMERS

"The best way to find yourself is to lose yourself in the service of others."
—Mahatma Gandhi

The primary focus of the books in this chapter is also related to the area of work. Fred Reichheld talks about the importance of asking customers for feedback. Geoffrey Moore discusses how different customers need different things. Jim Kalbach helps readers get clear on what the "thing" is. I also think there is a broader application to this chapter.

Everyone has customers they serve. Accounting serves the internal business functions. Churches serve their congregations. Parents serve their kids. Kathy Sierra's shift from creating better products to creating better users makes it easier to see this broader definition of customers and what we might do to be of service to them.

GROWTH: **CUSTOMERS**

❓ The Ultimate Question 2.0: How Net Promoter Companies Thrive in a Customer-Driven World
by Fred Reichheld with Rob Markey

"It always seemed to me that success in business and in life should result from your impact on the people you touch—whether you have enriched their lives or diminished them. Financial accounting, for all its sophistication and influence, completely ignores this fundamental idea."

ORGANIZATIONS develop standardized products and procedures with the intention of delivering value at scale. Fees and penalties become the methods to keep customers behaving in a way that works in their system. Net Promoter Score (NPS) gives companies the potential to see if the system is working for customers. When companies build systems that act in a generous way, customers in turn will be generous in their loyalty and their praise.

The NPS methodology is simple. After you have an interaction with a customer, follow up and ask them two questions: "What's the likelihood you would recommend us to a friend or colleague?" with the option to choose on a scale of 0 to 10, and "What is the primary reason for your score?" The magic of that simplicity is the insights it unlocks.

As a customer yourself, I am going to guess that you have been asked these questions. Financial services, airlines, technology, and even health care are just a few of the sectors that have adopted the methodology, and for good reason. Fred Reichheld and the folks at Bain & Company have deeply researched the connection between loyalty and growth for over forty years. "We first compiled data demonstrating that a 5 percent increase in customer retention could yield anywhere from a 25 percent to a 100 percent improvement in profits," says Reichheld. Follow-up research showed companies with highly loyal customers grew at twice the rate of their competitors.

The next step in the research was to look at the interactions between scoring and future behavior. Reichheld's research found three groups each with distinctive behaviors. Promoters, who gave scores of 9 or 10, showed the highest repurchase rates, are less price sensitive, and accounted for more than 80 percent of referrals. Passives, who gave scores of 7 or 8, acted like their label with 50 percent fewer referrals than promoters and easy switching when given a better offer. Detractors, which score companie between 0 and 6, account for 80 percent of negative word of mouth and consume more customer service resources complaining about their experiences.

This second edition of the book brings more nuance and useful advice to the methodology. Keeping surveys short can double participation rates. The exact scoring scale can be flexible, with some companies using a 0 to 5 scale and getting reliable results. The question itself should also be tested. Bain's research shows that business-to-business environments are better served with a question like "How likely is it that you would recommend that we do more of our business with Company X?" Avoid anonymous surveys and build mechanisms to follow up directly with unhappy customers. Use verbatim feedback whenever possible. Spending time and effort building reliable systems for collecting data will build confidence and internal buy-in. And finally, be careful of connecting financial incentives to NPS because of the risk that individuals start to influence customers and their responses.

NPS may sound like another marketing survey, but Reichheld implores practitioners to think of the measurement in the same regard as net income, as an operational metric to drive decision-making. Reichheld writes, "Line management has to take ownership of the tool and feel accountable for using it to improve performance." When that happens, the results are remarkable. Logitech has adopted an NPS milestone for new products, where devices may be delayed or even canceled if they don't meet a minimum NPS threshold. At Progressive, NPS has become a primary tool for evaluating improvements and connecting activities to retention. Apple reports that when store managers started following-up with detractors the company generated $25 million in additional revenue in its first year. Results like this reinforce the value of customer service when the finance function is often quick to view those activities as optional.

ESSENTIAL NPS ADVICE FOR PRACTITIONERS (AS FOUND IN THE BOOK'S APPENDIX):

- Close the loop with customers quickly.
- Focus on engaging with what your customers are really telling you.
- Link NPS to business economics.
- Build NPS into monthly financial reviews.
- Create transparency internally across the organization and externally with customers.
- Senior leaders need to take a leap of faith and not wait for glowing results.

Badass: Making Users Awesome
by Kathy Sierra

"We've been looking in the wrong place. The key attributes of sustained success don't live in the product. The key attributes live in the user."

I HAVE ALWAYS LIKED the startup adage, "If you want your product to be successful, make something people want." That obvious truth is easily lost in the pressure to build something and be successful. Kathy Sierra makes one more obvious step and says don't focus on creating great products—focus on creating great users. To do that, "Imagine that your competitive advantage is not how *you* compare to the competition but how your *users* compare to the competition's users."

The shift to a user focus solves some key problems. First, it helps us get clear on what the product should help the user do, whether that's taking better photos, writing better books, or making better cookies. Making better users creates people who want to talk about the successes they are having and how they have been helped. That talk leads to recommendations between friends, the most effective marketing a company could ask for.

When we build a product, all the talk tends to be about the features and what the product can do. When we change the focus to the user, the focus needs to shift to what the user can do. Expert users need to build expertise. They need new skills, and have to be able to acquire those skills. Sierra offers two options. First, users need to practice—and not just any kind of practice. They need to engage in *deliberate* practice. This points to the deep research by Anders Ericsson. Sierra says, "Design practice exercises that will take a fine grained task from unreliable to 95% reliability, within one to three 45–90 minute sessions." If the skill is too big, break it down into smaller chunks. If the skill is too complex, change the criteria for success. The whole point is to always practice in that spot that is just beyond our current abilities.

In a story from neuroscientist David Eagleman, he recounts how during World War II aircraft spotters in the United Kingdom were incredibly important in determining if incoming aircraft were friend or foe. But there were only a handful of spotters who were reliable at identifying high-altitude British aircraft, and attempts to teach the skill to others had failed. The British finally paired experts with novices and asked the beginners to just guess. Experts would provide an immediate yes or no, and eventually novices would acquire the same skills as the experts, not through defined criteria but by perceived knowledge. This method has been used by chicken breeders to determine the biological sex of chicks and by researchers to teach civilians how to read aircraft instrumentation without classroom training. So expertise can also be developed through exposure to a high quantity of high-quality examples and letting the brain do the pattern-matching.

Finally, we need to help users get through the tough times. Day two of snowboarding or learning Japanese are often the point when most people will give up. To create awesome users, we need to tell them when they are going to reach the hard parts and acknowledge how difficult it is. Honesty will keep users moving forward. Progress and payoffs will also keep them moving forward. Martial arts use colored belts. Video games use levels. In each case, the user is demonstrating acquired skills before they advance to the next stage of difficulty. That sense of progress changes how we feel and how we perform. What payoff can you give your novice user in the first thirty minutes of reading your book or using your tool?

Here is the opportunity that Sierra presents as she ends the book: "You have the chance to help people become more badass not only at using your tool within a meaningful context, but badass at life." That feels like a great goal for all of us.

MORE GREAT QUESTIONS ABOUT USERS:
- Where do your users get stuck?
- What did those who did become experts do differently from those who wanted to but didn't?
- How do we keep users moving forward?
- What can people now do *better* because of [X]?
- What can they now show others?

The Jobs to Be Done Playbook: Align Your Markets, Organizations, and Strategy around Customer Needs
by Jim Kalbach

"JTBD provides a way to understand, classify, and organize otherwise irregular feedback. It not only directs you to look at your markets differently, but it also provides a clear and stable unit of analysis: the job."

IF YOU ARE building new products and services, you are dancing with risk. You are trying to figure out what your customers need next. It is easy to deceive ourselves on the path to that answer. We ask leading questions to get the answers we want to hear, or maybe we don't even ask because we believe that we already know or know better. We need assistance to keep our sights straight. The Jobs to Be Done (JTBD) framework can be a real help.

A job is the core unit of activity—a specific task defined in functional terms. Jobs are performed and completed. Their descriptions contain a verb with an object (*prepare a meal, listen to music, get a promotion*). Once the job is defined, the customer need is created by adding a direction of change and unit of measure (*minimize the time needed to get a promotion*). The need gives us an indication of the progress that the customer wants to make. We might also add a clarifier at the end to further identify the circumstances (*minimize the time needed to get a promotion while staying at the current employer*).

Getting the need right is really hard. I chose Kalbach's *The Jobs to Be Done Playbook* because he explains and consolidates the various flavors of JTBD to provide a clear process to use in your own setting. Here are the five common JTBD principles that Kalbach believes are generally agreed upon:

1. People employ products and services to get *their* job done, not interact with *your* organization.
2. Jobs are stable over time, even as technology changes.
3. People seek services that enable them to get more of their job done quicker and easier.
4. Making the job the unit of analysis makes innovation more predictable.
5. JTBD isn't limited to one discipline; it's a point of view that can be applied throughout an organization.

Understanding jobs and their associated needs requires research. Interviews with customers and prospects let you understand the needs and assess customers' emotions with regard to their current options. Anthony Ulwick believes you should create a job map to identify what the job performer does at each stage of executing a job to determine the features needed. Bob Moesta and Chris Spiek propose what they call the "switch interview," where you start with the purchase and slowly work your way backwards through the purchasing journey, examining the decisions that led to the prior ones. No matter the method, the gathered information helps organizations assess value and see where the potential opportunities are to better help customers.

Instead of products or services, jobs can serve as defining the unit of value inside organizations. Companies structure employee positions and reporting structures around the jobs to be done. Organizational strategy might look at the amount charged in relation to the effectiveness of getting the job done. In the case of financial services provider USAA, they dropped traditional product management functions and created experience managers to manage the jobs their customers needed done. One job the company identified was daily spending, which led them to combine checking account and credit card functions under the same experience manager. These all are great examples of how JTBD gives you an amazing opportunity to better understand how to serve your customers.

OTHER BOOKS TO READ THAT EXPLAIN AND EXPAND UPON JTBD:
- *Jobs to Be Done: Theory to Practice* by Anthony Ulwick.
- *When Coffee and Kale Compete* by Alan Klement.
- *Talking to Humans: Success Starts with Understanding Your Customers* by Giff Constable.
- *Who Do You Want Your Customers to Become?* by Michael Schrage.

Crossing the Chasm: Marketing and Selling Disruptive Products to Mainstream Customers – Third Edition
by Geoffrey Moore

> "The place where most crossing-the-chasm marketing segmentation gets into trouble is at the beginning, when they focus on a target market or target segment instead of on a target customer."

IN 1962, Everett Rogers wrote the first edition of a book called *Diffusion of Innovations*. The book shared research that had been going on for over a decade and attempted to explain how products were adopted by markets. During this time, there was an enormous amount of innovation in the agriculture sector, so sociologists studied farmers and levels of acceptance to new varieties of potatoes and hybrid corn seed. *Diffusion of Innovations* has gone on to become the second most cited social science book in print. The book is technical but also highly readable. I highly recommend it, but for this collection, I'm going to recommend another book.

Geoffrey Moore's *Crossing the Chasm* captures the crucial points of Everett's work and extends it in important ways. The basis of all adoption theory is that there are five distinct groups of customers who each adopt to change with varying degrees of acceptance. New products and services are first enthusiastically embraced by a small group of leading-edge innovators who are always in search of what's new. They will try anything. Early adopters are also interested in innovation, but they "have the insight to match up an emerging technology to a strategic opportunity." They will take big risks for big returns. Over time, the innovation moves to the mainstream market and encounters the early majority. The early majority wants reliability, proof, and incremental improvements over the current status. The late majority waits for the inexpensive all-in-one option. Laggards wait until they don't have any other option.

Moore confirmed Rogers's research that showed a gap in adoption between each of these groups for adoption to move forward. Moore's important contribution was identifying that the gap between the early adopters and the early majority was much larger than previously thought. With the discovery of this chasm, Moore was finally able to explain the difficulties many early stage technology companies experience. Just as startups feel they are gaining traction due to success in those early markets, revenue growth flattens and companies start to burn through their raised capital. The early majority is not impressed by the reputation or the success with early adopters because their motivations differ. Early adopters see technology as the path to bring transformative change to the companies they work for. The early majority, in contrast, wants reliable components and moderate improvements.

To cross the chasm, Moore says the innovating company needs to marshal all of their efforts on a single destination. The potential customers in the early majority are quite satisfied with what they have. Focusing on a single niche with a small subset of customers creates a beachhead from which to operate. Other companies in the early majority start to feel comfortable with additional reference points. Further confidence is built by building alliances and bringing on partners to connect new innovations with existing ones. The early majority wants to buy new innovation from the proven market leader.

Here is some additional advice. Don't make the mistake of using the same marketing message you used in the early market when selling to the developing mainstream market. Customers in the early market are product-centric buyers who want unique functionality and ease of use. Mainstream customers are market-centric buyers who desire compatibility with standards, solid user experience, and fit for their purposes. At this stage, innovating companies actually *want* competition to show mainstream buyers that there is a market for the product. Publicity efforts should focus on the emergence of a new market rather than landing a company profile that impresses early adopters. As you build out into the mainstream market, always remember that the pragmatic early majority wants to back the market leader.

MOORE'S FILL-IN-THE-BLANK CROSSING-THE-CHASM ELEVATOR PITCH:

For [target customers—beachhead segment only]
who are dissatisfied with [the current market alternatives],
our product is a [product category]
that provides [compelling reason to buy].
Unlike [the product alternative],
we have assembled [key features for the product].

CHAPTER 14
INFLUENCE

"The way you treat people is your single greatest legacy.
Don't let it be an afterthought."
—Unknown

In psychology, there is a field of study that looks at the concept of compliance, where researchers study the circumstances when people are most likely to hear a request and agree to it. But we have all studied this field since the moment we were born. Our survival depended on it as babies. Our social life depended on it as teenagers. And in the world of work, success is in large part due to our ability to influence those around us.

These skills are also agnostic. They can be used to make the world a better place, and in another person's hands, they can be used to cheat and steal. Just a reminder that intention matters in this realm.

Influence: The Psychology of Persuasion
by Robert Cialdini

"I can freely admit it now. All my life I have been a patsy."

IF YOU CHOOSE only five books to read from the one hundred listed in this book, *Influence* should be one of them. I could spend this whole review talking about why and offering praise for what Robert Cialdini has done in this book. I can still remember reading it for the first time over twenty years ago and thinking the book was written by my favorite type of author—a researcher who understands the theories and steps out into the real world to see if those models are true. Cialdini validated his theories by applying for real-world positions ranging from selling vacuum cleaners door-to-door to doing fundraising at universities. He wanted to see if the influencing techniques these organizations taught in their training matched the existing academic scholarship.

The starting point for the techniques highlighted in *Influence* is that the world is full of too many decisions to bring careful consideration to each one. The way we cope as humans is through a set of built-in mental shortcuts that help us make decisions. Without those, we'd be paralyzed by the mountains of information and endless choices before us. These shortcuts are executed so quickly in our brains that we often don't even notice they happened. *Influence* slows down those processes, lets us see what is happening, and gives us the opportunity to both use the techniques on those we want to influence and protect ourselves from others who might try to take advantage of these subroutines.

In his latest version of *Influence* (568 pages in length), Cialdini offers a model from Gregory Neidert for how his original principles might be better organized given the kind of influence the situation requires. It starts when you first meet someone and there is a new relationship to cultivate. The most common and very natural technique is to see what you have in common with the other person. Cialdini calls this principle *unity*, and it is a new addition to the book. In my rereading of *Influence*, I found out Cialdini grew up in Wisconsin and has been a lifelong Green Bay Packers fan. He and I share both of those things in common and I could immediately feel myself smile when reading those words, appreciating the new connection we shared. It might sound obvious, but people *liking* you is also important early in a new relationship. Compliments to your new friend, frequent interactions with them, and finding ways to cooperate on a common problem builds familiarity and trust. That desire to cooperate also encourages a back-and-forth sharing through *reciprocity*. For example, grocery stores offer free samples to weekend shoppers, knowing that a small taste can often lead to a purchase. Cialdini both praises and warns about reciprocity, saying its power can make it a good method or a manipulative one and to be very aware when others use it.

The next phase of a relationship is often increasing confidence and reducing uncertainty. In the world of book publishing, these are frequent tools used to assure readers about new releases. Expertise is in full display as publishers work to establish *authority*. The author's biography is full of credentials. Notes on the cover indicate past professional and publishing successes. To evoke *social proof*, publishers provide praise and endorsements from reviewers at widely read publications and authors who have written similar books. It is no accident that each product page on Amazon has a section for purchaser reviews.

The last phase of influence is moving someone toward a specific action, maybe buying that book or signing a petition. The most common push is some way to make the offering contain *scarcity*. "Thirty units left in stock!" and "If you buy in the next thirty minutes, we'll include…" play to our high aversion to loss. Fear of missing out is real. A lesser-known tactic is creating *consistency*. Once we move down a path, we are reluctant to deviate. Car dealers do this when they ask a set of questions that have answers with an easy yes— "Do you like this car?" and "Would you buy the car if the price was right?" Even a telemarketer starting a call with a polite question like "How are you feeling tonight?" sets up a *commitment* to the conversation when you say "just fine" so that they can tell you about the people who are not fine and need your help.

The variations are endless. Knowing the techniques of influence will help you with the work you want to do and protect you from those who may not have your best interests at heart.

MORE ADVICE FROM CIALDINI ON INFLUENCE:

- **Unity:** "We-groups" favor the outcomes of fellow members, use their preferences to guide their own actions, and act to benefit the group.
- **Liking:** Build increased familiarity through repeated contact, deliver compliments to the person (and their peers about the person), and cultivate positive associations with complimentary people and organizations.
- **Reciprocity:** The desire to return a favor after receiving a gift is among the most powerful forms of influence. Making an initial concession can activate the same reciprocity with a return concession.
- **Authority:** Individuals with uniforms, titles, and trappings (like maybe someone who has written a book…) have been shown in studies to be given more obedience and deference by those they crossed paths with.
- **Social proof:** When multiple people are seen doing something, the action appears to be correct, valid, feasible, and socially acceptable.
- **Scarcity:** This technique works best when the desired object has become scarce and when we are competing with others for a limited amount available.
- **Consistency and commitment:** Consistency and commitment are most effective when they are active, public, effortful, and seen as internally motivated.

The Catalyst: How to Change Anyone's Mind
by Jonah Berger

"Behavioral scientist Kurt Lewin once noted, 'If you want to truly understand something, try to change it.'"

THERE IS OVERLAP between Jonah Berger's *The Catalyst* and Robert Cialdini's *Influence* (and I take Cialdini's endorsement on the back cover to mean little conflict as well). As humans, we are built in a certain way to hold beliefs, and if we are in the role of trying to bring about change, our most common approach is to push. We present evidence. We explain our position. We keep calling and trying to convince the other party. Berger says this puts the focus in the wrong place—on ourselves. He and Cialdini believe more success happens when you focus on the other person and on what has stopped them from changing already.

Sampling is often seen as activating the powerful effect of reciprocity in Cialdini's model, where Berger connects it with reducing uncertainty. I offer this comparison because you might think Berger has written the same book as Cialdini. That is not the case. Cialdini's objective was to share how people can take simple actions to gain compliance in others. As captured in the title and borrowed from the field of chemistry, Berger suggests finding catalysts that will lower the barriers to change through a different set of physiological features.

Berger offers five barriers to change that are summarized below. I am going to focus on one—corroborating evidence—in this review. It is natural to look for more information when making decisions. It is also well established that similarity (what Cialdini calls unity) matters in the opinions we value. Berger adds to this tenet, saying there are limits to who we value guidance from. In a study about political donations, additional donors to a campaign wanted to see donations from independent sources. Berger writes, "If one [donor] was a family member and another was a coworker, people were more than twice as likely to donate. But if they were two family members or two coworkers, multiple sources didn't have as much impact."

Timing is important in the value people assign to the evidence. Berger's own research into website user acquisition showed again that more invitations from friends matters to new users, but the closer in time between those invitations, the greater the impact. Addiction interventions often involve a dozen people (again, to bring a variety of sources) as they share their concerns all at the same time with the addict. The clear, consistent messages from concerned family members and friends can have profound impacts on the individual.

When and how we sequence evidence impacts how barriers to change are reduced. Change agents are often tasked with planning a widespread "sprinkler" campaign or something more focused within a group or region. Research suggests the best strategy depends on the strength of individuals' attitudes on the topic. "If a little proof is enough to drive action, then a sprinkler strategy is ideal. Go after each group simultaneously," Berger writes, "but when corroborating evidence is needed, concentrating resources becomes important." Anything that is expensive, controversial, time-consuming, or risky will likely require more proof.

Don't push harder. Don't keep asking. Don't expend more energy. Instead, look for the catalyst that can transform the situation with what is already there.

QUESTIONS TO HELP MINIMIZE BARRIERS TO CHANGE:
- **Reduce reactance:** How can you allow for agency? What questions can help people commit to their own conclusion?
- **Ease endowment:** What is the status quo, and what aspects make it attractive? Are there hidden costs of sticking with it that people might not realize?
- **Shrink distance:** Can you start by asking for less? Can you find a dimension on which there is already common ground to bring people closer?
- **Alleviate uncertainty:** Can you lower the barrier to trying it out? Reduce upfront costs? Make decisions reversible?
- **Find corroborating evidence:** How can you provide more proof? How can you concentrate that close in time?

Captivate: The Science of Succeeding with People
by Vanessa Van Edwards

"Every single interaction is an opportunity to understand more about yourself and the people you are with. Being curious about someone is one of the best ways to show you like them."

VANESSA VAN EDWARDS opens her book with a twenty-question quiz to test your level of interpersonal intelligence. She asks readers to evaluate the facial expressions in a series of photographs. She asks, when connecting with someone, if it is better to tell a story or pay a compliment. The last question asks if making someone feel "flattered/attractive/valued/powerful" is the best way to improve their mood. The survey gives you both an opportunity to assess your knowledge and get a sense of her approach in *Captivate*.

Van Edwards takes science-based findings from well-known researchers and her own lab, Science of People, and applies that directly to real-life situations of connection. The biggest strength of *Captivate* is its utility. Like me, there is a good chance you have heard about these researchers in other books or maybe even read their own works. Van Edwards's use of their work is pithy and succinct. The application of those findings makes the research easily applicable at work and at home. The book is divided into parts focused on making better connections when you first meet someone, how to better connect early on, and deepening the relationship over the long-term.

In this review, I am going to do something a little different and share some of the Van Edwards findings.

HERE'S SOME OF THE PROVOCATIVE RESEARCH ON CREATING CONNECTION

- Stanford researcher Van Sloan studied over 2,400 high school students and found the most likable students also liked the most other people, showing higher levels of friendliness and smiling at fellow students.
- Dr. Gary Chapman is a family therapist who noticed his clients showed different patterns of affection toward each other and developed the five love languages—words of affirmation, gifts, physical touch, acts of service, and quality time. These can help you identify how people might like to be shown appreciation.
- Social psychologist Dr. Uriel Foa believes that the value exchanged between people is a core dynamic in relationships—love, service, status, money, goods, and information.
- In a Science of People study, they found successful entrepreneurs got investment deals on the TV show *Shark Tank* when they used

- a unique pitch method 63 percent of the time. Some brought mascots. Others brought celebrities. A unique request or added interactivity improved their chances of success.
- This connects with researcher Dan McAdams's work on self-narratives. He found that knowing what we value can impart a sense of purpose in our life and work. Publishers might tell themselves that books enrich culture and make the world a better place.
- Psychologist Ellen Langer found that when you connect tasks with a purpose, people are more willing to help you reach your goal. You can do that by using the word "because" when you ask for something.
- Asking for advice helps you connect with people in three different ways—by softly admitting a vulnerability, by getting people talking, and by learning more about what matters to them.
- Dr. Paul Ekman studies microexpressions and says there are seven kinds that you should be on the lookout for—anger, contempt, happiness, fear, surprise, disgust, and sadness. These outward bursts can signal internal emotions.

Made to Stick: Why Some Ideas Survive and Others Die
by Chip Heath and Dan Heath

"Unexpected ideas are more likely to stick because surprise makes us pay attention and think. That extra attention and thinking sears unexpected events into our memories. Surprise gets our attention. Sometimes the attention is fleeting, but in other cases surprise can lead to enduring attention. Surprise can prompt us to hunt for underlying causes, to imagine other possibilities, to figure out how to avoid surprises in the future."

PROVERBS are the quintessential sticky ideas. In just a few words, a complex idea is conveyed in a simple and unexpected way. "A bird in the hand is worth two in the bush" is full of concrete elements (bird, hand, bush) that everyone knows. The lesson reminds us to value what we have over what we hope might be. And all of that philosophical complexity is delivered in one sentence with eleven words. This same proverb can be found in Spanish, Polish, medieval Latin, and a dozen other languages. Now *that* is a sticky idea.

You might ask: *Why measure ideas on their stickiness?* The answer is because the ideas that spread the furthest win. Sticky ideas are easy to remember. They possess an intriguing quality that makes us want to share them with others. Brothers Chip and Dan Heath believe you can engineer your ideas to be stickier and their framework can help you do that.

Creating stickiness comes from getting the audience to do these five things in connection with your idea:

1. Pay attention.
2. Understand and remember it.
3. Agree/believe.
4. Care.
5. Be able to act on it.

This list feels like a great set of steps, but the authors don't provide it until the epilogue at the end of *Made to Stick*. They believe that each of these steps matters, but we can easily get in our own way. They call this the curse of knowledge. They write, "Once we know something, we find it hard to imagine what it was like not to know it." We think *of course* people will pay attention, agree, and want to act. Our expertise in finding answers causes us not to see the equally difficult and wholly different problem of telling others. This is the villain that keeps us from building sticky ideas.

Simple, unexpected, concrete, credible, emotional, and stories—those are the qualities that sticky ideas have. These sound similar to the prior list, but they are more tangible, making them less susceptible to our curse of knowledge. Concreteness trumps the abstract. Internet memes and urban myths spread, in part, because of their specific details that involve other qualities like credibility and emotion.

We could talk about each quality individually (and we will shortly below), but they all get rolled together in the creation of great stories.

Stories, the authors say, act as flight simulators for the mind. Researcher Julian Orr demonstrated this through his observation of Xerox repair technicians and their group lunches. What at first looked like complaints shared among coworkers unfolded into a rich learning environment. Over the meal, each technician would share their latest tale of malfunctioning machines. As they did, their lunchmates visualized each problem, preparing themselves for their own future encounters. Further research has shown that visualizing the event activates the same parts of the brain as doing the physical activity and produces about two-thirds of the benefit of actual practice.

We all have the formidable challenge of selling our ideas to others. The startup CEO needs to sell their strategic course correction to employees and investors. Every day, medical professionals advise patients on healthier behaviors to improve quality of life. It's the same for parents, teachers, marketers, and managers. *Made to Stick* gives you the tools to create more traction for your ideas.

THE SIX PRINCIPLES OF STICKINESS:
- **Simple:** Find the core of your idea and determine the single most important thing about it. Then deliver it in the smallest package possible.
- **Unexpected:** Break the pattern of what people expect and create a mystery that makes people curious to find out the conclusion.
- **Concrete:** Write it like a fable and give the listener as many hooks as possible to help them remember it.
- **Credible:** Find a source to draw on—like personal experience, experts, vivid details, or statistics delivered in an accessible way.
- **Emotional:** Make people care by appealing to their self-interest and their identities.
- **Stories:** Stories are simulators for the mind. They help people know how to act and give them energy to move in a new direction.

GROWTH: **INFLUENCE**

How to Win Friends and Influence People: The Only Book You Need to Lead You to Success
by Dale Carnegie

"Dealing with people is probably the biggest problem you face, especially if you are in business. Yes, and that is also true if you are a housewife, architect, or engineer. ... [Our] research revealed that even in such technical lines as engineering, about 15 percent of one's financial success is due to one's technical knowledge and about 85 percent is due to skill in human engineering—to personality and the ability to lead people."

IN MY THIRTY YEARS of professional life, there is no book more read by those whose paths I've crossed than *How to Win Friends and Influence People*. I know that might be a bold claim, but the book has sold more than thirty million copies since its publication in 1936. It is still recommended to salespeople and at new employee orientations. Even my barber once asked for a book recommendation and then, before I could answer, quickly shared her love for Dale Carnegie. My guess is that you have read this book too.

The book continues to impact readers because its writing and its lessons are timeless. "Don't criticize, condemn, or complain." "Show respect for the other person's opinions." "Ask questions instead of giving direct orders." Carnegie's lessons fall at the intersection of kindness, lean-forward self-help, and the Golden Rule. You'll read anecdotes about Ben Franklin, Abraham Lincoln, and John Rockefeller, but that is the only way you might feel the book's age.

If you attempted to bundle all of the book's teachings into a single maxim, it would be "People want to feel important." Carnegie says to give honest and sincere appreciation. Remember a person's name and use it at appropriate points in conversation with them. Encourage others to talk about themselves and talk in terms of their interests. And of course, smile.

Robert Cialdini tells us that getting people to like us is a very important method of creating influence. Jeffery Gitomer says

"I like my sales rep" is the number one reason prospects will buy from you. Knowing the power these techniques have, it is always good to remember your intent: Am I doing things to help others or help myself?

QUOTES CARNEGIE USES TO ANCHOR HIS TEACHINGS:
- "The deepest principle in human nature is the craving to be appreciated." —William James
- "I will speak ill of no man, and speak all the good I know of everybody." —Ben Franklin
- "I consider my ability to arouse enthusiasm among my people the greatest asset I possess, and the way to develop the best that is in a person is by appreciation and encouragement." —Charles Schwab
- "If there is any one secret of success, it lies in the ability to get the other person's point of view and see things from that person's angle as well as from your own." —Henry Ford
- "It is the individual who has no interest in his fellow men who has the greatest difficulties in life and provides the greatest injury to others. It is from among such individuals that all human failures spring." —Alfred Alder
- "He who treads softly goes far." —Chinese proverb

CHAPTER 15
MARKETING

"The best marketing doesn't feel like marketing."
—Tom Fishburne

This is an interesting chapter. *100 Best Books* needed a chapter on marketing, and I wanted those books to be helpful in a variety of circumstances. The job of marketing is to create awareness, get people to raise their hand, and have them say, "I am interested."

Allan Dib's book provides the simplest process for building a marketing funnel. Donald Miller's book marries story theory with branding to create pitches that will work for you or your organization. And my choice from Al Reis and Jack Trout is their short classic on how to position yourself in the marketplace.

If you're serious about marketing, you should also read the books on influence from the prior chapter. And Mike Weinberg's *New Sales. Simplified.* in the next chapter, which talks about both marketing and sales. Read *Million Dollar Weekend* by Noah Kagan (Chapter 7) for ideas on scaling a new project. And Josh Kaufman (also in Chapter 7) devotes an entire section of *The Personal MBA* to twenty-one tactics to develop prospects.

The 1-Page Marketing Plan: Get New Customers, Make More Money, and Stand Out from the Crowd
by Allan Dib

"Remember, no one knows how good your products or services are until after the sale. Before they buy, they only know how good your marketing is. Put simply, the best marketer wins every time."

YOU COULD LOOK at the books in *100 Best Books* as examples for how you might write your own book. They address a core problem that many readers face. They provide leverage to make change easier for the reader. And these books provide a clear structure for how to implement the proposed solution. It is remarkable how few marketing books do this. Allan Dib's *The 1-Page Marketing Plan* is included here because it does all three of these things remarkably well.

Dib starts with every business's need to generate prospects. The objective in this first phase of acquiring new customers is to "get them to know you and indicate interest." While written for business owners, you might see how the same problem applies to a job search or community fundraiser. Spend time getting clear on your target market. Craft your message with a focus on why the prospect should buy and why they should buy from you particularly. After defining your market and message, you should focus on the best media for reaching your prospects. Dib encourages business owners to use paid media to create a reliable source of leads and force accountability on the return on investment. Remember, the objective is to get a prospect just to indicate interest.

That interest creates leads, but a good marketer knows that interest doesn't mean they are ready to buy. That makes building a system to capture those leads critical. You also need a system to nurture leads. The objective is to build a relationship. You want them to like you. You want to be a clear option when they are ready to buy. Dib writes, "In marketing, the money is in the follow-up." In this process of nurturing, you build a regular cadence of outreach that provides values and highlights your expertise. Blog posts, white papers, email sequences, lead magnets, handwritten notes—these are all potential assets for your nurturing system. At Bard Press, there is a point in the nurturing cycle when we offer to send potential authors a package with a selection of our books. They see our work and start to envision what their book might look like if they publish with us. As Dib says, "Positioning yourself correctly will make the sales conversion process easy and natural for both you and your customer."

There is an equally powerful marketing opportunity after leads become customers. I really like this piece of advice from Dib—"Tell your audience about all the effort that goes into your product or service." We are often too modest and lose the opportunity to show points of differentiation. Nurturing customers creates opportunities to work with them again and increases value for them and for you. Many businesses depend on referrals, and Dib says you need a system here as well, one that encourages the referral and is specific enough to encourage customers to take action. Be clear who you want to be referred to and how you can help. Consider other partners who work with your customers before or after you as another source for referrals.

All this marketing advice might sound obvious, but how much of it do you do now? How well are you doing it? The answer to those questions will determine if this is your next read.

OTHER MEMORABLE THOUGHTS FROM DIB:
- "By far the biggest leverage point in any business is marketing. If you get 10% better at marketing, this can have an exponential or multiplying effect on your bottom line."
- A good customer pitch addresses the problem, the solution, and the proof. Dib's formula is "You know [problem]? Well, what we do is [solution]. In fact, [proof]."
- "The purpose of any new technology in your business is to eliminate friction. We want the fastest and easiest path to the sales, while increasing customer satisfaction."
- "I always say to have an unlimited budget for marketing that works. ... Once you have a winner that pulls in more than it costs you, crank up the marketing spend and hence the speed of your legal money printing press!"

GROWTH: **MARKETING**

Building a Storybrand 2.0: Clarify Your Message so Customers Will Listen
by Donald Miller

"A story identifies an ambition or objective the hero wants to accomplish, then defines the challenges that are keeping the hero from getting what they want, then provides a plan to help the hero conquer those challenges so they can survive and thrive."

DONALD MILLER believes story is the missing structure from most marketing messages. "When we define the elements of a story as it relates to our brand," he writes, "we create a map customers can follow to engage our products and services." The same is true for employees and partners. When they understand what you do, they also know how their work aligns with helping others.

Miller says you have to start with your customers, and the key is to make *them* the hero of the story, not you. Focus on what they want. The characters in all of our stories desire something, and that something is connected in some way to their survival. The obvious desires are accumulating resources and building social bonds to ensure safety and prosperity. We might also sell methods to be more efficient with our resources or paths to gain more status among the tribe. As we move up Maslow's hierarchy of needs, we also want to offer ways to be generous or find a greater sense of purpose in our lives.

If we are not the hero, that means we are the guide. With all of the desires listed above, there will be a problem or a villain that is keeping the hero from their desires. We can help identify what is in the way. Miller says when brands act as guides, they communicate using empathy and authority. You want to empathetically identify with the customer's dilemma and show you have the experience to help them on their way. Answer the hero's questions: "Can I trust this person?" and "Can I respect this person?" Finally, guides provide plans that make it clear how the hero will succeed.

If you have studied storytelling, you know that there is always a call to action. "In stories, characters never take action on their own. They have to be challenged to take action," Miller writes. Being passive about our company offerings helps neither our customer nor our business. Some businesses can use direct calls like "Schedule an appointment" or "Register today." Other businesses are better served with a series of transitional calls with things like free information, testimonials, and samples of the product or service.

Remember that heroes want to succeed on their quest. Mentors remind their mentees what's at stake and what is to be avoided. Miller says that success is some combination of three things. First, heroes desire status by winning position or power. Second, they desire something external to make them feel whole. Third, heroes desire the moment of reaching their full potential. Build those endpoints into conversations with your customers and you will succeed too.

THREE CRUCIAL QUESTIONS TO ASK YOURSELF WHEN BUILDING YOUR STORYBRAND:
1. What does the hero want?
2. Who or what is preventing the hero from getting what they want?
3. What will the hero's life look like if they do (or do not) get what they want?

22. The 22 Immutable Laws of Marketing: Violate Them at Your Own Risk!
by Al Reis and Jack Trout

"The essence of marketing is narrowing the focus. You become stronger when you reduce the scope of your operations. You can't stand for something if you chase after everything."

AL REIS AND JACK TROUT developed the concept of "positioning" in the 1970s. They have long held the belief that successful brands are relentlessly focused. In their worldview, the objective is to always be first in the consumer's mind for a given task. You want to own a word—like Volvo for safety or ChatGPT for AI. The duo wrote *Positioning: The Battle for Your Mind* in 1982. Ten years later, they wrote another book and distilled the lessons down to twenty-two short essays on how to manage a brand in a sort of executive summary of their prior work.

In *The 22 Immutable Laws of Marketing*, you get a core set of truths about the world of customer psychology, intermixed with additional counter-truths. You might group a subset of truths under their original banner of positioning. Be first. First to market imbues leadership. First in mind is even better. "The most powerful concept in marketing is owning a word in a prospect's mind" reads their Law of Focus. And according to their teachings, maintaining that leadership and focus will require you to resist the urge to extend that success beyond your original space. You'll undoubtedly cede ground to competitors. But being first is everything, because it will mean that your sales will be double the number two brand and four times the number three brand. Be first.

The counter-truths are just as important. Don't try to own another brand's word. It won't work. Your competitor already owns that space in the customer's mind. Find another space. Set up a new category you can own. Wait for the category to split and build a position in the new space. The leader is going to own some attribute that the customer values. "For every attribute, there is an opposite, effective attribute," the authors say in their Law of Attributes.

If you find yourself as something other than the market leader, Reis and Trout also have advice. Where you are on the ladder of recognition will determine your strategy. Popular products with strongly felt need will have more rungs (cars and clothing) than once-in-a-lifetime purchases (caskets). At most, there will be seven slots in the high-interest categories. Most markets will consolidate into a two-horse race (like Apple and Samsung). "A good No. 2 can't afford to be timid," the authors write. "When you give up focusing on No. 1, you make yourself vulnerable not only to the leader but to the rest of the pack."

GROWTH: **MARKETING**

READERS BEWARE:
"Thus are you duly warned. If you violate the immutable laws, you run the risk of failure. If you apply the immutable laws, you run the risk of being bad-mouthed, ignored, or even ostracized. Have patience. The immutable laws of marketing will help you achieve success. And success is the best revenge of all."

CHAPTER 16
SALES

"Most people think 'selling' is the same as 'talking.' But the most effective salespeople know that listening is the most important part of their job."
—Roy Bartell

Everyone is selling something. Don't fool yourself into thinking otherwise. Sales is somewhere in your work—the promotion, the project approval, even getting the best caterer for the holiday party. Selling isn't pushing products or opinions. Selling is listening for commonalities and how you might help someone else. Bring your expertise and your insight to those conversations. And don't underestimate the work it takes to stay motivated and stay positive in the face of resistance to change.

The Little Red Book of Selling: 12.5 Principles of Sales Greatness— How to Make Sales FOREVER
by Jeffrey Gitomer

"Liking is the single most powerful element in a sales relationship. ... Like leads to trust. Trust leads to buying. Buying leads to relationship."

THE LITTLE RED BOOK OF SELLING is the best-selling sales book of all time. The book is full of cartoons, one-liners, affirmations, and lots of lists. Since good book reviews reflect the book they are examining, I'm going to share using the same bite-sized explanations he uses.

GITOMER'S 12.5 PRINCIPLES OF SALES ARE AS FOLLOWS:

1. **Kick Your Own Ass:** Study the basics; talk to your five best customers and have them evaluate you; hang around positive, successful people; avoid negative talk and negative people like the plague; and celebrate effort, not victory.
2. **Prepare to Win, or Lose to Someone Who Is:** Be prepared! Do your homework on your prospects—ask their competition how they win business, ask their customers how it is to work with them. "The workday starts the night before."
3. **Personal Branding Is Sales:** It's not who you know, it's who knows you; prospects buy the salesperson *first*; establish yourself as an expert; be seen and known as a leader; stay in front of the people you want to do business with; and position more to compete less.
4. **It's All About Value, It's All About Relationship, It's Not All About Price:** Writing creates a perceived leadership position; give speeches, create handouts, record the speech, and figure out what your customer wants (hint: more sales, better image, loyal employees, no hassles, more free time).
5. **It's Not Work, It's Network:** Networking eliminates cold-calling and leads to referrals. Create a *great* thirty-second commercial; spend 75 percent of your time with people you don't know; invite a prospect to dinner, and then invite a prospect for them.

6. **If You Can't Get in Front of the Real Decision Maker, You Suck:** Don't sell the product or service, sell the appointment; start higher than you dare; offer answers, not pitches; and ask, "How will the decision be made?" and then ask "Then what?" over and over until you discover the real decision maker.
7. **Engage Me and You Can Make Me Convince Myself:** Ask questions! Ask questions that make them evaluate new information; ask questions about improved productivity, profits, or savings; ask questions about company or personal goals; and get every prospect to say, "No one has ever asked me that before."
8. **If You Can Make Them Laugh, You Can Make Them Buy:** Making people smile puts them at ease. Keep the lines real clean, poke fun at yourself, and look for humor in everyday life. Laughter is universal.
9. **Use Creativity to Differentiate and Dominate:** Pay attention; write ideas down; use the book *Thinkertoys* and its model of "substitute, combine, adapt, modify, maximize, or minimize." Creativity is a science that can be learned.
10. **Reduce Their Risk and You'll Convert Selling into Buying:** Eliminate the risk! Hesitation comes from cold feet, their "gut" saying no, fear of the unknown, not enough information, and lack of confidence or trust in the salesperson/company/product. Counter risk with reward.
11. **When You Say It About Yourself, It's Bragging; When Someone Else Says It about You, It's Proof:** Testimonials are key! Who is better at selling your product, you or your customer? The most powerful person on your sales team is your customer; sharing the buying motivation of customers is a thousand times more powerful than selling skills.
12. **Antennas Up!:** Be aware of your confidence, determination, achievement, winning, and success. What is your focus factor? Where is your attention?
12.5. **Resign Your Position as General Manager of the Universe:** "The less time you spend on other people's business, other people's problems, and other people's drama, the more time you'll have for your own success."

The Challenger Sale: Taking Control of the Customer Conversation
by Matthew Dixon and Brent Adamson

"Over half of customer loyalty is a result not of what you sell, but how you sell it."

THE CHALLENGER SALE has sold the most copies of any sales title in the last decade. There are many good reasons for that. Authors Matthew Dixon and Brent Adamson make good arguments for what has changed in the world of sales—rise of consensus-based sales, greater demand for customization, increased use of third-party consultants. Their research at the Corporate Executive Board into sales skills and behaviors led to a set of unexpected findings around what creates success in sales today. Their member-based advisory firm gave them access to over six thousand salespeople for their study and a wide array of firms that reported on their activities with customers.

Their research identified forty-four different attributes that represent skills and behaviors that sales reps engage in to be successful. Dixon and Adamson are careful to say they focused their research on actions one might take and not personality types or personal strengths. Through statistical analysis, they identified five groups of attributes that naturally arose. These groups became profiles, and when comparing the performance of core sales team members, each of the profiles performed at a similar level.

Now, when star sales performers were compared, one profile jumped out, representing almost 40 percent of all high performers—the Challenger. The following attributes showed up as significant for this profile:

- Offers the customer unique perspectives
- Has strong two-way communication skills
- Knows the individual customer's value drivers
- Can identify economic drivers of the customer's business
- Is comfortable discussing money
- Can pressure the customer

The Challenger rep wins more deals for several reasons. Fundamentally, Challengers help their customers think differently about their business. This helps clients make progress on their goals. And as deals become more complex, Challengers are better at promoting systemic change over simply convincing a client to purchase from a new source. The authors say this comes from the ability to teach, tailor, and take control.

The Corporate Executive Board's research confirms that customers deeply value being taught unique perspectives on the market, navigating alternatives, and avoiding potential pitfalls. Challengers tailor those insights not just to a company or industry but down to the individual role. In taking control, the rep leads and simplifies by suggesting who should be involved in the purchase process. All of these steps take both the rep and the organization working in concert to be successful.

The authors end the book with a chapter for everyone, whether you work in sales or not. They believe the Challenger approach applies to everyone who serves clients (which is everyone). HR recruiters can act as strategic advisors on current trends in the labor market. Customer service representatives can change their data from call center incidents to "complaint-to-market impact" that assesses the financial consequences for increased call volume. R&D engineers can better align with market outcomes. Legal counsels could better assess probabilities for litigation and suggest proactive action to mitigate risk. The point is, all functions have the opportunity to provide insights and challenge clients to make changes for the better.

HERE ARE THE FIVE SALES PROFILES:

- **The Hard Worker:** Shows up early, stays late, and is always willing to put in extra effort.
- **The Relationship Builder:** Nurtures advocates by being generous with time to ensure customer needs are met.
- **The Lone Wolf:** Follows instincts over rules and often succeeds in spite of themselves.
- **The Reactive Problem Solver:** Reliable and detail oriented, they love customer service.
- **The Challenger:** Debaters who are assertive and not afraid to share views that are controversial.

GROWTH: **SALES**

New Sales. Simplified.: The Essential Handbook for Prospecting and New Business Development
by Mike Weinberg

"Proactively pursuing new business is not complicated. Prospective customers have needs. We have potential solutions for those needs. When charged with developing new business from new accounts, our job is to engage with potential customers to determine if what we sell aligns with what these prospects need. It's that simple."

THERE ARE SOME BUSINESS BOOKS that just tell you what you need to do to be successful. These "cookbooks" identify the ingredients and describe the best methods for getting a great outcome. Many will argue that too many things in business don't have repeatable outcomes. I don't think that's true, especially when you are close to the problem you are trying to solve.

Weinberg provides a recipe for new business development in *New Sales. Simplified.* Any business that wants to grow or recover from slow growth needs a process for bringing in new business. Weinberg believes there is a process that can do exactly that.

Weinberg opens the book with a chapter on all the reasons that prospecting fails at most businesses. See if any of these sound familiar:

- Salespeople never had to or didn't need to prospect.
- Poor target account selection.
- Salespeople can't tell the company story.
- Salespeople can't conduct an effective sales call.
- Too much effort spent on existing accounts.

If none of those quite fit, Weinberg provides eleven more reasons why efforts fall short.

The basic plan for success boils down to three steps: Select targets, deploy sales and marketing devices, and execute the plan. At that level, the plan sounds easy and maybe obvious, but Weinberg's recipe is more detailed, more nuanced, and more helpful than that.

In selecting new prospects, the target list needs to be finite and written down. The list has a set number of companies. Defining the list creates a commitment to develop relationships and gain traction with these new opportunities. The list should focus on a market segment that aligns with your company's strengths or one you believe could succeed with the right sales strategy. "Find the path of least resistance and then focus like mad on that very path," says Weinberg. Also, choose a handful of dream clients, knowing that they need their own plan and the high-risk, high-reward nature of these prospects.

Weinberg catalogs twenty different devices that salespeople can use to gain attention and build trust with new clients. The list details a host of marketing and sales tactics ranging from voicemail to white papers to facility tours. Over the course of two chapters, Weinberg describes the tactic he believes is the most important—the sales story. His treatment of the topic is as good as any I have read on positioning or brand, with an important focus on how salespeople develop stories that effectively introduce their companies.

The back half of the book contains more of that advice from Weinberg on being effective in various prospecting scenarios. When making cold calls (and yes, he believes they are still critical), he suggests starting with "Let me steal a minute" to politely acknowledge the intrusion and then saying "I head up X" to communicate the importance of your role. The only goal is to get a face-to-face meeting. When overcoming buyer resistance, top performers believe every sales call is an opportunity for a sale. When asked to give a sales presentation, ask for a face-to-face meeting first, and if that can't be arranged, avoid an opening monologue during the presentation and start with a dialogue to gather more information about the prospect.

Prospecting is a game of math. Each phase of the process has some conversion rate, and starting with closed deals, you need to work back through the steps in the sales pipeline to see how many prospects are needed on the initial list. Like I said, business is more predictable than people think. A book like *New Sales. Simplified.* improves your chances of creating success.

WEINBERG'S QUESTIONS FOR REFLECTION:
- If you sat down with a few key executives and salespeople from your company and asked each of them to share your company's story, what would you hear?
- Do you see yourself as an important businessperson calling your prospects because you might be able to help them? If not, what can you do to change your mindset about making calls?
- How might you differently position yourself, physically and verbally, to come across as more of an ally than an adversary during sales calls?
- If your current pipeline of sales opportunities is not full, moving, and balanced, what can you begin doing immediately to restore it to health?

The SPIN Selling Fieldbook: Practical Tools, Methods, Exercises, and Resources
by Neil Rackham

"Remember, questions are the secret of sales success. Studies show that high-performing salespeople ask more questions. If you don't ask questions, you won't sell effectively. This book will help you build your seeking skills."

NEIL RACKHAM'S first book, *SPIN Selling,* is still famous for changing how sales is practiced. Look up any list of must-read books on sales and you will find it there. I think what he teaches is important, not just for sales professionals but also for anyone who is involved in business development, client management, or entrepreneurship. I also think there is a better book for the wider audience I am trying to reach in *100 Best Books*. So, let me suggest Rackham's follow-up book *The SPIN Selling Fieldbook* as the more approachable, better synthesized version of his work.

If you are reading this section or this review, my guess is that you have been on sales calls, and you've seen how easy it is to spend all the time talking about your organization and its offerings. The first finding that Rackham's research reinforces is that successful sales calls happen when *the buyer* does the majority of the talking. And the way salespeople do that is by asking questions. If you master that concept, that alone will drastically change your outcomes and help you find even more ways to help your new clients. Successful salespeople ask more questions.

Rackham writes that when given a choice, experienced salespeople ask for more training in asking questions. A question-based approach shifts the focus from persuading a buyer to understanding them better. Asking more questions also shifts the seller's approach from leading with their solutions to uncovering what the buyer needs. Rackham's research from 35,000 observed sales calls has much more to say about the questions to ask and when to ask them.

HERE ARE FOUR TYPES OF SALES QUESTIONS:

1. **Situation questions** gather facts and information about the buyer. Do your homework and use these sparingly to find out only what you couldn't through your research.
2. **Problem questions** uncover difficulties and dissatisfactions of the buyer. Successful salespeople ask more of these questions to help discover problems to connect their solutions with and deepen the seriousness of the situation for the buyer.
3. **Implication questions** shift the focus to the effects and consequences of the problem. How often does that cause...? Does that ever lead to...? These questions are particularly effective if the problems are significant, unclear, or require redefinition. Seek to understand more. That in turn will help the buyer see their implicit needs even more clearly.
4. **Need-payoff questions** do what they say—ask about the value and importance of a solution. How much would you save if...? If we could shorten the time, then...? With these questions, you are helping the buyer express their desire for the solution and the benefits they will get.

SECTION FOUR
LEADING

CHANGE
LEADERSHIP
MANAGING
TEAMS
HIRING

CHAPTER 17
CHANGE

"When we are no longer able to change a situation, we are challenged to change ourselves."
—Viktor Frankl

The biggest problem with change is us. Our most common reaction to change is fear, even when it is change we wish and hope for. A new job creates new possibilities and brings the need to learn the preferences of new colleagues, new expectations from your boss, and new processes for just about everything else. Maybe you have been hired to bring about change, and now it's not just you. You have to bring everyone else along on a journey into the unknown.

My hope for this chapter is that more of us become students of change. William Bridges provides a useful model for seeing how change unfolds. Robert Kegan and Lisa Laskow Lahey describe in detail what makes it hard for us to change. John Kotter writes about a process that can accelerate change. And Pema Chödrön counsels us that change is in the nature of everything, and how we handle today's change will set the stage for what tomorrow will bring.

Managing Transitions: Making the Most of Change
by William Bridges

"The beginning will take place only after they have come through the wilderness and are ready to make the emotional commitment to do things the new way and see themselves as new people. Starts involve new situations. Beginnings involve new understandings, new values, new attitudes, and—most of all—new identities."

TRANSITIONS ARE HARD, period. As I write this review, I have two sons who just left for their first year away at college. I just hired my first employee, and I am starting to facilitate a class that has been mapped out to run over the course of the next five years. Beginnings, endings, and the neutral zones in between all carry challenges and opportunities.

Not managing transitions comes with a host of ill effects. The science says people in transition are stressed by changes and more likely to become ill or get injured. Being unclear about the future creates anxiety. Individuals' fields of view narrow as they become self-absorbed with the issues directly affecting them. All of these lead to guilt in those who initiated the changes and even more guilt from those who are left to deal with the aftereffects. As these emotions rise, everyone starts to feel angry and resentful about the changes, even when everyone might agree the changes will help in the long term.

So let's start with endings. "Changes cause transitions, which cause losses, and it is the losses, not the changes they're reacting to," writes William Bridges. In acknowledging the loss, we might consider how to compensate for those losses. We could make clear what is over and what isn't; we respect the part that is. Expect grief. Expect overreaction. Address it, in the open, in a way that people see your concern and feel acknowledged. Be clear: "I know there is loss. I am sorry there isn't another way." And move on with a clear-to-everyone ending.

The next part is the hardest—the "nowhere between two somewheres." Bridges quotes André Gide, who said, "One doesn't discover new lands without consenting to lose sight of the shore for a very long time." While difficult, fewer anchoring points allow for more creative perspectives on what is to come. Bridges calls it the winter before spring's new growth. Flexibility gains in value during this time. Extra connections temporarily substitute for standard operating procedures. The time spent in this neutral zone makes room to notice old habits and develop new patterns more appropriate for the context.

"The beginning will only take place after they have come through the wilderness and are ready to make the emotional commitment to do things the new way and see themselves as new people," says Bridges. He suggests that you have four Ps ready: the Purpose, a Picture, the Plan, and a Part to play. Sell the problem and communicate it as you define the purpose. Paint a simple picture of what things will be like now. Make a *transition* plan that focuses on where people are and where they will be at each point along the way. And describe their "part to play," or how their role changes and what new relationships are needed as things begin anew.

BRIDGES'S FIVE LAWS OF ORGANIZATIONAL DEVELOPMENT:
1. Those who were most at home with the necessary activities and arrangements are the ones who are the most likely to experience the subsequent phase as a severe personal setback.
2. The successful outcome of any phase of organizational development triggers its demise by creating challenges that it is not equipped to handle.
3. In any significant transition, the thing that the organization needs to let go of is the very thing that got it this far.
4. Whenever there is a painful, troubled time in the organization, a developmental transition is probably going on.
5. Not making a transition when the time is ripe for one to occur will cause a developmental impairment in the organization.

LEADING: **CHANGE**

Immunity to Change: How to Overcome It and Unlock The Potential in Yourself and Your Organization
by Robert Kegan and Lisa Laskow Lahey

> "The psychologist William Perry once said there are two important things to know about people you are trying to help change: 'What do they really want, and what will they do to keep from getting it?'"

IMMUNITY TO CHANGE takes a certain level of commitment to read. At 323 pages, the book is not an airplane read, even if you are on a transoceanic flight. At several points, the authors warn readers not to read straight through but instead take time to work with the concepts presented. That's exactly why I chose *Immunity to Change* for this chapter. Robert Kegan and Lisa Laskow Lahey bring some much-needed depth to the topic of change. Their approach addresses how we can't separate the spheres of our lives and how the changes we need to make in our personal lives are the same ones we most likely need to make in our professional lives.

Is change possible? Can you teach old dogs new tricks? That's where the authors' research starts and builds on that of others before them. The ability to enact change in our lives is a function of our "mental complexity." This is our ability to make sense of the complex and contradictory world we live in. The research shows our level of mental complexity increases with age, but there is wide variation within any age group, and that development comes in a sharp period of growth followed by long plateaus of stability. Each new plateau provides a new mindset for a broader, more accurate ability to make sense of the world:

1. **The socialized mind** emphasizes communication that aligns one with the group, but it often builds inaccurate meaning beyond what is truly there.
2. **The self-authoring mind** places more value on sharing what is needed to positively influence the group and move forward their agenda, but internal filters still influence receiving information and lead to inaccurate mental models.

3. **The self-transforming mind** looks beyond the filters and also sees the filters; it deeply realizes that interpretations are incomplete and continually seeks to add information to create better worldviews.

Now, I'm only describing the first thirty pages of the book, but this is important context because more complexity in the world requires deeper mental complexity to understand it. Further studies show that more than 60 percent of people align with the socializing mind, 35 percent of the population understand the self-authoring mind, but less than 1 percent can deeply operate from the self-transforming mind.

To see past the filters, we need to slow down and examine the perceptions that influence our behavior. It is precisely these perceptions that make us immune to change. The authors write, "The immune-to-change technology enables the development of a more complex self, which...is always a matter of being able to look *at* something that, before, we could only look *through*. That is why the 160 pages of cases in the middle of the books, about people from all different levels of authority and organizations, are so important. We really have to slow down to see what keeps us from what we really want."

I have given a short description below of the full process that you will find in Chapter 9 of *Immunity to Change*. The remainder of the book is about building a way to monitor your progress on making that change or working on a group's immunity to change. In any case, deep work is required, but if you have the patience, *Immunity to Change* provides a master class in doing that work.

CONSTRUCT YOUR *IMMUNITY TO CHANGE* MAP:
1. Choose one big goal that is important to you, that you feel you *need to* get better at, and that is accomplished through changes you are going to make.
2. Generate a list of all the things you are doing and not doing that work against your goal. Bring in feedback from partners, bosses, peers, and reports to build out other impediments to change.
3. Dig deeper for a more hidden level of competing commitments that keep you from doing what is needed to work toward

your goal. There is likely a conflict being avoided or a persona that is embraced that needs examination.
4. Identify the core assumptions that sustain your immunity to change and start to test those assumptions with new actions and behaviors.

Leading Change
by John Kotter

"A useful rule of thumb: Whenever you cannot describe the vision driving a change initiative in five minutes or less and get a reaction that signifies both understanding and interest, you are in for trouble."

IN THE 1995 *Harvard Business Review* article "Why Transformation Efforts Fail," John Kotter enumerated an eight-point framework for creating major change in organizations. You can look at them as errors that occur during large-scale change efforts or opportunities to focus on. Kotter says an arc of their overlapping enactment is what is required for success. For this review, let's look at each point and what makes them work:

1. **Establishing a sense of urgency:** Use customers, consultants, and suppliers with their external data to counteract insider myopia. Create initiative by taking bold and even risky actions to show leadership. Eliminate symbols of excess. Raise goals and expectations that make change necessary.
2. **Creating the guiding coalition:** Gather a team built on trust and a common goal. The right members will have positional power, various expertise on the challenge, credibility in the organization, and proven experience in driving change. New decision-making acknowledges that any one person doesn't have all that is needed to drive change.

3. **Developing a vision and strategy:** Confusion, disagreement, and disbelief are why a clarifying vision is important. Strong clarity establishes priority with regard to resources, which is often at odds with the competing interests of customers, employees, and stockholders. Effective visions are imaginable, desirable, feasible, and flexible. Be sure to include both head and heart.
4. **Communicating the change vision:** The success in sharing a vision involves the success of the prior three points around urgency, coalition, and clarity. Communicate using simplicity and concrete metaphors and analogies. Use company meetings, weekly newsletters, social media, and one-on-ones. Repeat and repeat, again and again. The coalition's changed behavior can do more to communicate than a hundred-page manual ever would.
5. **Empowering broad-based action:** The new vision is going to collide with structural barriers. Align systems from IT to HR to support and reinforce new desired behaviors. Train everyone adequately, appropriately, and when it is most useful for them. Don't avoid honest and needed dialogue with the resistance.
6. **Generating short-term wins:** Big changes take time; small wins show progress. The unsure want evidence the changes will work. Those same gains reward early supporters. The pressure for those near-term connects with a sense of urgency. Better is hard to argue with, but be sure the improvements continue to be seen by all.
7. **Consolidating gains and producing more change:** To quote Kotter here: "Whenever you let up before the job is done, critical momentum can be lost and regression may follow." Interdependence starts to show at this point. Where can those linkages be eliminated to support the progress being made? That means more leadership, more management, and more help, too.
8. **Anchoring new approaches in the culture:** The change strategy becomes a changed culture. New practices replace old ones as the results clearly show the improvement. Those who supported the effort are promoted, and they hire the next wave. The communication never stops. Culture is the last step, not the first.

HERE ARE SOME OTHER BOOKS BY KOTTER TO HELP WITH CHANGE:

- *Our Iceberg Is Melting*: Written with Holger Rathgeber, this business fable version of *Leading Change* takes readers through the same eight points.
- *A Sense of Urgency*: Kotter takes the first step of his change process and gives it a book-length treatment to cover its importance.
- *Buy-In*: I like this book's approach, in which the reader walks through leading an imagined community project and is offeredcommon objections and responses to help your good ideas succeed.

When Things Fall Apart: Heart Advice for Difficult Times
by Pema Chödrön

"We're always trying to deny that it's a natural occurrence that things change, that the sand is slipping through our fingers. Time is passing. It's as natural as the seasons changing and day turning into night. But getting old, getting sick, losing what we love—we don't see those events as natural occurrences. We want to ward off that sense of death, no matter what."

OUR PROBLEM WITH change arises because it is largely an existential one. Religion and philosophy have long tried to advise us on how to deal with our discomfort. They all point to the need to examine our experience outside of the rational, easily explainable ruts of habitual energy or institutional inertia. They often use nature as a metaphor. The world outside your window reminds you daily of how much things change as the sunlight slowly shifts and the noises grow and fall as the unseen passes by. But as many reminders as we have of the changing nature of all things, we seem to ignore it. Pema Chödrön would take everything said in this chapter on change and turn it a bit. That's why I include her book here.

"[Things] come together and they fall apart. Then they come together again and fall apart. It's just like that," she writes. The weekly project review is also just like that, with its gathering and dispersing members, each time a little different (if we notice). When my children were younger, I remember traveling for a week, returning back, and noticing small changes in them—a new phrase, a touch taller. Read this review twice and tell me you don't notice something different in what I say, or maybe a subtle shift in your reaction to what I am saying.

Everything is impermanent. Sit with that for a minute. The food in your refrigerator, the flowers in the park, the job you have right now, your neighbors, the page or screen you are reading this on—all of it. And as Chödrön says in the opening quote, we are very uncomfortable with this truth. "We take no delight in it; in fact, we despair of it. We regard it as a pain. We try to resist this by making things that will last," Chödrön writes.

That leads us to do many things that hurt ourselves and others. We seek out pleasure to soothe and mask the grief of continual loss. We express anger at the unfairness of the situation. When everything falls apart, we attempt to return things to the way they were, even though we already know they will never be the same. These are all habits and resistance to the natural ways the world works. All of that suffering is just as true as impermanence itself.

Chödrön is a Tibetan Buddhist nun, so her advice for us is based in meditation, awareness, compassion, and seeing what's true. We don't know what is going to happen next, as much as we think we do or wish we did. It is that very activity that keeps us from the joy that arises when things come together in each moment. Someone once told me that "impermanence makes everything possible." If we saw change in that way, imagine how much more (we could achieve) would be possible.

SOME FINAL WORDS FROM CHÖDRÖN:
"When we find ourselves in a mess, we don't have to feel guilty about it. Instead, we could reflect on the fact that how we relate to this mess will be sowing the seeds of how we will relate to whatever happens next. We can make ourselves miserable, or we can make ourselves strong. The amount of effort is the same."

CHAPTER 18
LEADERSHIP

"To handle yourself, use your head; to handle others, use your heart."
—Eleanor Roosevelt

Leadership is commonly defined as activity in relationship to others. Leaders make people want to follow them. Leaders move people in the direction toward a common purpose. Leaders make progress on the toughest challenges and create new paths for others.

Holding those definitions in mind, the books in this chapter have a strong emphasis on the internal work you need to do to become a better leader. You'll read about the qualities that are respected in leaders and need to be developed. You'll hear that the limiting beliefs we carry, if unaddressed, will eventually impact those who follow us. And you'll be asked to examine your life and build more alignment among its components to fuel your work as a leader.

The results are clear: Individuals collectively improve when they work with effective leaders. So do your work so that others can do theirs.

The Leadership Challenge: How to Make Extraordinary Things Happen in Organizations
by James Kouzes and Barry Posner

"How do you get other people to want to follow you? How do you get other people, by free will and free choice, to move forward together on a common purpose? Just how do you get others to want to do things?"

I HAVE A FRIEND WHO, after graduating from university, went to work for the national office of his college fraternity. He and a group of new employees would gather at six o'clock each morning at the invitation of a willing mentor to discuss *The Leadership Challenge*. That friend can still fondly recount the practices and commitments that make up the book. I love that story because I think this is the perfect first book everyone should read to learn about leadership.

The Leadership Challenge is now in its seventh edition (yes, I own all seven). The opening quote is from the first page of the first edition, published in 1987, and provides an opening query exploring the core of leadership. Their most recent definition of leadership is more elegant—"the art of mobilizing others to want to struggle for shared aspirations." Their findings on how to practice the art of leadership are based on two vectors of research.

One approach was to ask people, "What values, personality traits, or characteristics do you look for and admire in a leader?" Over time, their research narrowed to twenty characteristics that were used to poll respondents. While every characteristic gets votes in each round of research, four qualities consistently get the majority of votes: honest, competent, inspiring, and forward-looking. James Kouzes and Barry Posner point out that in what feels like an increasingly more uncertain post-pandemic world, these qualities resonate even more strongly with respondents. These same characteristics correspond to credibility as well. Successful news reporters, physicians, politicians, and priests all rate highly as reliable sources for information, particularly their ability to be forward-looking. The authors summarize it this way: "If you don't believe in the messenger, you won't believe the message."

The second approach started with a question: "What do people do when they are at their personal best as leaders?" The research led to the development of a twelve-page survey with thirty-eight open-ended questions, which focuses on capturing everything from location, timing, project type, scope of responsibility, size of group, and lesson learned. Five thousand surveys later, the authors have come to two conclusions: First, that everyone has a personal-best leadership story to tell, and second, that leadership is an identifiable set of skills and abilities available to anyone.

Kouzes and Posner present the identifiable skills as a five-practice model: Model the Way, Inspire a Shared Vision, Challenge the Process, Enable Others to Act, and Encourage the Heart. There isn't enough room here to talk about all of these practices, so let me focus on the one that I have always started with.

"When we reviewed the personal-best leadership experiences," the authors write, "it became evident that every single case involved some kind of challenge." They further describe challenges as "the common denominator" for personal-best leadership stories. They cite research in the "Challenge the Process" section that has connected successful change and innovation with the energy, ideas, and methods that leadership supplies. New processes require risk. Effective leaders are proactive; they don't wait for permission or instruction. New perspectives require experimentation. "The only way people learn is by doing things they've never done before."

I'll end by saying that the seventh edition of this classic is filled with an enormous amount of research and personal-best case studies. The book is so full, in fact, that it is starting to read like a textbook or title written for professionals. This might turn some away, and that is not my intention. As a first read on leadership, you still won't find a better choice than *The Leadership Challenge*.

THE BOOK'S TEN COMMITMENTS OF LEADERSHIP ARE:

- Clarify values
- Set the example
- Envision the future
- Enlist others
- Search for opportunities
- Experiment and take risks
- Foster collaborations
- Strengthen others
- Recognize contributions
- Celebrate the values and victories

The Speed of Trust: The One Thing That Changes Everything
by Stephen M. R. Covey

"Nothing is as fast as the speed of trust. Nothing is as profitable as the economics of trust. Nothing is as relevant as the pervasive impact of trust. And the dividends of trust can significantly enhance the quality of every relationship on every level of your life."

I COULD PLACE a book about trust in any number of chapters in *100 Best Books*, and the way that Stephen M. R. Covey writes about trust makes the book even more encompassing. At the same time, there isn't a strong cultural definition for trust. Covey's organization will often do an exercise at their live events where they ask that very question—"What is trust?"—to each table of participants. Of the ten words that each person writes down as answers, Covey reports that only one or two will be the same among the group. Let me confound this even further, because the answer to the question "Do you trust your boss?" has been found to be the best predictor of team performance and organizational success, according to FranklinCovey research. How can we build "trust" if we can't even agree on a shared meaning for what it is?

The value of *The Speed of Trust* is helping create a variety of meanings that work across a range of situations. Covey believes there are four key elements that are interconnected. Integrity is what we most often think of first as we consider whether someone is honest. Covey adds courage, humility, and congruence to the list under integrity. Intent is next, and this is because for us to build trust we consider a person's motivation, agenda, and behavior. These first two qualities point to credibility, while the next two highlight competence.

Capability is Covey's third core element of trust, along with all the things needed to perform a task well. He uses the acronym TASKS to help us remember the role of talents, attitudes, skills, knowledge, and style. You could consider "your ability to establish, grow, extend, and restore trust" as a capability to invest in. Results are the final element. In other settings, we might call this execution or accountability.

In his definition of leadership, Covey says it's "getting results in a way that inspires trust." *What* results are achieved matters, but *how* those results are reached is just as important. Employees, partners, and customers who trust you, make getting those results easier. This is the speed that Covey connects trust with.

If you need more convincing about the power of trust, consider all of these sources and studies. The Great Place to Work Institute reports that "trust between managers and employees is the primary defining characteristic of the very best workplaces." For their letter of recommendation, Harvard Business School requests examples of behavior that inspires trust and confidence. Mercer reports that "only forty-four percent of workers trust that senior management communicates honestly." Leadership experts James Kouzes and Barry Posner (from the previous review in this chapter) say, "Trust is the most significant predictor of individual satisfaction within their organization." A Watson Wyatt study reports that "high-trust organizations outperformed low-trust organizations in total return to shareholders (stock price plus dividends) by 286 percent." Further, Russell Investments Group studied *Fortune*'s "100 Best Companies to Work for in America" and found those companies "earned over four times the returns of the broader market over a prior seven-year period." Trust constitutes nearly two-thirds of the criteria for making that list.

My emphasis in this chapter has been on our work life, but I hope you can see the same dividends that are possible in all parts of our lives if we build trust in all of our relationships.

TRUST TIPS FROM COVEY:
- Show respect by sending thank you notes, making calls, and sending notes of concern. Match what you feel with what you do.
- To build transparency, ask yourself if you are holding onto information that should be shared.
- Next time you make a mistake, notice how you respond. Do you ignore and justify it or quickly admit it and do what you can to resolve it?
- You can also reframe that mistake as feedback and see it as an opportunity to learn and grow.
- When you are improving your listening skills, know that people

communicating with high emotion do not yet feel understood. And if they do not feel understood, they are not yet in a place to take advice from others.

Total Leadership: Be a Better Leader, Have a Richer Life
by Stewart Friedman

"If you're going to make a difference, thinking of yourself as a leader will make it more likely that your legacy turns out to be the one you really want."

LET'S START WITH Stewart Friedman's description of leadership—"Being a leader means inspiring committed action that engages people in taking intelligent steps, in a direction you have chosen, to achieve something that has significant meaning for all relevant parties." That matches well with the common definition found in this chapter's books and many others. From there, most authors in the leadership space will then describe the strategies and techniques that will best engage followers to move toward the desired goal. Friedman takes a different approach. Being a better leader requires internal work.

First, you have to figure out what is important to you. That passion is where you are going to find the energy to pursue work and a life that is fulfilling. As leaders, this authenticity is what engages others. Friedman provides exercises to help. He suggests writing your life story with the four or five plot points that made you who you are. He then asks you to write the vision for fifteen years from now and describe how you became that leader. Chapter 4, "Personality," and Chapter 6, "Purpose," here in *100 Best Books* can also help with this discovery. He ends the chapter with the question, "What changes might you make to live more closely in accord with what really matters to you?" This is the throughline of the whole book.

Friedman believes we really become the best leader when we create alignment between all domains of our life—work, home, community, and self. He asks the reader to think of each of the four areas as a circle and draw the Venn diagram of your life. Where do you place the domains on the page? Where do the domains intersect? How much do they overlap and support each other? Rather than seeing these domains as separate slices that compete for time and energy, look for opportunities to be more authentic and find more ways to integrate them.

That integration requires that we look more deeply at the domains of our life. As a leader, we have stakeholders—our partner, family, coworkers, fellow volunteers—that hold varying levels of expectations. They want some form of our time and energy in support of the lives they want to live. The interference of one domain with another is where we feel suffering and grief. And often our assumptions are wrong because we haven't asked others about them or others have changed since we last asked. When we understand these needs, we have the opportunity to explore the boundaries between the domains. How permeable are they? Where is there flexibility? As a leader, the work to better engage with those who are important to us makes us more whole.

We will undoubtedly find areas of our life that need change. Friedman proposes that we design experiments to explore what might change to create more alignment. It's best to treat this process like an experiment by making a hypothesis about the outcome and what we need to do to create the best probability of success. You'll need some way to measure the results. Friedman writes, "[Leaders] aim to make the world better for the people around them, as you are now doing in your experiments. In what might seem paradoxical, the more you take self-interest out of the picture and instead *do for others*, the more you end up benefiting your own interest, in both the short and the long term."

EXPERIMENTS YOU CAN RUN:
- **Tracking and reflecting:** Record your thoughts and feelings to build self-awareness and keep priorities clear.
- **Rejuvenating and restoring:** Attend to yourself with intention and priority.
- **Revealing and engaging:** Share more of yourself with your stakeholders so they can support you.
- **Exploring and venturing:** Use new activities to move toward a life that better aligns with your core values and vision for leadership.

Reboot: Leadership and the Art of Growing Up
by Jerry Colonna

"Time and again I've watched hearts break open, so that true and authentic leaders can emerge. But that process depends on a brave first step: facing the reality of what is and not being deluded by the powerful, seductive dreams of what can be."

JERRY COLONNA says early in *Reboot* that he has "a well-earned reputation for making people cry." It's interesting because the question he asks to open the book seems straightforward: What do I believe to be true about work, leadership, and how we may live our lives?

Colonna tells the stories of founders who are living out stories—stories they created, internalized, and believed to be true. Karma and lifelong conditioning contorts our perception of the world. And then we act out in work and life. We lead others colored by those misguided interpretations.

We cry because there is no veil when Colonna speaks about his life. He is raw and honest. He talks about his attempted suicide, his time in a locked psychiatric ward, growing up with a mother who suffered from mental illness, and the unspoken burdens of generational expectations. Jerry also helmed a technology magazine, ran successful venture funds, and helped lead the organizing committee that tried to bring the 2012 Olympics to New York City. He lays all his cards on the table, and he says, "OK, what have *you* got?" with his Brooklyn accent that practically comes through the words on the page. That raw honesty is what makes him such a great coach.

I cry because I can't help but remember my own leadership mistakes. My first position of real responsibility only lasted eight months before I blew it up with demands for more compensation and a return to aggressive growth, all while ignoring how the owners were still reeling from the gut-retching decision to shut down decades-old divisions in hopes their business would survive the Great Recession. In my next leadership position, I was important and helpful, until circumstances changed and I wasn't important or helpful anymore. "Read the room!" I tell myself now. I think of the pain I caused. You can't save yourself from the things you can't see.

I share all that because that is what Colonna asks for in *Reboot*. He both nudges and provokes readers to engage in radical self-inquiry. What hidden patterns are we bringing to our roles as leaders? Colonna writes, "Power in the hands of one afraid or unwilling to look in the mirror perpetuates an often silent and always seething violence in the workplace." As a leader, our behavior doesn't just impact our friends or a partner, it multiplies as it affects our kids, our employees, and our communities.

We all want love, safety, and belonging. And we have told ourselves stories about which of those we deserve and under what conditions. I'll say it one more time: Those stories confine us. "Great leaders look unflinchingly in the mirror and transform untamed hungers and unruly compulsions into moments of self-compassion and understanding." May we take responsibility for the leader we are and direct a portion of that responsibility for how we hold ourselves for the benefit of all.

JOURNALING INVITATIONS FROM JERRY:
- How was my relationship to money first formed?
- At the end of my current tenure in my position, what would I like to feel about myself?
- While growing up what is the story my family told me about being real, being vulnerable, and being true?
- What am I not saying that needs to be said? And once I recognize that, what now?

CHAPTER 19
MANAGING

"The conventional definition of management is getting work done through people, but real management is developing people through work."
—Agha Hasan Abedi

Management seems to sit in the long shadow of leadership. Managing is perceived as boring and uninspired, and yet it is the essential activity of successful projects and growing organizations. We easily forget all the roles that the modern manager is asked to fill, often needing to switch between them many times each day. No wonder new managers feel overwhelmed when they take the position for the first time. Let's take a moment and honor the work of organizing, orchestrating, and keeping the trains running on time.

LEADING: **MANAGING**

The Making of a Manager: What to Do When Everyone Looks to You
by Julie Zhuo

"So, what is the job of a manager? Without understanding this deeply, it's hard to know how to be good at it."

A FEW PAGES AFTER Julie Zhuo writes the question above, she answers with a straightforward definition of management: "to get better outcomes from a group of people working together." She says everything flows from that. Managers need to prioritize purpose, people, and process. Zhuo distinguishes management as a role separate from leadership, which is about guiding and influencing others. She also addresses whether management is the right career path for you: Do you like talking to people? Can you provide stability? Are you about outcomes or serving a particular role?

That opening arc takes us through the first thirty pages and sets the tone for the rest of the book. Rather than looking at management as a set of skills to be described and learned, Zhuo presents the topics in the order that new managers will likely encounter them. Even the second chapter, titled "Your First Three Months," breaks out the variety of situations a new manager might find themselves involved in. You might be starting a brand-new team, taking responsibility for an existing group, or acting in a new role with a new team that grew out of a former group. Each scenario has its own unique set of challenges. Zhuo quotes Linda Hill, who says, "Ask any senior executive to recall how he or she felt as a new manager. If you get an honest answer, you'll hear a tale of disorientation and, for some, overwhelming confusion. The new role didn't feel anything like it was supposed to. It felt too big for any one person to handle."

Even a small team of four or five people brings new challenges. How do you stay connected? How do you best surface the tough issues your reports are dealing with? How do you clearly communicate performance issues that need improvement? I really like Zhuo's diagnosis that if you are having problems with an employee you are likely dealing with lack of motivation, lack of skills, or both. The new manager needs to build many early communication and evaluation skills to be successful.

The second half of the book provides chapter-length discussions of key topics that affect every manager. Managers have to be good at meetings, and Zhuo says there are only a handful of good reasons to hold them: to make a decision, share information, provide feedback, generate ideas, and strengthen relationships. In the next chapter, Zhuo writes, "At a growing organization, hiring well is the single most important thing you do." Managers also have to make things happen, and I like her point on perfect execution over perfect strategy: "The most brilliant plans in the world won't help you succeed if you can't bring them to life." Zhuo ends the book with the bigger topics of building a growing team and nurturing culture.

Sometimes, the way you tell the story makes all the difference. I am choosing to start this chapter with *The Making of a Manager* because Zhuo reveals the art of management in a way that matches how a manager experiences the new role. That alone is valuable.

TEST YOURSELF WITH THESE THREE STATEMENTS:
- My reports regularly bring their biggest challenges to my attention.
- My reports and I regularly give each other critical feedback, and it isn't taken personally.
- My reports would gladly work for me again.

Leading from the Middle: A Playbook for Managers to Influence Up, Down, and Across the Organization
by Scott Mautz

"A study of 320,000 employees found that the bottom 5 percent in terms of engagement and happiness levels weren't the people with poor performance ratings or those so new they hadn't moved on yet from an ill-fitting job, but five- to ten-year tenured employees in mid-level roles with good performance ratings."

THROUGH HIS RESEARCH, Scott Mautz has identified twenty-one roles that middle managers are expected to fill in the normal course of their duties: translator, converter, strategist, catalyst, designer, implementer, decision-maker, resource allocator, synthesizer, intrapreneur, bridge builder, framer, sense-maker, champion, facilitator, buffer, straddler, accountability czar, communicator, coach, and team builder. Take a minute and read back through that list. Think about all the switching back and forth between perspectives and positions that is needed in the course of a day or a week. Each moment calls for new role.

The book's big idea is that there is a multiplicity to one's job as middle manager and that it is worth exploring the breadth of that. "Playbook" really is a great description for Mautz's approach. You will find lots of lists to describe the work of middle managers. Sometimes, the lists are presented in the form of acronyms like AMPLIFY, DRIVE, or EMC2.

Most management books, like others in this chapter, focus on the relationship between the manager and their employees. And Mautz addresses working with reports. Quoting a meta-analysis of 133 studies, he cautions that feedback can easily hurt subsequent performance. Data from Gallup confirms the same thing, reporting that only 26 percent of employees believe that feedback "helps them do their work better." Mautz suggests an improved feedback framework using the acronym SHARES—describe the Situation, Halo with support, Articulate with details, Share the result, give an Example, and Solicit the report's point of view.

Managing up also requires the attention of the middle manager. McKinsey reports that the relationship with your manager is "two times more critical for your career success than any other relationship." Mautz more accurately points out the interdependence, saying, "You need your boss, and they need you." And yet the power dynamic easily gets in the way. You focus too much on their approval or you get too caught up in disagreements. Mautz again offers good questions that can create better alignment with your boss, like "These are my top priorities, are they consistent with yours?" and "What measures does your boss mostly frequently discuss with you?"

That leaves peers. Coworkers make or break success when you engage in cross-functional initiatives. Mautz quotes author Dan Schwartz and suggests using influencing tactics like caring, listening, giving, and teaching. Be willing to help. Link your agenda to theirs. Admit past mistakes. Work together on a common problem. All of these foster collaboration with equals. This sums up to Mautz's belief that others-oriented leadership is how you are going to thrive as you lead from the middle.

MAUTZ AND COLLABORATOR MARK POWERS ON EMBRACING UNCERTAINTY:
"In the face of uncertainty, simply observe the uncertainty, don't overreact to it. Acknowledge its presence, don't attempt to control it by filling the unknown with misinformation and assumptions. Recognize that impermanence is inevitable (solidity is an illusion, fluidity is real) and revel in the benefits uncertainty spurs like creativity, resilience, and agility."

Becoming the Evidence-Based Manager: Making the Science of Management Work for You
by Gary Latham

"Good management always requires a lot of hard work and sustained effort, but once evidence-based techniques are mastered, it also can become fun, because employees respond so well to this approach. With employees inspired and engaged, managers don't have to battle to get desired results; they just happen."

WE ARE GOING TO lean more into a science-based approach on how to be a better manager. Our guide here is Gary Latham. You might recognize his name from his research with Edwin Locke on the effectiveness of goal-setting (see Chapter 8, "Goals," for more references). Latham brings that same research-based perspective to the practice of management; as he says in the introduction, "Most books on management only focus on the art." We want skills that we can teach and transfer to others that get superior, repeatable results. Let's use the more than fifty years of research, backed up with over thirty pages of notes and references, to get better.

Latham covers almost a dozen management practices. He moves fast and assumes a certain proficiency as a manager and familiarity with the topics that are key to effectiveness. I am putting this title at the end of the chapter hoping the other books will introduce the knowledge you need for this one. You might also want a grounding in theories on goal-setting, motivation, and decision-making provided in other chapters of *100 Best Books* before you dive deeply into *this book*.

The chapter from *Becoming the Evidence-Based Manager* I talked about with other people the most was how to develop and train a high-performing team. I am sure you can envision a variety of techniques you might use, but I wonder if any of Latham's suggestions are on your list. He first suggests that you instruct employees in functional self-talk. This technique builds awareness around one's internal dialogue replacing negative chatter with positive thoughts. Reducing negative self-talk with unemployed managers allowed 95 percent of them to find new jobs within nine months. Only 12 percent of the managers in the control group that went untrained found new employment over the same period. He recommends visualization to improve confidence in unfamiliar situations and developing self-awareness to identify limiting problems.

DAILY QUESTIONS TO ASK AS A MANAGER:
- Do you find ways to inspire your employees?
- Do they trust you?
- Do you provide them daily support?
- Do you give them autonomy?
- What about recognition for a job well done?
- Are you perceived as fair and as having high integrity?
- Have you ensured that they have the resources needed to perform their job?

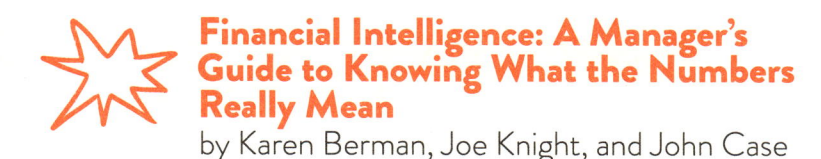

Financial Intelligence: A Manager's Guide to Knowing What the Numbers Really Mean

by Karen Berman, Joe Knight, and John Case

"The fact is, accounting and finance, like all those other business disciplines, really are as much art as they are science."

I AM GOING TO ASK for a small indulgence by including *Financial Intelligence* among these best books. Some among you might resist reading a book about accounting principles, and I would encourage you to examine that resistance. No matter the organization you work for, we are all playing a game and most of us don't know how the score is kept. A little more knowledge about the numbers means more understanding and better decisions about the business. Let me give a few examples.

Take the opening quote about accounting being as much art as science. This is surprising and sometimes frustrating when people first hear this. The reality is that the finance statements for an organization are developed to reflect as best as possible what is going on in the organization. Given the wide variation in the nature of businesses, there is variation allowed in how those businesses make decisions about their accounting. Take sales for example. Revenue transactions are the lifeblood of a business, and the timing for when you record a sale can vary. Some choose to record the revenue when the contract is signed. The most common method is to recognize the sale when the product or service is delivered. You could also choose to count the sales when the invoice is sent or bill is paid. You can see that this sole decision can have a huge impact on "the score."

In an effort to create financial statements that accurately reflect the organization, accountants generally follow a concept called the "matching principle." The goal is to match sales with the appropriate expenses. Recording material and labor costs in the same time period as the sale happened is a straightforward starting point. But what about machinery and equipment used to create those sales? Accountants will often spread out those larger capital costs over many time periods to reflect a portion of expense in each period. This is called depreciation and it again brings the art of accounting to the forefront. What is the right amount of time to depreciate a computer? One year? Five years? Now, imagine companies making decisions on forklifts, office furniture, and brewery vats. The timing of these cost allocations can significantly impact the profit a company reports.

For the purposes of this review, I will leave you with one last concept that confuses many and is a bedrock accounting principle for leaders to understand—profit does not equal cash. There can be a huge difference between when you record the revenue and when you get paid by a customer. In book publishing, I generally wait 120 days to get paid for books that are shipped to retailers. And those books were purchased months (or even years) prior to shipment, so we also spent cash far in advance to purchase that inventory. Spending cash and receiving cash can often look very different from when the profit is recorded.

What I love about *Financial Intelligence* is that it is all taught without technical language from the world of accounting. The objective of the book is to teach leaders how to understand the numbers and ask better questions. Even small accounting decisions can create significant ripple effects, influencing how various departments interpret their success. The key is understanding all the assumptions and implications and knowing how to improve together.

WISE WORDS FOR EVERYONE READING THIS BOOK:
"No, we don't expect everyone to become Wall Street analysts or accountants. We just think that if the financials are out there and the key concepts repeatedly explained, every employee in the place will be more trusting and more loyal, and the company will be stronger for it."

CHAPTER 20
TEAMS

"Sticks in a bundle are unbreakable."
—Unknown

Every team has an operating system that exists to get work done. That operating system consists of how the team communicates, the processes that are used to complete the work, and the measurements used to track progress.

An operating system always exists, whether it was created intentionally or arose haphazardly over time. The purpose of this chapter is to highlight the qualities and characteristics of a great team and the aspect of a smooth operating system to give you the opportunity to build an upgrade to the "software" that runs your organization.

LEADING: **TEAMS**

The Five Dysfunctions of a Team: A Leadership Fable
by Patrick Lencioni

> "If you could get all the people in an organization rowing in the same direction, you could dominate any industry, in any market, against any competition, at any time."

PATRICK LENCIONI opens his book with the above quote from a friend who founded a billion-dollar company. The statement seems obvious. Strong alignment creates strong results. Also notice the founder started by saying, "If you could … ". That kind of collaboration is rare. *The Five Dysfunctions of a Team* proposes a model to make it much more common.

The first dysfunction is lack of trust. There are whole books written on the importance of trust. Lencioni boils the problem down to a lack of vulnerability with fellow members. When individuals can't share mistakes or weaknesses, there is no basis on which to build trust relationships amongst team members. Exercises like sharing personal histories or behavioral assessments can accelerate the process.

Without trust, team members fear engaging in conflict. There is an illusion of agreement around important issues, but the more important quality of alignment is lacking. "Teams that engage in productive conflict know that the only purpose is the best possible solution in the shortest period of time," Lencioni says. Team members need to look for buried points of conflict and, when conversations become heated, remind each other that raising the heat is necessary.

Without conflict, team members lack commitment to the plan. Team members need to be bought into the decisions that the group makes. The commitments need to be clear for the team and for others who are affected by those decisions. Lencioni warns against a goal of consensus. He instead says that great teams create the opportunity for all members to genuinely share their views with the goal of everyone's buy-in around the final decision.

Without commitment, it is easy to avoid accountability. This is where the agreed goals become progress through action. Tolerating poor performance hurts the team. This is an easily confused point.

People often believe pointing out missed deadlines will negatively impact their relationship with other team members. In the moment, it might, but if the team has done the work to build trust, engage in healthy conflict, and align around commitments, that call out to a team member is just reinforcing the shared agreements of the team. Age-old tactics of published goals and progress reviews build processes to support collective accountability.

Without accountability, the results got lost. And the results are the whole point! All the steps leading to this point create a shared priority for everyone on the team to achieve those results. This is where individuals often have to drop their own ego or shift away from their own success to serve the greater goals of the team they are a part of. "Who do you consider to be your first team?" Lencioni asks through the new CEO, Kathryn, in the fable portion of the book. Publicly declared outcomes and tying rewards to team goals are just a few ways to put the focus back on the results.

In all honesty, I have never been a fan of this book's title. It's too negative for me. In Lencioni's other work, he talks about organizational health. I hope you'll quickly see these five qualities in that same positive light as the "the five capacities of a thriving team."

THE CAUSES AND EFFECTS OF THE FIVE DYSFUNCTIONS:
- Absence of trust → Invulnerability
- Fear of conflict → Artificial harmony
- Lack of commitment → Ambiguity
- Avoidance of accountability → Low standards
- Inattention to results → Status and ego

Traction: Get a Grip on Your Business
by Gino Wickman

"You must have one abiding vision, one voice, one culture, and one operating system. This includes a uniform approach to how you meet, how you set priorities, how you plan and set your vision, the terminology you use, and the way you communicate with employees."

EVERY TIME I PICK UP *Traction*, I have a hard time reading it. I can open it up to almost any page, read a few paragraphs, and immediately start thinking about how I might run my business better. That's pretty remarkable. It speaks to the topics that Gino Wickman chooses to cover in the book and how he focused on the best solution to each topic.

Wickman quotes a client who says, "I used to worry about a hundred different things," but now they only worry about six things: vision, people, data, process, issues, and traction. Wickman calls this the Entrepreneurial Operating System (EOS). There are other books in other chapters that deal with these subjects in more detail. The benefit you get from a book like *Traction* is a set of pieces that are designed to work together.

Now, those main topics are presented in a logical order from big (vision) to small (issues), but Wickman suggests in the final chapter of the book that there might be a different order to implement EOS in your business. First, you clear up people's responsibilities and determine who is accountable for the major functions of the business—marketing/sales, operations, and finance. "The reason we start here with every client is that [it] goes to the root of most issues," Wickman says. At the same time, you make sure you have the right people to match the company's culture and the right people in the right positions.

Next, Wickman suggests looking at priorities to gain traction. He borrows an anecdote from Stephen Covey and asks the reader to imagine filling a large glass container with big commitments, smaller day-to-day responsibilities, and the unexpected demands that appear in the normal workday. Which do you put in first?

The big rocks, says Wickman. Choose three to seven key priorities—your "rocks"—and set ninety-day commitments for everyone in the organization.

With responsibility and priority established, you next want to build rhythm to reinforce both of those initial aspects and gain more traction. Wickman says, "For now and forever, let's dispel the myth that all meetings are bad, that meetings are a waste of time, and that there are already too many of them." He says every company needs a "meeting pulse" that involves a weekly gathering and a quarterly summit. Every seven days, the leadership team needs to meet for ninety minutes to quickly cover key data, share progress on the big rocks, and share good news. Then spend the most amount of time in the meeting solving issues that are impacting the organization. The quarterly meeting should be a full day meeting with a review of all the performance numbers and all of the ninety-day rocks.

Like me, you might be wondering why he doesn't recommend starting with vision. It is the first item that Wickman talks about in *Traction*. Wickman says, "The truth is, most organizations have a pretty good idea where they're going already. After all, they're not exactly starting from scratch. ... Where will you get the most impact in the shortest period of time? What I've learned over the last decade with over 400 companies is that this approach is it."

WICKMAN'S OTHER GREAT BOOKS IN HIS TRACTION LIBRARY:
- *Rocket Fuel: The One Essential Combination That Will Get You More of What You Want from Your Business*: Learn about the powerful combination of visionary and integrator in any business.
- *What the Heck Is EOS?: A Complete Guide for Employees in Companies Running on EOS*: Here's the book to teach everyone in your organization about running the EOS.
- *How to Be a Great Boss*: Help managers at all levels get the most from their people.
- *Get a Grip: An Entrepreneurial Fable... Your Journey to Get Real, Get Simple, and Get Results*: If fiction works better for you than non-fiction, this book is the one for you.

The 4 Disciplines of Execution: Achieving Your Wildly Important Goals
by Chris McChesney, Sean Covey, and Jim Huling with Beverly Walker and Scott Thele

"Think of 4DX like the operating system on your laptop. You need a powerful operating system to execute whatever programs you choose to install. ... Likewise, without an operating system for executing your goals, no matter how beautifully designed your strategy, it won't work consistently. Even if you achieve the results, you won't be able to sustain them or surpass them, year after year."

TELL ME IF YOU have heard this one: A consultant walks into a boardroom and says, "I can make all your dreams come true in four simple steps. All you need is to do is establish a goal, measure the goal, post your progress, and celebrate the successes." If you have ever been at the kickoff to a new initiative or started reading a new business book, you were likely given a similar story. Fast forward six months and little or nothing has changed. *The 4 Disciplines of Execution* takes the same four-step process and examines it in fine detail to determine how to really make it work.

In this framework, each step is a practice to be improved. The first discipline is bringing "focus to the wildly important." We all have the day-to-day responsibilities that keep organizations running. The authors refer to this as "the whirlwind." When you want a breakthrough that will change things, you need focus. They quote Sean's father, Stephen R. Covey, who says, "You have to decide what your highest priorities are and have the courage—pleasantly, smilingly, unapologetically—to say no to other things. And the way you do that is by having a bigger 'yes' burning inside." You are looking for leverage in this stage—"What is the smallest number of battles necessary to win the war?" Your Wildly Important Goal (WIG) needs to be clearly measurable and connected to a deadline (like "Generate preorders for ten thousand copies for *100 Best Books* by its publication date on October 7, 2025"). And to keep that focus, each person only gets one WIG to work on at a time.

Many measurements that get attention, like revenue or profit, indicate success or failure, but only weeks after the actions are taken. The second discipline is to act on lead measures. The authors tell leaders to look upstream to the actions that will influence those downstream measures. What can be done today to influence the measures of tomorrow? Lead measures must be both predictive and influenceable. Sometimes, organizations know what will move the needle and simply haven't focused on it. Think keeping shelves stocked in retail stores. Other times, experimentation is needed to find those actions that will make the impact. A large shoe retailer tested over a dozen potential lead measures and unexpectedly found that measuring people's feet was the best one.

The third discipline is to keep a compelling scoreboard. Lack of engagement is what kills most change efforts. Scoreboards provide simple, visible means to share information about measures. Lag and lead measurement should appear. The existence of the scorecard separates out the breakthrough you are looking to create from the daily whirlwind that consumes so much activity and attention. Scoreboards create the visible sense of progress and "enables you to set up a winning game."

The fourth principle is creating a cadence of accountability. "Each week, every member of the team makes personal commitments to the entire team that will move the score forward," the authors write. Those commitments are given in a weekly WIG session, held on the same day and at the same time every week, without exception. The only thing talked about in the session is progress on the WIG. The agenda is as follows: Report on last week's commitments, review the scoreboard, and plan the coming week's commitments. The session lasts twenty to thirty minutes. The process emphasizes creative commitments that connect to the current situation and current state of learning, rather than elaborate planning that takes the responsibility away from the individuals engaged in the work.

In the second and third parts of the book, the authors further address how frontline leaders and the leaders of leaders interact differently with the 4DX process. Presented as a difference in authority, that division also illustrates the tactical aspects versus conceptual aspects of 4DX. As a reader, you get to see conversations at WIG meetings and many examples of organizations who adopted 4DX. All of these finer details are what makes this book so different and so valuable to your next change efforts.

GREAT QUOTES THE AUTHORS USED IN
THE 4 DISCIPLINES OF EXECUTION:
- "I define a leader as anyone who takes responsibility for finding the potential in people and processes and who has the courage to develop that potential." —Brené Brown
- "When leaders define clear ownership and invest in others, they have sown the seeds of success and earned the right to hold people accountable." —Liz Wiseman
- "Leadership is communicating to people their worth and potential so clearly that they come to see it in themselves." —Stephen Covey
- "Without clear visible measures, the same goal will mean a hundred different things to a hundred different people." —Jim Stuart
- "If your entire paycheck was based on this one commitment, two things would happen automatically. You would be careful in making the commitment, and you would be absolutely certain to follow through." —Hyrum Smith
- "Intent is more important than technique." —Mahan Khalsa

Good to Great: Why Some Companies Make the Leap...and Others Don't
by Jim Collins

"The good-to-great companies did get incredible commitment and alignment—they artfully managed change—but they never really spent much time thinking about it. It was utterly transparent to them. We learned that under the right conditions, the problems of commitment, alignment, motivation, and change just melt away. They largely take care of themselves."

JIM COLLINS has been studying the operating systems of companies for over three decades. *Built to Last*, which Collins wrote with Jerry Porras, studies visionary companies in a search for timeless fundamental principles that explain their enduring success. In *Great by Choice*, which he wrote with Morten Hansen, Collins seeks to explain the extraordinary growth of startups within turbulent environments. Collins also wrote a handbook on the decline of great companies, even chronicling a few of his past shining examples, in *How the Mighty Fall*. The Collins book I chose for this collection, however, starts with the most widely applicable question of his works.

In the opening to *Good to Great*, Collins tells a story about a dinner where one of his readers shares their admiration for *Built to Last* but laments its limited applicability. "The companies you wrote about, for the most part, were always great," they said. "Can a good company become a great company, and if so, how?" Collins could have taken the comments lightly and moved on. But he didn't. Collins spent the next five years researching that question, trying to find out if companies can go from good to great.

In recent years, Collins has created a framework called The Map to connect the ideas from all of his books and continues to use three divisions he presented in *Good to Great*. Disciplined People is the first stage. In Collins's research, Good to Great companies were found to be run by Level 5 leaders. These executives build "enduring greatness through a paradoxical blend of personal humility and professional will." In the media coverage of these CEOs, journalists consistently used words like quiet, humble, gracious, and understated. Equally important was a "ferocious resolve, an almost stoic determination to do whatever needs to be done to make the company great." The next thing Level 5 leaders do is "get the right people on the bus," to use one of Collins's now famous phrases from the book. "Who?" comes before "What?"—that is, deciding on people comes before deciding on the company's direction. In Collins's research, the less successful comparison companies did the opposite—started with vision and then recruited a team to execute the vision.

Stage Two of the Map Framework is Disciplined Thought. Collins tells all leaders to find ways to build a culture that confronts brutal facts. In his research, he never found one company to have better information than another. Instead, CEOs continually ignored changes in the market and what the future held for them. Imagine leading Kroger in the 1970s and realizing that every store needed to be replaced—and then having the courage to follow through on doing it. Collins also talks about the power of focus, which we see appear in several places in *100 Best Books*. His formula, the Hedgehog Concept, works at the intersection of what you are most passionate about, what you can be best in the world at, and what drives your economic engine. He writes that the Hedgehog Concept is not a goal, strategy, or intention to be the best: "it is an *understanding* of what you *can* be the best at."

The third stage is Disciplined Action. In his current Map framework, Collins still promotes the Flywheel effect—"Tremendous power exists in the fact of continued improvement and the delivery of results." The most remarkable insight from his research is how smoothly the good-to-great companies built momentum. Leaders didn't spend time on motivation, alignment, or big change efforts. Results inspired people and naturally created more alignment and more momentum. Let all the teachings in *Good to Great* do the same for your efforts to succeed.

THE TWO OTHER METHODS OF DISCIPLINED ACTION FROM COLLINS'S *GREAT BY CHOICE*:

- **The Twenty-Mile March** asks companies to hit regular milestones with great consistency over long periods of time. The effort teaches individuals and organizations that success arises from their actions, not the conditions they are experiencing.
- **Fire Bullets, Then Cannonballs** emphasizes the power of acting experimentally. Successful companies tried lots of small things and informed their big launches with the information they learned. The lack of experimentation and the lack of big launches both severely limited the upside that high-growth companies experienced.

CHAPTER 21
HIRING

"A small team of A+ players can run circles around a giant team of B and C players."
—Steve Jobs

Here is the thing with talent—being around it makes you better. You probably already know the line that you are only as smart as the five smartest people around you. If you are a manager, great talent creates better results.

Finding that talent is the challenge. The books in this chapter highlight how poor we are at evaluating and hiring great people. Intelligence and personality tests are faulty predictors of long-term success. The questions we often ask in interviews don't uncover the information to determine if the individual is a good fit. I included *Moneyball* by Michael Lewis in this chapter to show how professional sports used to evaluate talent and how it was revolutionized by new data-driven analytics.

Alongside all the problems, the books listed here also provide solutions for evaluating and hiring talented people that will make your company better.

LEADING: **HIRING**

Talent: How to Identify Energizers, Creatives, and Winners Around the World
by Tyler Cowen and Daniel Gross

"Just about everyone is on a quest to find talent in others or to show off their own."

TYLER COWEN AND DANIEL GROSS both run organizations that are constantly searching for and evaluating talent. As they evaluate proposals ranging from establishing think tanks in Indonesia to asteroid mining in outer space, they are always asking, "Who is going to do this?" People who can execute those kinds of big ideas are rare. The opportunity that the authors see is that the methods we use to evaluate talent are weak. We miss potential, both hidden and in plain sight. "The world's inability to find and mobilize enough talent [is] one of the most significant failures of our time," they write.

Cowen and Gross also identify another aspect of talent that is often overlooked. Salary and location are important in choosing a job, but each of us benefits from being around strong talent. During the Renaissance, the city of Florence, Italy, produced a long string of stand-out artists, including da Vinci and Michelangelo, even though the population of the area was sixty thousand people. Germany outperformed the world in classical music over a two-hundred-year period with Bach, Handel, Beethoven, Wagner, Brahms, and so many more. My first job out of college was with GE during the peak Jack Welch years, and the talent that existed there at that time forever changed the trajectory of my life. Good people around us make us better.

What you read *Talent* for is the authors' survey of common truths and the limitations on what can be believed. Take intelligence. Most would agree that they want to hire and work with smart people. In some professions, like that of inventor, IQ is incredibly important, but for most positions it doesn't explain why the successful are successful. A Finnish study found IQ only explained 8 percent of success in doctors and 5 percent in lawyers. Another study found that intelligence was a very poor predictor of lifetime earnings. The authors even note that the National Association of Colleges and Employers, a group that might be motivated to emphasize the importance of intelligence, listed ten qualities in their 2020 job survey, seven of which had nothing to do with intelligence. The authors write, "Intelligence clearly matters; it simply does not dominate in relevance."

Cowen and Gross do the same thing to the five-factor personality theory, which they say creates a good vocabulary for groups but provides weak predictive qualities, with the potential exception of conscientiousness. They introduce their own factors to consider like rate of self-improvement, ability to understand complex hierarchies, adhesiveness in teams, and "fun-ness."

For me, the book truly shines in its chapters on disabilities and minorities. The term "disability" is a misnomer from their perspective and another example of how easily talent can be overlooked. Research suggests individuals with dyslexia are more likely to become entrepreneurs. Ed Catmull, the former president of Pixar, rose to the top of his field while having a condition called aphantasia, which is the inability to visualize images in one's mind. To better identify autistic candidates for programming roles, Microsoft adapted their interview process to "allow email to replace the phone call, [give] individuals the chance to do a practice interview first, and [give] individuals the option to code using their own laptops instead of having to do whiteboard work in front of other individuals."

Talent in female and Black, Indigenous, and people of color (BIPOC) candidates is just as poorly assessed. Cultural differences and gender bias create more formal interchanges, so candidates feel less able to share and take fewer chances. So much potential is missed. Women are better at assessing intelligence than men; Y Combinator reports women being better at detecting deceitful founders in the interviewing process. And talent in BIPOC communities is completely overlooked. "It is remarkable how many people still have not even arrived at the stage of having any consciousness of the underlying problem."

And that's the point in this book—there are incredible people being misjudged from so many directions. Opportunity abounds if you can get better at assessing talented individuals and hiring them for your organization.

MORE INTERVIEW QUESTIONS:
- Give me an example of a time you went above and beyond? And then ask seven more times to thoroughly get past all of the expected responses.
- If we looked at your Netflix, what sorts of movies would be recommended?
- What have you achieved that is unusual for your peer group?
- What is one mainstream view that you wholeheartedly agree with?
- Which of your beliefs are you most likely wrong about?
- How ambitious are you?
- What skill do you work on every day to improve?
- What criteria would you use for hiring?
- How do you think this interview is going?

Who
by Geoff Smart and Randy Street

"Who is your number-one problem. Not what."

SOMETIMES when you read a book, it's helpful to know its origin story. That's the case with *Who*. Geoff Smart is the son of Brad Smart, the author of *Topgrading*. With his father, Geoff co-created the Topgrading methodology that was a highly influential talent management process in the 2000s with Fortune 500 companies. Geoff went on to found his own company ghSMART and focus on management assessment for CEOs and investors. That final audience is important for two reasons.

First, the authors of *Who* write primarily from the perspective of executive search. The supporting quotes come from private equity investors and large company CEOs. Don't let that dissuade you, because the book is also designed to be an airplane read that executives will get through. All readers benefit from a simplified interviewing process with the best components of Topgrading in a better ordered process. Some will still want the three hundred pages of deeper detail in *Topgrading* (and you can see it recommended below).

Who's primary complaint is that people spend too little time truly evaluating candidates. Some depend too much on instinct (the art critic). Some spend too much time selling the opportunity (the suitor). Others use puzzles or gimmicks to tease out useless information (the prosecutor and the trickster). The authors call these "voodoo practices" that don't assess the individual's fit for the position. The authors write, "According to the four thousand studies and the meta-analyses we have examined, traditional interviewing is simply not predictive of job performance."

First, get a clear mission, outcomes, and competencies for the position. How can you hire the right person without understanding what they need to be doing? "You'll know you have a good mission when [people] understand what you are looking for without having to ask clarifying questions," write the authors. Outcomes with specific goals and definitive timelines lead to a clear list of competencies. Smart and Street provide a list of potential ones that could be helpful for your scorecard, but tucked at the back of the book is an insight from research they did with the University of Chicago by looking at over three hundred CEO interviews. CEOs who excelled in the soft skills of listening, giving feedback, and showing respect with people succeeded 57 percent of the time in their new position. CEOs who were decisive, persistent, and set high standards succeeded 100 percent of the time and created significant value for shareholders. Remember, and the authors also point this out, to make sure to build a job profile that matches the culture of your company.

After building a strong pool of candidates from referrals, recruiters, and researchers, you need to start interviewing. The authors suggest four different interviews "to collect facts and data about somebody's performance that spans decades." The screening interview is done over the phone and takes less than thirty minutes, with the purpose of narrowing down the list. The Topgrading interview digs deep, can take a few hours, and walks chronologically through a candidate's career (see the questions below). The focused interview, which can take place after the Topgrading interview, goes further and specifically targets the outcomes and competencies for the position. The final step is interviewing references (and the authors suggest that interviewers ask candidates to help with scheduling these).

When the authors asked leaders about talent that contributed to business success, the leaders reported that 52 percent of that success came from the quality of their talent.

FIVE INTERVIEWING QUESTIONS:
1. What were you hired to do?
2. What accomplishments are you most proud of?
3. What were some of the low points during that job?
4. Who were the people you worked with specifically?
   What will they tell me your greatest strengths and weaknesses were?
   How would you rate the team you inherited?
   And how would you rate it again when you left?
5. Why did you leave that job?

Work Rules!: Insights from Inside Google That Will Transform How You Live and Lead
by Laszlo Bock

"The question is not what management system is required to change the nature of man, but rather what is required to change the nature of work."

THE OPENING QUOTE for this book might sound like it came from an early nineteenth-century Enlightenment philosopher debating the best way to consider the slowly industrializing world. Instead, it is from a twenty-first century HR leader named Laszlo Bock. Rather than making sense of steam engines and railroads, Bock spent a decade at Google during its largest periods of growth, when they were adding as many as ten thousand people *a year*. Now, imagine a company with very smart people building world-changing technology, and take their deep desire to learn and point it at figuring out the best ways to build an organization.

There are books upon books where researchers share their laboratory findings and observational studies on psychology and sociology. Those researchers and (more often) other authors then translate those insights into better ways to run the workplace. Imagine how much better it would be if you could build a living laboratory with workers and real work that needed to be done. That's essentially what Google did with their own company. They embedded researchers in their People Operations (HR) group to determine the best ways to operate their growing company. Bock's approach in the book is essentially describing Google's A/B testing of established norms against newer theories in organizational management.

Let's start with hiring. Google added roughly five thousand people every year, and to get there they started with one to three million applicants. That makes hiring both a volume problem and a selection problem. To meet the volume, they treated it like a search engine problem. They built enormous lists of potential Googlers through LinkedIn and university alumni lists. Consider this statement from Bock: "In fact, it is now possible to identify virtually every person working in a particular company or industry." They found referrals from internal employees to be very effective as well. The trouble was the hiring process itself.

Google selected less than 0.25 percent of applicants, and when they started, it would take as many as twenty-five interviews over several months to determine if a single applicant was a good fit. Applicants are always interviewed by a group of employees, including one person from outside the job function. The interviews are heavily structured with questions that have been tested for particular job functions. "Until we hit about twenty thousand employees, most people in our company spent four to ten hours per week on hiring, and our top executives would easily spend a full day each week on it," Bock writes. Referrers didn't want to put their friend through that process. So, Google researched how the company could keep hiring successful candidates but reduce the time spent interviewing. Their team found they could reduce the number of interviews to four and still determine hireability with an 86 percent confidence. They saved massive amounts of time devoted to recruiting and improved the experience for applicants.

Google has applied the same methodology to employee performance reviews by improving job function profiles through studying their highest performers. They did the same thing with clarifying the functions of a manager that actually improve employee performance (yes, managers really matter). *Work Rules!* is included here because we all have the opportunity to improve the workplace for employees. Experiment more!

MORE MANAGERIAL INSIGHTS FROM GOOGLE'S PROJECT OXYGEN:

1. Be a good coach.
2. Empower the team and do not micromanage.
3. Express interest/concern for team members' success and personal well-being.
4. Be very productive/results-oriented.
5. Be a good communicator—listen and share information.
6. Help the team with career development.
7. Have a clear vision/strategy for the team.
8. Have important technical skills that help advise the team.

Moneyball: The Art of Winning an Unfair Game
by Michael Lewis

"If gross miscalculations of a person's value could occur on a baseball field, before a live audience of thirty thousand, and a television audience of millions more, what did that say about the measurement of performance in other lines of work?"

IT'S REALLY HARD to overstate how perfect Billy Beane is as the protagonist in *Moneyball*. Beane is recruited into professional baseball using scouting techniques that favor physical characteristics and institutional illusions of talent. After forgoing college and being drafted by the Mets, Beane failed to make any impact during his seven years in MLB. He retires as a player and asks to become a scout, unheard of among former major leaguers. Beane then pioneers the use of a statistics-based approach for evaluating talent that allows the Oakland A's to compete successfully against teams, like the New York Yankees, that spent three times the A's budget on player salaries.

In the past two decades, data and analytics have come to be a part of every form of professional sports. In the NBA, that meant more three-point shots. In the NFL, more teams attempted fourth down conversions than even before. "Moneyball" itself has become a term that has entered the vernacular as the approach one takes to finding undervalued talent or approaches. As I was looking at selections for this chapter, I wondered if all of the lessons from the book had been extracted and accounted for in today's world. I promise they haven't.

When you watch the 2011 movie version of *Moneyball,* you get the impression that Beane stumbled upon sabermetrics after talking to an unknown assistant. But in real life when Beane entered scouting, the A's were already a decade into thinking about a more objective approach to player evaluation. By the time he took over as general manager in 1997, Beane had read all twelve of Bill James's *Baseball Abstracts,* the publications that popularized a host of new measurements that better predicted the performance of baseball players.

In *Moneyball*, we follow Beane through the A's' 2002 season. At this point, he has fully embraced these new metrics and that goes against all the established norms for the sport. This allows him to get better talent for less money, a strategy critical for his small-budget team. Beane drafts college players with demonstrated talent versus high-sought after high school players. He pursues players late in their career who other teams have given up on because the statistics show they maintain their value on offense. And he actively works on acquiring players later in the season that he couldn't have hoped to afford on opening day. Michael Lewis picked a great year to profile the team. After a slow start to the season, the A's go on a twenty-game winning streak and win their division.

Lewis says all of his books in some way are about people who see an opportunity in a market that no one else can see. In the case of *Moneyball,* you might add "…and the courage to act on it." There were individuals who saw a completely different way to evaluate talent, but didn't try it. What Lewis does so well is show how difficult it is to have the courage to adopt a new paradigm. Even after Beane starts implementing his new strategy, there are still coaches and players on his team who can't believe the traditional truths he has abandoned. Seeing it all play out in over three hundred pages gives time for the nuances of creativity, conflict, and courage to play out when someone tries to introduce a change that so many believe won't work.

HERE ARE SOME MORE OF LEWIS'S PIECES ON TALENT:

- **"Coach Leach Goes Deep, Very Deep":** This 8,700-word article profiles former Texas Tech football coach Mike Leach and his game-changing view for how college football should be played. (*The New York Times Magazine,* December 4, 2005)
- **"The No-Stats All-Star":** This 9,000-word story centered on the Houston Rockets' Shane Battier and his almost unmatched ability to make his team better when he is on the court—and not through offense. (*The New York Times Magazine,* February 13, 2009)
- **"Commie Ball":** "There's at least a half a billion dollars of baseball players in Cuba right now and probably a lot more." (*Vanity Fair,* July 2008)

SECTION FIVE
CONNECTION

RELATIONSHIPS
GENEROSITY
CONVERSATIONS
COACHING

CHAPTER 22
RELATIONSHIPS

"In every relationship, the work is never just in fixing what's broken. It's in nurturing what's beautiful."
—Unknown

With both work and life, we are in relationships with others. I couldn't envision this book not having a chapter on how to be better within those relationships. The first two books in this chapter teach us how important the quality of our relationships is to our health and well-being. We often can't see the effects we are having on others or that they are having on us, but they are powerful. The other two books are about improving the quality of those relationships. They show us how and where to invest our time and energy.

Reading any book in this entire section on generosity, coaching, and conversations is an investment in improving the relationships in your life.

CONNECTION: **RELATIONSHIPS**

The Good Life: Lessons from the World's Longest Scientific Study of Happiness
by Robert Waldinger and Marc Schulz

THE BOOK PUBLISHER in me believes someone buried the lede in titling this book. Yes, there are many lessons that can be found in *The Good Life,* but the headline is really this (found on page 10):

"If we had to take all eighty-four years of the Harvard Study and boil it down to a single principle for living, one life investment that is supported by similar findings across a wide variety of other studies, it would be this: Good relationships keep us healthier and happier. Period."

The Harvard Study of Adult Development is a three-generation, 1,300-person longitudinal study that started with the intention of finding what "made human beings thrive." Up to that point, the primary interest in the field of medicine was to find what caused people to fail. This study found that yes, exercise, diet, and income matter, but social connections matter just as much.

In a meta-analysis conducted by Julianne Holt-Lunstad and her colleagues, they examined 148 studies from countries all over the world that included 300,000 people in total. Their conclusion: "Social connection increased the likelihood of surviving any given year by more than 50 percent." It is rare to see such profound effects in research studies. In this case, the effects of positive relationships on your health are equivalent to the effects of quitting smoking.

What I like about this book is the coverage of all different kinds of relationships, with each given a chapter or more. With intimate partners, the authors advise cultivating affection and empathy. With family members, they suggest you notice when you want someone to be different from who they are. They quote Gallup research that shows people who have a best friend at work are more likely to be engaged in their job. For women, the friend effect doubles their engagement likelihood. Friendships of varying depths can also be beneficial. "Some of the most beneficial relationships can be with people we don't spend a lot of time with or don't know very well," the authors write.

For me, the most important question the book offers is this: What action could I take today to give attention and appreciation to someone who deserves it? The book ends with an answer to this advice: "Think about someone, just one person who is important to you. ... Now think about what you would thank them for if you thought you would never see them again. And at this moment—right now—turn to them. Call them. Tell them."

HERE ARE THREE SUGGESTIONS TO ENERGIZE YOUR RELATIONSHIPS:

1. **Generosity:** Relationships are reciprocal systems. Research shows helping others benefits givers and receivers equally.
2. **Change things up:** Find ways to move past trauma and disappointment and open yourself to new experiences with others.
3. **Curiosity:** Open up new conversations and expose new knowledge that you never knew was there.

Connected: The Surprising Power of Our Social Networks and How They Shape Our Lives
by Nicholas Christakis and James Fowler

"Social networks are creative. And what these networks create does not belong to any one individual—it is shared by all those in the network. In this way, a social network is like a commonly owned forest: We all stand to benefit from it, but we also must work together to ensure it remains healthy and productive."

CONNECTED is a different take on relationships. The book reads more from the popular science genre than business or self-help, yet the findings deserve our attention. The book looks at linkages and the networks that form from them. They also look at what is passed along those connections. In the post-pandemic world, we might think of germs being shared, but their research finds that happiness, violence, fashion, and obesity also get passed along those same pathways. And in the same way that it can be hard to see how we got sick from those around us, the authors show that things like emotions and behaviors can move just as easily between those who are connected to one another.

The research from Nicholas Christakis and James Fowler that is probably most remarkable is that a broad range of contagions don't just affect family, friends, and acquaintances. The broader experiments in mapping social networks now show effects that can cascade out two or three connections beyond you. Take smoking and its decline from 45 percent to 21 percent of the US population over the course of the last fifty years. The authors' research shows that when one person quits smoking, there is a ripple effect that rolls out to friends, friends of friends, and friends of friends of friends. In this case, cultural norms heavily influenced the acceptance of this behavior. Education also played a role, both in seeding smoking's original US adoption in the early twentieth century among the highly educated and its mass cessation later in the same century by the same group.

With *100 Best Books'* focus on work and life, we can find many examples of how connections are constantly at work in our lives in interesting ways. Mark Granovetter found that if you ask someone who helped them get their last job, they will very likely say it was a person they occasionally or rarely see, highlighting the power of weak ties in one's network. Brian Uzzi found that the most successful teams in Broadway productions were formed by having members that previously worked together mixed with some new members. That combination of strong and weak ties balanced easy communication with enhanced creativity. And consider this research about piano teachers in Tempe, Arizona: "38 percent of the [customer referrals] came from people who were three degrees removed from the piano teacher."

So let us invest in the important relationships around us, but I am also left with this thought from the authors: "On a human level, social networks affect every aspect of our lives. Events occurring in distant others can determine the shape of our lives, what we think, what we desire, whether we fall ill or die. In a social chain reaction, we respond to faraway events, often without being consciously aware of it."

MORE HIDDEN WAYS RELATIONSHIPS INFLUENCE US:

- **Reduce disease spread:** Immunize acquaintances of randomly selected individuals, because those nominated are more likely to have more links and be more central to a network. With this approach, you can immunize 30 percent of the population and get the same protection that would normally require 99 percent immunization levels.
- **Loneliness:** "At the periphery, people have fewer friends; this makes them lonely, but this also tends to drive them to cut the few ties they have left. But before they do, they may infect their friends with the same feeling of loneliness, starting the cycle anew."
- **Emotions in families:** "The strongest path was from daughters to both parents while conversely the parents' emotional state appeared to have no effect on their daughters. Fathers' emotions affected their wives and their sons but not their daughters."

The Power of Vulnerability: Teachings on Authenticity, Connection, and Courage
by Brené Brown

"How-to doesn't work. If how-to worked, we would not be the most obese, in debt, medicated, and addicted adults in human history. If how-to worked, we wouldn't be struggling as much as we are with feeling lonely and disconnected. ... [If] how-to be happy worked, all of us in the room, myself included, would not struggle all the time with feeling like we are enough."

BRENÉ BROWN'S work could go in any number of chapters in this book. Her research touches on some of the most fundamental qualities of being human. At its core, she is teaching us how to connect, reconnect, and stay connected. Vulnerability is required for all of those. Shame gets in the way.

Brown has sold more books than any other non-fiction author in the last twenty years, and I am going to go against the millions of people who love her titles to recommend something else. *The Power of Vulnerability* is a set of live sessions that were recorded in 2010. She is speaking after her breakout TEDxHouston talk and her closing TED Talk on the main stage in 2012, just before *Daring Greatly* was published. She says in the performance, "This is the first and only place when all of my work has really come together. I have never talked about the shame work, the wholeheartedness and the vulnerability, all in one place before."

In summarizing her work, the arc would go something like this. Love and belonging are irreducible needs of every human being. Fitting in or the inability to connect with others becomes the barrier to that real belonging. This is where her emphasis on shame comes in. The shame scripts are either "Never good enough" or "Who do you think you are?" Why does all of this matter? Well, as she says, because "shame is highly correlated to addiction, depression, suicide, bullying, aggression, violence, and eating disorders."

In Brown's research, she found people with a deep sense of love and belonging believe that they are worthy of love and belonging. These folks are what she called the wholehearted, and the wholehearted talk constantly about vulnerability. And vulnerability is the bright light that withers shame away. We see things from others' perspectives. We pass fewer judgments on others. We identify with others' emotions, we share back what we are seeing, and we say, "Me too. I've been there."

I absolutely love this line of Brown's, and it fully explains why I put this recording in the chapter on relationships: "Shame happens between people, and it is healed between people."

There is something special in these six hours of talks. Brown admits, "I write because it is a necessity, I speak because I love it. But I can't go around everywhere, so I put my stuff in books. I enjoy it sometimes, but writing it is tough for me." So go read *Daring Greatly*, but that love for speaking and teaching comes through so strongly in *The Power of Vulnerability* that I have to suggest this as the best way to experience Brown and her work.

BOOKS BY BRENE BROWN THAT YOU CAN READ:
- *Gift of Imperfection* (2010) - Choose authenticity over perfection
- *Daring Greatly* (2012) - Choose vulnerability over shame
- *Rising Strong* (2015) - Choose resilience over defeat
- *Braving The Wilderness* (2017) - Choose belonging over fitting in
- *Dare to Lead* (2018) - Choose courage over comfort

The Seven Principles for Making Marriage Work
by John Gottman and Nan Silver

"Only 40 percent of the time do couples divorce because they are having frequent, devastating fights. More often marriages end because, to avoid constant skirmishes, [partners] distance themselves so much that their friendship and sense of connection are lost."

JOHN GOTTMAN is another person Malcolm Gladwell made a household name. Gladwell opened his book *Blink* with the story of the Love Lab at the University of Washington and Gottman's ability to predict in minutes whether a couple would still be together years later. That remarkable feat is worthy of praise, but we're not going to start using high-speed cameras to capture microexpressions on our partners' faces. Gottman's lifetime of research into relationships is what we should focus on.

Gottman says that when negativity finds its way into the heart of a relationship, it often proves lethal to a marriage. He refers to these specific qualities as the "Four Horsemen." Criticism arrives first, as rebukes focus on the person, rather than the situation. Next, contempt appears, as one partner believes they are superior to the other. That's followed by defensiveness, which seems understandable given the downward trajectory, but it serves as an accelerant. Defensiveness places the blame right back on the other partner. The difficulty and strife of the first three horsemen usher in the final arrival—stonewalling. Partners stop communicating "as though [they] could care less" about what each other is saying.

Gottman's research keeps pointing back to one insight: Most marital arguments cannot be resolved. Take a minute with that one. Most of the conflict in your most important relationship will not go away. Gottman says 69 percent of marital conflict has this perpetual nature. He identifies the primary cause as unexpressed dreams, with each partner holding a differing value or moral around an important topic. Gottman encourages couples to explore those dreams and make those beliefs known. The objective is to find the areas that are non-negotiable and define those areas in as small a range as possible. At the same time, look for the areas of compromise and make those possibilities as broad as possible. These conversations will be difficult but fruitful if handled with care.

I would argue that the next six principles are meant to create space for less negativity around avoidable conflict and creating more engaged, loving relationships. Gottman says you should continually invest in "love maps" and build on the knowledge you have of your partner's life. As an antidote to contempt, you can "get in the habit of scanning for qualities and actions that you can appreciate." Another technique is to simply turn toward each other in the small moments that happen throughout the day. Build rituals and traditions around things like weekly date nights or yearly celebrations.

Gottman gives readers lots of recommendations, questions, and exercises to work on improving the quality of marriages. He ends the book with great advice on making change: "Being able to say 'I'm sorry' and mean it is a pretty great gift to give your spouse—and yourself as well. The more you can imbue your relationship with the spirit of thanksgiving and the graceful presence of praise, the more profound your life together will be."

FIVE QUESTIONS TO IMPROVE POSITIVITY AND CONNECTION:
1. I can list my partner's three favorite movies. True or False?
2. I am really proud of my partner. True or False?
3. We just love talking to one another. True or False?
4. I feel confident we can resolve most issues between us. True or False?
5. We have ways of becoming renewed and refreshed when we are burned out or fatigued. True or False?

CHAPTER 23
GENEROSITY

"No one has ever become poor by giving."
—Unknown

I once heard that courtesies like holding the door for someone or saying "thank you" were small acts of generosity. Offering that helping hand is a habit-building reminder of how to put someone else's needs above our own. Those reminders activate the brain's other scripts that see the benefit of working with others. This is important because our brains are wired to see scarcity and feel pain in the event of loss. Sharing creates safety. Asking for help creates connection. The books in this chapter show us how to be generous and the broader benefits we gain from that.

CONNECTION: **GENEROSITY**

Give and Take: Why Helping Others Drives Our Success
by Adam Grant

"The researchers created an energy network map, which looked like a model of the galaxy. The takers were black holes. They sucked the energy from those around them. The givers were suns: They injected light around the organization."

I ORIGINALLY READ *Give and Take* in 2015, after the book came out in paperback. My copy is filled with highlighted passages that caught my attention. In a blog post, I raved about it as one of the best books I had read in years. And then I asked a female colleague about the book, and she said, "I felt like I knew all of this already." That put me into a bit of a spiral. Should I know all this already? Was I not a giver? Was I a taker? Or maybe a matcher?

Adam Grant writes about these three styles and shows how each acts when put into different situations with each other. My favorite shortcut to describing a giver comes from entrepreneur Adam Rifkin— "You should be willing to do something that will take you five minutes or less *for anybody*." How does that land for you? Do you feel a strong yes to Rifkin's statement or do you feel some hesitation?

In a study of pharmaceutical salespeople assigned to a new product, giving was the only characteristic that could predict performance. Givers are more likely to admit mistakes and release their attachment to prior commitments, making them less susceptible to the sunk-cost fallacy. Givers tend to create psychologically safe environments where people learn better and innovate more. Even NASA sees the value of giving on space flights, encouraging "expedition behavior" where individuals put "the group's goals and mission first and [show] the same amount of concern for others as you do yourself." The case is pretty clear for the positive effect of giving, but let's give one more interesting example.

You may be familiar with the power of asking others for advice. Researcher Katie Liljenquist has identified four benefits of seeking advice. First, the asker learns things they didn't know. Second, it encourages others to see things from another perspective. Third, asking for advice builds commitment on the part of those who are asked, since it is their ideas that form the next potential steps. Finally, when we ask for help, we show others that we "respect and admire their insights and expertise." Asking advice is effective with all three styles. "Giving advice makes takers feel important, and it makes givers feel helpful. Matchers often enjoy giving advice...[because] it's a low-cost way of racking up credits that they can cash later," Grant writes.

What's interesting is that givers are just as likely to be at the top of a graduation class as they are to be at the bottom. There can be serious emotional and energetic costs to being a giver. Grant provides some antidotes. Givers often self-sacrifice for others to the point of burning themselves out. The research shows that successful givers need an equally high interest in themselves and should engage in activities that they personally find fulfilling to maintain their motivation for all activities. The prescription is specific: two hours per week in a different domain. In negotiations, givers can be at a disadvantage, but the tables turn when they change their perspective and imagine themselves representing a friend, allowing their giver tendencies to positively serve themselves.

ACTIONS THAT CONNECT PEOPLE AND CREATE IMPACT:

- **Run a reciprocity ring:** Gather a group that makes requests and helps one another fulfill them.
- **Practice powerless communication:** Shift from talking to listening, from self-promoting to seeking advice, and from advocating to inquiring.
- **Help fund a project:** Use Kickstarter or Kiva and help someone create their dream.
- **Seek help more often:** "Help generously and without thought of return, but also ask often for what you need."

The Go-Giver: A Little Story about a Powerful Business Idea
by Bob Burg and John David Mann

"Every giving can happen only because it is also a receiving."

WE CAN LEARN a lot from Pindar, the fictional mentor in *The Go-Giver*. He is advising Joe, the down-on-his-luck salesman who isn't going to make his quota this quarter. Pindar agrees to meet with Joe the next day, on a Saturday. He tries to reset Joe's mindset from that first encounter. "You and I are coming from two different directions when it comes to wealth creation," Pindar says. Joe has already been described as a go getter, but Pindar cautions him that success doesn't come from making lots of money. He says it comes from giving, from being a go-*giver*.

Each day for a week, Pindar meets with Joe for lunch and introduces him to a new go-giver to show him another facet of the power of giving. Pindar places one condition on this mentoring: For each new lesson, Joe needs to practice the lesson before they meet the next day. We could all use pushes like this to put what we learn into practice quickly. Joe sees a new vision of success in each new introduction, but it's the translations that Joe makes that shows where the lessons are really learned.

If I say much more I am going to give away the story and the real opportunity to learn from *The Go-Giver*. Take its inclusion in this collection as signal enough that it is worth your time for its lessons in generosity.

THE GO-GIVER'S FIVE LAWS OF STRATOSPHERIC SUCCESS:

- **The Law of Value:** Your true worth is determined by how much more you give in value than you take in payment.
- **The Law of Compensation:** Your income is determined by how many people you serve and how well you serve them.
- **The Law of Influence:** Your influence is determined by how abundantly you place other people's interests first.
- **The Law of Authenticity:** The most valuable gift you have to offer is yourself.
- **The Law of Receptivity:** The key to effective giving is to stay open to receiving.

CONNECTION: **GENEROSITY**

Setting the Table: The Transforming Power of Hospitality in Business
by Danny Meyer

"I don't believe that the principle of erring on the side of generosity is inherently superior to the principle of fiercely protecting yourself in order to make as much money as possible. But generosity is the way I choose to do business in my restaurants, and so far it has always contributed mightily to our success."

IN NEW YORK CITY, if you have eaten at Union Square Cafe, The Modern, or Gramercy Tavern, you have eaten at Danny Meyer's Union Square Hospitality Group. If you have eaten a burger at Shake Shack, you have enjoyed the food at Meyer's most successful global venture.

Setting the Table details Meyer's first twenty years in the restaurant business. The book itself could be categorized to appear in a number of different chapters in *100 Best Books*. There are big leadership lessons to be found in its pages. Meyer is a product developer, and this book could be placed alongside discussions in the Customers chapter. He is very savvy with marketing and publicity, both of which have served his businesses very well over the years. The book is also a biography about Meyer's life and his restaurants' origins. Some sorting and skimming are required to find the best of his advice. At its core, though, the book is about the magical power of hospitality.

Meyers writes: "Understanding the distinction between service and hospitality has been at the foundation of our success. Service is the technical delivery of a product. Hospitality is how the delivery of that product makes its recipient feel. Service is a monologue—we decide how we want to do things and set our own standards for service. Hospitality, on the other hand, is a dialogue. To be on a guest's side requires listening to that person with every sense and following up with a thoughtful, gracious, appropriate response. It takes both great service and great hospitality to rise to the top."

I put *Setting the Table* in this chapter because of the insights Meyer shares about what generosity looks like in practice. In one section, Meyer writes about the list of qualities that he looks for in the managers they hire for his restaurants. He wants his managers to hold a charitable assumption about guests—like assuming the best if they arrive late to their reservation. Meyers asks the managers to work from a sense of abundance. When Union Square Hospitality Group participates in New York City's Restaurant Week, they create a special $20 lunch like other participants, but they also give each patron a $20 gift certificate to return again. He asks managers to work from a place of trust, rather than fear. He asks them to think about words like listening, empowering, hopeful, and giving.

At Meyer's restaurants, they have an established process for addressing mistakes made with customers. First, you need to have awareness of the mistake, because many mistakes go completely unnoticed. You then need to acknowledge the mistake and apologize without excuses. That is followed by action and "[saying] what you are going to do to make amends." The end of their process always includes additional generosity—a complimentary dessert or possibly even a free meal. I remember my mentor Jack Covert telling me that mistakes always created amazing opportunities for showing even more care in the response.

Let me end with two quotes from Meyer: "Hospitality is hopeful, it's confident, thoughtful, optimistic, generous, and open hearted." And "No amount of generosity has so far succeeded in putting us out of business!"

MEYER'S TRAITS THAT TURN GREAT MANAGERS INTO GREAT LEADERS:

- Honor
- Discipline
- Consistency
- Clear communication
- Courage
- Wisdom
- Compassion
- Flexibility
- Ability to love (and be loved)
- Humility
- Confidence (to possess it and to inspire it in team members)
- Passion for the work and for excellence
- Positive self-image

CHAPTER 24
CONVERSATIONS

"A great conversation requires a curious mind, an open heart, and a willingness to be changed."
—Unknown

Four out of five of the books in this chapter have the word "conversations" in their titles. That made the title for this chapter easy. I worried a little that readers might think these books are about casual conversations, like teaching someone how to engage in small talk—no, that is not what you will find here!

These books teach us how to have the conversations that are hard, the ones where facts are disputed and feelings are hurt. We have probably contributed to both situations. Now we are unsure what to say. We are unsure what we want. But, as Susan Scott says, "The conversation is the relationship." No conversations, no relationships. Let these books give you both the skills and the courage to have the conversations you need to have.

Crucial Conversations: Tools for Talking When Stakes Are High

by Joseph Grenny, Kerry Patterson, Ron McMillan, Al Switzler, and Emily Gregory

"Most of us make a 'Fool's Choice'—we think we have to choose between 'telling the truth' and 'keeping a friend.' Skilled communicators resist this false tradeoff and look for ways to do both."

CRUCIAL CONVERSATIONS starts by defining what one is. A crucial conversation exists when opinions vary, stakes are high, and opinions are strong. That definition is helpful. We have all found ourselves in those situations, or found ourselves avoiding those exact conversations. The ability to resolve conflict is the difference between healthy relationships and strained relationships. As the authors point out, we are either going to "talk it out" or "act it out."

When faced with an unsafe situation for a patient, nurses speak up less than one in twelve times. In this case, the action is *not* taking action. Consider the potential outcome for the patient and the stress that puts on the nurse. In a survey of over four thousand respondents, 93 percent said their organizations employed colleagues who were "bullying, conniving, dishonest, or incompetent," and those people were "untouchable." And, in a study of over 2,200 projects, the authors could predict with a 90 percent accuracy rate whether the project would fail based on whether people could have the crucial conversations needed. Silence was the most common chosen route when the crucial moment arrived. Communication skills are not soft or optional skills.

As the "Tools for Talking" subtitle signals, *Crucial Conversations* feels the most like a handbook of all the selections in this chapter. Let's highlight a few of its suggestions. The authors say to choose the right topic to focus the conversation. "What do I want?" is an effective starting point. When people get stressed, they start to jump around. Choose the conversation you are going to have up front. You might focus on the immediate problem in need of solving. You might raise the conversation up a level by pointing out a string of events and talking about a pattern that is appearing. You could elevate the conversation to yet another level and focus on the relationship. The authors write, "Relationship issues get to deeper concerns about trust, competence, and respect." Success comes from keeping the conversation focused. Be careful to notice when that focus shifts and be prepared to "bookmark" a raised concern to satisfy your desire for resolution now and the potential need to return to a sensitive topic later.

Our work at improving dialogue with others often requires work with the dialogue we are having with ourselves. The authors warn of three stories we tell. We might say, "I am the victim here." This story discounts our own role in the conflict and is resolved when we admit the part we play. We might lay blame on another and make them the villain of our story. The antidote here is to see the enemy as human and fallible as you are. The final story is one of helplessness, believing there is nothing that can be done. The authors recommend returning to the "What do I want?" question and write, "When you refuse to make yourself helpless, you're forced to hold yourself accountable for using your dialogue skills rather than bemoaning your weakness."

The whole point of crucial conversations is to stay engaged when conflict arises and stay in dialogue around the things that matter.

HERE ARE SOME MORE TIPS FOR YOUR CRUCIAL CONVERSATION:
- **Care about their concerns:** Build safety by showing that you have a mutual purpose.
- **Care about them:** Build more safety by showing mutual respect.
- **S.T.A.T.E. your path: S**hare your facts. **T**ell your story. **A**sk for others' facts and stories. **T**alk tentatively. **E**ncourage testing.
- **Be curious:** Look for the underlying source of pain or discomfort that is affecting the dialogue.

Fierce Conversations: Achieving Success at Work and in Life, One Conversation at a Time
by Susan Scott

"Often the real trouble is that the conversation hasn't been allowed to find its subject; it isn't yet about what it wants to be about."

I CAN STILL REMEMBER reading *Fierce Conversations* for the first time over twenty years ago. As I reread it for this review, I was surprised how much of the book continues to stay with me. Susan Scott writes with urgency. She believes people desperately want to have better conversations with those around them. The authors of *Crucial Conversations* say that the lag between knowing and resolving conflict is what increases the conflict. Scott takes that fact and uses it as the emotional starting point for her book. It is very simple—the conversation is the relationship. No conversation, no relationship. It's obvious, and our lives are full of places where conversations lack the depth needed to support us and those around us.

Scott brings the same lens of self-reflection to her book as the other titles in this chapter. If we are going to speak with integrity, then we need to know the values and the beliefs we hold. We are also going to need courage to speak honestly about those values and beliefs. If we can't have those conversations, then we can't explore the collective truth of that moment. All of our experiences are filtered through those values and beliefs. The engineering department is not going to look at a problem the same way manufacturing or marketing will. A new transit line may create accessibility and equity for some residents but noise and displacement for others. Our ability to have the conversation is the key. As Scott says, "If a problem exists, it exists whether we talk about it or not."

Every book is unique to its author. Scott loves fiction. The pages of the book are filled with character descriptions from other works. This is a clever device for bringing insights from other authors into her book. I offer several quotes below as proxy descriptions for the seven principles Scott uses to organize her book.

Scott also spent more than a decade as a coach to CEOs. Her coaching conversations bring stories of people struggling with alcoholism, dissolving marriages, and failing businesses, all because conversations weren't happening. Sometimes those conversations unfolded in a single encounter, while others took months to take place. The stories speak to the possibility in every conversation and the persistence often needed to get to "ground truth."

I am going to end with a beautiful metaphor that Scott uses for the opportunity we have in every conversation. She uses the image of a crucible, a vessel that can carry all that is needed for that conversation to take place. She says, "My job is simply to hold, to withstand, so whatever needs to be said, what needs to be heard, can safely be said and heard." Later she says, "Each of us is a place where conversations occur. You are a physical, emotional, spiritual, and intellectual place where conversations happen. ... You do not need a diploma to be a human being, to be a friend. What is needed is *you*, willing and ready, available, clear, and clean." That is the urgency and the aspiration that makes this book so good.

FICTIONAL CHARACTER QUOTES THAT DESCRIBE SCOTT'S SEVEN PRINCIPLES:

1. "It wasn't a real conversation, just the batting of a ball of words from one mouth to the other." —Barney Norris, *Five Rivers Met on a Wooded Plain*
2. "Knowing something's easy. Saying it out loud is the hard part." —Nicholas Evans, *The Horse Whisperer*
3. "I always thought it was what I wanted: to be loved and admired. Now I think perhaps I'd like to be known." —Kristin Hannah, *The Nightingale*
4. "If Barbara can't find it in herself to work not only as a member of a team but also as an individual whose responsibility carries the weight of certain behavioral requirements, then she needs to find another line of employment. Frankly, I can come up with several but most of them have to do with sheep and the Falkland Islands and my guess is that lacks a certain appeal." —Elizabeth George, *A Banquet of Consequences*

5. "My instincts were many. I was full of penetrating insights. But they led to nothing except an ever-growing private collection." —Steve Tesich, *Karoo*
6. "If you want to build a ship, don't gather your people and ask them to provide wood, prepare tools, assign tasks. Call them together and raise in their minds the longing for the sea." —Antoine de Saint-Exupéry, *Citadelle*
7. "What does it mean, knowing how to keep silent? What kind of silence would this be? How does this particular silence contrast with being morosely mute? What is a knowledgeable silence? How would we know or for that matter recognize this knowledge?" —Charles Baxter, *The Feast of Love*

Difficult Conversations: How to Discuss What Matters Most
by Douglas Stone, Bruce Patton, and Sheila Heen

"As a rule, when something goes wrong in human relationships, everyone has contributed in some important way."

WHEN I THINK ABOUT having a difficult conversation, my primary concern is that I will say the wrong thing. I fear I will be misunderstood. I wonder if I will make the other person upset. At the core, there is something I want—maybe a completed contract or a repaired relationship—and that requires resolving conflict. Since my worry is in the words, I often think I just need some tips or a better set of scripts to use in those tough interactions. *Difficult Conversations* suggests there is deeper work to be done.

These authors' work is deeply influenced by their efforts at the Harvard Negotiation Project. You might know *Getting to Yes* by William Ury, the cofounder of the Harvard Negotiation Project. That book and the organization's research has always emphasized finding shared interests when working to resolve conflict. This core tenet lies at the heart of *Difficult Conversations*. Rather than scripts (which I admit I'd hoped for), three-quarters of the book describes the work you need to do to determine what you are bringing to the conversation and uncovering the same in your partner, colleague, or friend.

What they mean is that every conversation is actually made up of three intertwining conversations. The first conversation is about the details of what actually happened. Even though people might be talking about the same situation, both sides never have exactly the same information about the events that transpired. There are always other outside parties or prior histories that factor into the present moment. When conflicts arise, it is incredibly important for both sides to see as many of those components as possible. When that discovery process is done well, there is an opportunity to put aside blame and instead explore how each side contributed to the perceived failure.

I use the word "failure" specifically because alongside the "facts" of the situation are also the feelings that come from what has happened. This is the second conversation. There are many settings where expressing feelings may seem inappropriate. The reality is that we are expressing them whether we realize it or not. The authors offer research that shows people are very astute at perceiving when someone else is "distorting, manufacturing, or withholding an emotion." Withholding emotion also impacts our ability to listen and further explore the conflict because we are too consumed by the stories playing out in our head. Those unexpressed feelings can easily take the form of judgments—for instance, anger becomes blame. That doesn't mean that you vent everything you are thinking. To be effective, it is important to connect it to the conflict at hand. Use simple statements that start with "I feel."

Conflicts also threaten our identity, leading to the third conversation. If this seems like a difficult topic to enter into, the authors offer three common identity issues: Am I competent? Am I a good person? Am I worthy of love? We have all suffered from not being able to answer yes to these queries, but we also suffered because these answers are rarely binary or permanent. We miss deadlines. We say the wrong thing. We contribute to the problems around us. Letting ourselves exist in a more complex world of intentions. As Morihei Ueshiba, founder of aikido said, "I am constantly losing my balance. My skill lies in my ability to regain it." This is also great wisdom from the authors: "Our advice is not to turn off your internal voice, or even to turn it down. You can't. Instead, we urge you to do the opposite—turn up your internal voice, at least for the time being, and get to know the kinds of things it says."

This is another book in *100 Best Books* that excels at the resources it gives readers. The entire final chapter is the full text of a difficult conversation, interspersed with coaching interactions that encourage and redirect the participants toward a better outcome. The last section in the newest edition of the book is a Q&A that explores topics like power differentials, bad intentions, and mental illness. My favorite question is "Who has time for all this in the real world?" and you already know the authors' answer—*you* are spending time and energy dwelling on the conversation you should have, and that spent energy is actually making the problem worse. Instead, go have the difficult conversation that you need to have.

QUESTIONS THAT CAN HELP DEEPEN ALL THREE CONVERSATIONS:
- Can you say a little more about how you see things?
- What information might you have that I don't?
- How do you see it differently?
- What impact have my actions had on you?
- Can you say a little more about why you think this is my fault?
- Were you reacting to something I did?
- How are you feeling about all of this?
- Can you say more about why this is important to you?
- What would it mean to you if that happened?

Nonviolent Communication: A Language of Life
by Marshall Rosenberg

"Time and again, people transcend the paralyzing effects of psychological pain when they have sufficient contact with someone who can hear them empathically."

IN THIS CHAPTER, *Nonviolent Communication* is both the simplest and the hardest title for me to work with. Marshall Rosenberg's lifetime of teachings boil down to a few simple lessons, but the lessons are so counterintuitive that they are almost foreign. It is striking how poorly we form our thoughts and express them to others. But you'll recognize themes from the other titles I've reviewed, and you'll see how Rosenberg's work cuts to the core, if you accept his premise.

Rosenberg starts with the truth that humans are naturally compassionate and want to move through the world sharing and expressing that innate quality. You will often see Rosenberg's work also described as "compassionate communication." The trouble we quickly recognize is that we are not communicating with care. Our conversations are full of judgment, blame, and comparison directed at others. And we just as often direct these at ourselves.

Rosenberg raises the stakes for our conversations. He sees these habits of judgment as harm we are perpetuating upon each other. Rosenberg quotes research from O. J. Harvey, who studied the relationship between language and violence. Harvey took random samples of literature from countries around the world and, through textual analysis, determined the frequency of classifying and judging people. "His study shows a high correlation between frequent use of such words and frequency of [violent] incidents," writes Rosenberg. "It does not surprise me to hear that there is considerably less violence in cultures where people think in terms of human needs than in cultures where people label one another as 'good' or 'bad' and believe that the 'bad ones' deserve to be punished."

The nonviolent communication process described below aspires to keep us connected to our conversations and encourages us to express what we need:

1. **Observe** the concrete actions that are affecting our well-being.
2. Express our **feelings** in relation to what we observe.
3. Share our **needs** that create those feelings.
4. **Request** the concrete actions that we need to enrich our lives.

Each step is given a chapter from the perspective of the communicator and then from the perspective of the listener. Observations should be communicated back like the event was reported from a video recording. At the end of each chapter, there is an exercise with a set of statements to help the reader see where they might be misinterpreting the situation. Often we substitute a judgment for a feeling or need. "I feel you don't love me" is a judgment. "I'm feeling sad that you are leaving" is a genuine expression of feeling. We get into further trouble when we can't connect the feeling expressed with the underlying need. Rosenberg writes, "The more directly we can connect our feelings to our needs, the easier it is for others to respond compassionately."

Through the book, Rosenberg describes how versatile this process is. We can use this approach to express appreciation for another's actions. We can deeply listen for feelings, needs, and requests that the counterparty may not consciously realize. We can use this framework to resolve external conflict and just as effectively resolve distress from inner dialogue with ourselves. We can use this approach to settle disputes between other parties by facilitating a discussion that gets people to truly share their feelings and needs. We can express anger more fully and explore depression with self-empathy.

If there is any book featured in *100 Best Books* that I would return to regularly, it would be *Nonviolent Communication*. As I finish this review, I am recommitting myself to return to the book on a yearly basis to see what other lessons I can draw out.

HERE'S A LIST OF FEELINGS AND NEEDS TO THINK ABOUT USING TO ENGAGE OTHERS:

"I feel ... " joyful, moved, eager, fulfilled, curious, relieved, affectionate, exhilarated, alert, calm, safe, hopeful, worried, anxious, overwhelmed, lonely, bored, exhausted, resentful, alarmed, sad, hopeless, torn, embarrassed

" ... because I need ... ?" empathy, intimacy, affection, warmth, kindness, agency, independence, honor, security, trust, reliability, partnership, collaboration, acknowledgement, belonging, participation, purpose, efficiency, order, celebration, mourning, play, joy, honesty, creativity, peace, completion, food, water, rest, movement, touch

The Conversation: How Seeking and Speaking the Truth about Racism Can Radically Transform Individuals and Organizations

by Robert Livingston

"The first step in producing profound and sustainable change is raising awareness of the existence of a real problem. Otherwise, the solution will seem like the problem—and resistance will follow."

OUR MOST IMPACTFUL and consequential learning occurs through our relationships with other people. We are much more likely to talk to, listen to, influence, and be influenced by those who are part of our familial, social, or professional networks.

Robert Livingston says his book is "a road map and compass for our shared journey towards a more racially just and equitable destination." Livingston's approach is different from bestsellers like Ta-Nehisi Coates's *Between the World and Me* and Ibram Kendi's *How to Be an Antiracist*. The additional reader's note on the book cover gives a clue, saying "A Science-Based Approach."

Livingston says "racism occurs when individuals or institutions show more favorable evaluation or treatment of an individual or group based on race or ethnicity." Most dictionaries would provide a similar definition. The real conversation begins when we start to discuss how prevalent racism is in the world or whether we as individuals evaluate and treat others in a racist manner. Rather than writing a memoir or sharing the stories of the lived experiences of individuals affected by racism, Livingston shares a vast array of psychological and sociological findings that show racism as anchored in biases and beliefs. The book's forty page bibliography details the research that shows both how pervasive racism is and how difficult it can be to see those biases.

Take Black job candidates. Field research continues to show that Black applicants get fewer interview requests than identical White candidates. Economists Marianne Bertrand and Sendhil Mullainathan conducted a resume study in 2004. Simply changing a first name on a resume (say from Emily to Lakisha) shifts perception and showed dramatically lower interview callbacks for Black candidates. Bertrand and Mullaninathan estimate the benefits of being White is equivalent to eight years of additional work experience. Devah Pager also looked at the impact of a prior criminal record to see how Black and White applicants fared in the job market. The starkest finding in Pager's work is the fact that White felons get more callbacks for interviews than Black non-felons (17 percent versus 14 percent). I would encourage you to stop and read that last sentence one more time and just take a minute to reflect on that.

These are just facts—facts about the nature of the job market—based on race. Livingston says sharing facts and research and correcting cultural and historical representation is the first step to look more deeply at how different racial groups are treated and address racism.

The next step is concern. In Livingston's model, we have to ask ourselves if we care about the problem and the people it harms. And then we have to ask ourselves if we are going to change and correct the problems of racism as individuals and as organizations. Discussions about race are not easy, but *The Conversation* provides a roadmap for you to explore your views on racism and continue to challenge the organizations we work in to do better.

FOUR RULES FOR A PRODUCTIVE CONVERSATION THAT ADVANCES POSITIVE SOCIAL CHANGE:

1. **Gather the facts … and make space for the feelings:** Make room for both. His rule is 70 percent facts, 30 percent feelings.
2. **Make people feel affirmed when possible:** White people are likely to be triggered by information that suggests they might be racists. Black people are more likely to be triggered by information that indicates they are not to be respected.
3. **Focus on the problem, not the person:** Keep the focus on the broader system or culture rather than on someone else in the room.
4. **Show curiosity, not animosity:** Focus on inquiry that involves seeking new information, pondering new possibilities, asking questions, and listening to others.

CHAPTER 25
COACHING

"The best coaches give their players a sense of their own greatness and the belief that they can achieve anything."
—Phil Jackson

Those who engage with coaches are actively asking "How can I get better?" There is a gap to close. There is a desire to learn. The authors of *Co-Active Coaching* believe those people want a better quality of life.

The primary perspective for this chapter is that of the coach. Doug Silsbee says coaching is taking responsibility for the long-term development of another. All the books here caution against mistaking what we want for what is best for those being coached. Good coaching adapts to what is needed in the moment, and both parties are left better from the effort.

Helping People Change: Coaching with Compassion for Lifelong Learning and Growth
by Richard Boyatzis, Melvin Smith, and Ellen Van Oosten

"To help other people, we have to focus on them, not on our vision of how we think things should be."

THAT QUOTED LINE ABOVE is the reason I included a chapter on coaching in this book. I deeply believe that if we brought a coaching mindset to more conversations, we would transform our relationships with others. The authors ask readers to think of the word "coach" as a verb, not a noun. "Coach" is something you do rather than something you are. This creates the opportunity for parents, nurses, counselors, teachers, monastics, and managers to engage with family members, clients, or students in a very different way. If we do this, we would transform the people we interacted with and we would be successfully helping people change.

I am going to quote Richard Boyatzis, Melvin Smith, and Ellen Van Oosten to push this point a little further and ask you to think about those around you that you are trying to help: "In our attempt to coach a person seeking help, most of us naturally take a problem-centered approach, focusing on the gaps between where we are and where we think they could or should be. We are trying to *fix* them. This does not work well, if at all, to motivate sustained learning, change, or adaptation."

The motivation that draws people into coaching is the gap that people perceive between what the authors call "the ideal self" and "the real self." The source of tension can be hard to identify. Many haven't done the work to get clear on a shift in values or see a new calling they have in their life. The same kind of honest work is needed to assess their current state of strengths and weaknesses. Good coaching helps create more honest insights on both fronts. A great coach works with the coachee to identify newly needed skills and experiment with those as they work to close the gap.

As suggested in the subtitle, the authors put a strong emphasis on compassion in the coaching relationship. They write that too many coaching interactions rely on negative emotions for motivation. Negativity narrows focus and makes it harder to see potential options in moments of change. Asking positive coaching questions activates the parasympathetic nervous system, which triggers renewal hormones and a state of openness and hope. Research from Case Western also suggests that activities like actively listening, asking someone for help, and helping others engages our brain's empathetic network. This combination of functions keeps us open to the emotions of others, helps us see things from others' perspectives and helps us appreciate the impact of our decisions on others.

OTHER INTERESTING INSIGHTS ON COACHING:
- Scott Taylor's research suggests a good measure of one's own self-awareness is their *prediction* of how others see them against how others *actually* see them.
- Using a variety of renewal techniques is more effective at battling stress. And small dosages of activities like exercise, family time, and meditation spread out over the whole day is better than one single block.
- Successful goal-setting varies by context. When the task is complex and requires adaptation, learning goals lead to better performance. When the task is simple or routine, performance goals inspire greater performance by providing direction and clarity.
- "What else?" is one of the authors' favorite coaching questions because it invites coachees to share the "thoughts beneath their thoughts."

Co-Active Coaching: The Proven Framework for Transformative Conversations at Work and in Life

by Henry Kimsey-House, Karen Kimsey-House, Phillip Sandhal, and Laura Whitworth

"Sometimes, people want more from life: more peace of mind, more security, more impact in their work. And sometimes they want less: less confusion, less stress, less financial pressure. In general, they come to coaching because they want a better quality of life."

WHEN I REACHED OUT to my coaching friends to get suggestions on the books in the field, every list came back with *Co-Active Coaching*. I was a little surprised because I had never run across the book in my travels. "The bible of coaching guides" is trumpeted from the front cover in a quote from Stephen Covey. After reading it, I see what they all see—a model for using coaching in a wide array of scenarios, from formal coaching engagements to manager-employee conversations to parent-child relationships. *Co-Active Coaching* has a multipart framework, and in this review, I am going to focus on three core principles of co-active coaching to both illustrate the targets for good coaching and show how we might better coach ourselves.

"Think about your own life for a moment," the authors write early in Part 3 of the book. "What is your vision of a really fulfilling life?" I think most of us find this a hard question to answer, and the authors confirm this: "In our experience, it takes tremendous courage and commitment on the part of the coachee to really choose and keep choosing a course of fulfillment." Good coaches help people maintain a view of the alignment between their values and their actions. The authors suggest that this is a process to both see what is alive in that moment and how it shifts over time. They also suggest flexibility in how one chooses their values, because language is imprecise. Combining values into clusters can bring more clarity. For myself, success, competitiveness, and leadership blend into a single group.

The next principle is balance. "When it comes to balance, what coachees want is the ability to juggle the precious priorities of their lives," the authors write. The big warning here is that most people don't immediately see balance as a problem. They might say they are out of options or feel trapped in a repeating loop. "You will hear the harshness of unchangeable circumstances and unyielding boxes." Good coaching helps people see possibilities again. It's about seeing new choices and committing to change. This is where the daily string of what we say yes and no to sets the path for both success and fulfillment.

The authors describe the third principle as process, and they say the goal for this kind of coaching is to "enhance the coachee's ability to be aware of the moment and name it." Listening and observing closely, we can look for (or notice for ourselves) a tense facial expression, a sharp verbal response, or a racing heartbeat. Coaches can see that tension and work with the coachee to become aware of it. That recognition starts a shift and creates new movement. The energy there is no longer stuck. That release opens new paths and resources for the coachees.

And that's the whole point of coaching—helping someone see their life, come to believe what is possible, and take action to lean into that potential.

THE FOUR CORNERSTONES OF CO-ACTIVE COACHING:

1. **People are naturally creative, resourceful, and whole:** Believe in the capability of the coachee and become a champion on their behalf.
2. **Focus on the whole person:** Keep a broad, attentive focus on all aspects of the person sitting across from you.
3. **Dance in the moment:** Be very present to what is happening in this moment and respond to only that.
4. **Evoke transformation:** Pursue what leads to a life fully lived in whatever area coachees find important.

The Coaching Habit: Say Less, Ask More, and Change the Way You Lead Forever
by Micheal Bungay Stanier

"Coaching is a foundational skill for every manager and leader. When people make coaching an everyday way of working, they create more focus, more courage, and more resilience. They help others (and themselves) work less hard and have more impact."

I BELIEVE that in great books you will always find a single page that makes owning the book completely invaluable. There might be a single statement on that page that shifts your perspective. Or you find an image that fully encapsulates all the teachings the author has offered. And sometimes, it is a question that you continue to ponder long after you put the book down.

In *The Coaching Habit*, that is page 200, and it is not one question but seven questions that the book is built around to help you quickly become a better coach to others. On that magical page, Stanier lists each situation and the question to best use in that particular situation. It is the kind of page that you could tear out, tape to your computer monitor, and forever be better at helping others find their way.

When I tell people about my one-page rule, they will sometimes think that you could just collect all of those pages into another book and instantly have the best book ever. It is a bit like saying that just by owning this book, you wouldn't ever need to read another book again. In the case of all of those single pages and their associated unread books, you'd lack the context to appreciate and best apply those learnings. The magic of books is how they create the space and time to contemplate new ideas and connect them to what you already know.

This point is important, because Stanier connects points and contexts really well in *The Coaching Habit*. Many books, including other selections in *100 Best Books*, present an idea and support it with the stories and experiences of the author. That can be a great path to learning. *The Coaching Habit* is particular in how it teaches you about these better coaching questions but also about why the wording matters, what people often use to less effectively do the same thing, and what are acceptable alterations for the situation you might find yourself in. *Tiny Habits* and *The 4 Disciplines of Execution* use that similar approach of picking a particular target and fully exploring the pros and cons of various techniques to best hit the mark.

You may feel like I tricked you with this review, talking about books in general but not addressing this one directly. But Stanier reveals his questions in a way that I want to keep a surprise. I want you to experience firsthand how he teaches the art of opening a coaching conversation, guiding someone to the heart of their challenge, and reinforcing what they've learned.

HERE ARE FOUR WAYS FOR COACHES TO ASK QUESTIONS BETTER:
1. Ask one question at a time.
2. Cut the introduction and just ask the question.
3. Focus on questions that start with "What...?"
4. Acknowledge the answers you get with replies like "Fantastic," "Nice," and "Yes, that's good."

The Mindful Coach: Seven Roles for Facilitating Leader Development
by Doug Silsbee

"[Coaching is] that part of a relationship in which one person is primarily dedicated to serving the long-term development of effectiveness and self-generation of the other."

DOUG SILSBEE does two things in *The Mindful Coach* that make it a great book on its own and a great book on which to end this chapter. First, Silsbee bases his coaching framework on the idea that we can only become better coaches through the same work required when going through coaching. We have to search out our limiting beliefs, pay attention to when we are triggered by the same challenges as those with whom we are helping, and discern when we are being pushed and pulled by our preferences rather than by what is best for the client. Look at Chapter 2, "Mindfulness," for more *100 Best Books* that can help with these challenges.

The second reason I like Silsbee's book is the identification of the various roles that a coach plays in the course of helping another. Silsbee prefers the term "voices" and writes, "When we're in tune with our clients, when our own conditioned patterns are set aside and we are fully present, we are able to choose the voice that's most appropriate and most helpful at a particular time." There are seven voices in his model, each providing a different approach for helping the client.

In the realm of coaching, it is easy to recognize certain voices. The Investigator Voice asks questions to shift the client's understanding and generate next courses of action. The Partner Voice establishes the structure for the relationship and offers suggestions for the path that the coaching relationship might take. The Contractor Voice establishes agreements and holds the client accountable. Those are all common components in other coaching methods.

There are three modes that Silsbee calls the "Sharpener Voices." These lenses focus on seeing ourselves accurately by "developing a different and clearer understanding of [the] situation (as opposed to an outcome or action)." The Reflector Voice provides missing information to the client or directs them toward known information that supports their potential to change. The Guide Voice encourages action and offers options, while still giving the client room to self-generate their own path. The Teacher Voice provides knowledge, challenges faulty interpretations, and exposes the coaching process itself for examination and improvement.

The entire book is a course in self-discovery. In several exercises throughout the book, Silsbee stops and asks the reader to think about how they can better apply a certain aspect of a voice. He even asks the reader to consider if they are reading the book too fast and not getting the full benefit. The final chapter has even more encouragement. Create an audio or video recording of a session and examine it for patterns. Notice when you shift voices and see what the implications are for the rest of a coaching session. Make a list of traits in your clients that you judge or resist and notice how it manifests in you. Read this one for you, for the coach you want to be, and for all the people you will be able to better help.

A FINAL TRUTH FROM SILSBEE:

"We are conditioned beings.
Every small moment
of self-awareness,
of noticing
a judgment or an urge
or an attachment
or an aversion,
is a small awakening.
The goal,
and the only measure of success,
is our commitment
to doing this work,
to paying attention."

Acknowledgements

I WANT TO START BY THANKING the authors and the publishers whose books are featured in *100 Best Books for Work and Life*. As an author and a publisher, I am inspired by their work and their commitment to help readers live happier and more fulfilling lives.

I want to thank Jack Covert who picked up my cold call that started a seven-year professional relationship that I still cherish. He described himself as a merchant—a record store owner and then a bookseller. To me, Jack was a mentor, a reluctant co-author, and a friend. I miss him.

I want to thank Ray Bard. We have a friendship that I deeply value. It started in our shared love of books and publishing. He trusted me to continue the legacy of Bard Press, the company he founded over thirty years ago. I take that responsibility seriously, and I hope this book is another example of that work.

I didn't reach this point without so many other people in the world of book publishing. Sally, Meg, Aaron, Dylan, Roy, Ryan, Zach, Todd, and all the others at Porchlight Books are amazing. The folks at Portfolio like Adrian Zackheim, Will Weisser, Adrienne Schultz, and Maureen Cole who helped Jack, Sally, and I release *The 100 Best Business Books of All Time*. Christy Fletcher gave me a place to hang out a shingle as an agent (and had patience when it didn't really work). Erin Edmison helped me navigate literary scouting. Gene Kim hired me to help him publish a book and then run IT Revolution. Many others have influenced my journey, and while this list is incomplete, I deeply appreciate each of them: Seth Godin, Richard Nash, Brian O'Leary, Hollis Heimbouch, Mark Bloomfield, Todd Berman, Erin Brown, Susan Williams, Johanna Vondeling, John Moore, Jackie Huba, Barbara Cave Henricks, Mark Fortier, Matty Goldberg, Jason Brockwell, Josh Kaufman, and Jonathon Flaum.

I want to thank the authors who have engaged Bard Press to publish their amazing books. Our process lets us get to know our authors, professionally and personally. I value each of those relationships. In recent years, Bobby Herrera trusted us with his first book which was also my first book at Bard Press. Ed O'Malley cold-emailed me and now we have done two books together.

Julia Fabris McBride co-wrote with Ed and is now working on another book with Kaye Monk-Morgan, both on the Bard Press imprint. Mo Bunnell trusted Bard Press to publish his second book and is about to start the third with us as well. Cyril Peupion, based in Australia, has started writing his Bard Press debut book. And for those who sign with us after I write this, thanks to you as well.

Extra special mentions go to: Tim Grahl who found me at SXSW twenty years ago and now we both have found our way to the right places. Charlie Gilkey moved to Portland the same summer I did, and our friendship has only grown more with each BookGym. And Jamey Stegmaier whose thoughtful writing and conversations have inspired me and the projects I have done.

Let me conclude by recognizing the three people who make Bard Press awesome:

Anne Ugarte keeps everything running behind the scenes, overseeing operations with care and precision. The timing couldn't have been better—just as she was looking for a new opportunity, Bard Press was ready for more help. She brings passion, dedication, and a constant drive to improve, and I'm grateful to have her on our team.

Joy Panos Stauber and I have worked together for almost twenty years. Her design and communications work have shaped every major book project I've been a part of. We even convinced our publisher in 2009 to use her designs for *The 100 Best Business Books of All Time*. And everything you see in *100 Best Books for Work and Life* is Joy's work as well. This acknowledgment is just one more way to express how much I value her partnership.

Finally, I need to thank Amy Buckley. As my wife, she's had a front-row seat to my entire professional journey over the past thirty years. She helped me publish my first book back in 2005 and has supported me through every success and challenge since. With *100 Best Books for Work and Life*, I'm thrilled that she's no longer just watching from the sidelines—she's now fully involved in Bard Press as our Managing Editor.

A Bard Press Book

Publisher: Todd Sattersten, Bard Press
Managing Editor: Amy Buckley, Bard Press
Director of Operations: Anne Ugarte, Bard Press
Illustrator: Alexa Buckley, Bard Press

Jacket Designer: Joy Panos Stauber, Stauber Brand Studio
Text Designers: Joy Panos Stauber and Richard Weaver, Stauber Brand Studio
Copyeditor: Sarah Currin, Currin Editorial
Proofreaders: Monte Lin and Melissa Ousley, Indigo: Editing, Design, and More
Indexers: Kevin Broccoli and Jennifer Broccoli, Indigo: Editing, Design, and More

THE SAPLING PROGRAM
National Forest Foundation nationalforests.org

Bard Press is committed to planting trees forward. For each tree we use to print our books we plant two new trees through the US National Forest Foundation's Sapling Program. These trees are planted in non-commercial, US National Forests, and provide fresh air, clean water and habitat protections. To learn more go to BardPress.com/SaplingProgram.

Copyright

100 Best Books for Work and Life: What They Say, Why They Matter, and How They Can Help You, by Todd Sattersten

Published by Bard Press, Portland, Oregon, USA
Copyright © 2025 Todd Sattersten
All Rights Reserved.
Printed in the United States of America.
Permission to reproduce or transmit in any form or by any means—electronic or mechanical, including photocopying and recording, or by an information storage and retrieval system—must be obtained by contacting the publisher.

Bard Press Contact Information:
info@bardpress.com www.bardpress.com

Ordering Information:
For additional copies, contact your favorite bookstore or email info@bardpress.com. Quantity discounts are available.

First printing—October 2025

Publisher's Cataloging-in-Publication
(Provided by Cassidy Cataloguing Services, Inc.)

Names: Sattersten, Todd, author.
Title: 100 best books for work and life : what they say, why they matter, and how they can help you / Todd Sattersten.
Other titles: One hundred best books for work and life
Description: Portland, Oregon : Bard Press, [2025] | Includes bibliographical references and index.
Identifiers: ISBN: 9781959472230 (hardcover) | 9781959472247 (ebook) | 9781959472254 (audio)
Subjects: LCSH: Best books. | Self-actualization (Psychology)--Bibliography. | Self-culture--Bibliography. | Success in business--Bibliography. | Career development--Bibliography. | Leadership--Bibliography. | Problem solving--Bibliography. | Habit--Bibliography. | LCGFT: Bibliographies. | Reference works. | BISAC: BUSINESS & ECONOMICS / Reference. | BUSINESS & ECONOMICS / Management. | BUSINESS & ECONOMICS / Personal Success.
Classification: LCC: Z1035 .S38 2025 | DDC: 011.73--dc23

Index

Abedi, Agha Hasan, 181
accountability, 190–191, 195
accounting, 187–188
Achor, Shawn, 90–92
Adamson, Brent, 155–156
adoption theory, 130–132
advice, asking for, 140, 221–222
agreeableness, 38
Alder, Alfred, 144
Allen, David, 109–110
Amabile, Teresa, 84, 88–90
amusement, emotion of, 91
anger, 55, 56, 171, 232, 235
apologizing, 225
appreciation, expressing, 7, 144, 176
Ariely, Dan, 29–31
Aristotle, 93
art. *See* creative work
attention. *See* focus; mindfulness
authenticity, 177, 215–217, 223
autonomy, 24, 85, 87, 90, 186
awareness. *See* mindfulness
awe, 91

Bacon, Francis, 44
Banaji, Mahzarin, 31–33
Bard Press, 70, 147
Bartell, Roy, 152
Beane, Billy, 6, 206–207
Beck, Martha, 54
Beeman, Mark, 29
beginner's mind, 21
belonging, 215, 217

Berger, Jonah, 136–138
Berman, Karen, 187–188
Berry, Bertice, 53
Bertrand, Marianne, 236–237
better, getting, 5–14
  by doing less, 12–14
  mindset for, 6–7
  by practicing, 8–11
  by prioritizing, 12–13
  talent and, 10–12
biases, 31–33, 67, 236–237
Blackburn, Barbara, 8
Bock, Laszlo, 204–206
books, learning from, 12
Bossidy, Larry, 106
Boyatzis, Richard, 239–240
brain, workings of, 27–29, 68–69
Bridges, William, 163, 164–165
Brooks, David, 69
Brown, Brené, 196, 215–217
Burg, Bob, 223
Burnett, Bill, 57–59
business. *See also* teams; work
  fundamentals of, 66–67
  goal-setting in, 78–80
  starting, 70–71

Cain, Susan, 39–41
Campbell, Joseph, 22
career. *See* work
Carnegie, Dale, 39, 143–144
Case, John, 187–188
Case Western, 240
Catmull, Ed, 201
change, 25, 121, 163–171. *See also* better, getting; coaching
  awareness as catalyst for, 242

252 100 BEST BOOKS FOR WORK & LIFE

belief in ability to, 6–7
common reactions to, 163
immunity to, overcoming, 166–168
as inevitable, 171–172, 185
in leadership, 64–65
leading, 168–170, 174
making most of, 164–165
managing, 164–165
mindfulness and, 25
Chapman, Gary, 139
Charan, Ram, 106
Cheryan, Sapna, 33
Chödrön, Pema, 78, 163, 170–171
Christakis, Nicholas, 213–215
Cialdini, Robert, 134–136
Clear, James, 98
CliftonStrengths assessment, 42
coaching, 206, 238–245
   co-active, 241–242
   compassion in, 240
   determining strengths and weaknesses, 239
   effect on skill building, 11
   mindfulness in, 244–246
   problem-centered approach, avoiding, 239
   roles played in, 245
   using questions in, 243–244
cold calls, 158
collaboration, 13
Collins, Jim, 7, 50, 196–198
Collins, Marva, 7
Colonna, Jerry, 179–180
commitment, 11, 30, 136, 190–191
communication. *See* conversations, difficult

compassion, 15–16, 225, 233–236, 240
concentration, 20, 23, 105, 106. *See also* focus
conflict, 190–191, 217–219. *See also* conversations, difficult; relationships
confusion, 33. *See also* thinking
connection. *See* coaching; conversations; generosity; relationships
conscientiousness, 37
contribution, 105–106
conversations, difficult, 226–237. *See also* relationships
   about racism, 236–237
   compassion in, 233–236
   emotions in, 232, 234–235
   finding shared interests, 231–232
   as foundation of relationships, 229–230
   honesty in, 227–228
   identity and, 232
   in marriage, 217–219
   nonviolent, 233–236
   opportunity in, 230
Corporate Executive Board, 155–156
Covert, Jack, 225
Covey, Sean, 102, 194–196, 244
Covey, Stephen M. R., 175–177, 192–193
Covey, Stephen R., 100–102, 194, 196, 241
Cowen, Tyler, 200–202
Coyle, Daniel, 5, 10–12
creative work, 113–121
   all work as, 120

audience of, 120–121
daily routine and, 118
process-oriented approach, 118, 120
projects in, 114–115
roadblocks in, 116–117
shipping, 120–121
criticism, 17, 34, 143, 217. *See also* feedback
Csikszentmihalyi, Mihaly, 22, 85
Cunningham, Bill, 119
curiosity, 29
   in conversations, 213, 226, 228, 235, 237
   influencing others and, 138
   purpose and, 59
   relationships and, 69
   stickiness of ideas and, 142
customers, 123–132. *See also* marketing
   acquiring, 70–71
   adoption of products or technology by, 130–132
   broad definition of, 123
   challenging to make changes, 155–156
   changing mind of, 136–138
   connecting with, 138–140
   encouraging repeat business from, 147
   helping to become experts, 126–128
   influencing, 134–136, 143–144
   Jobs to Be Done (JTBD) and, 128–130
   loyalty and satisfaction of, 124–126

   making hero of marketing stories, 148–149
   mistakes made with, 225
   referrals from, 147
   selling ideas to, 140–142

Davidson, Bill, 79
de Bono, Edward, 33–35
deadlines, 30
Deci, Edward, 83, 84
decision-making, 91
   biases around, 31–33
   effectiveness and, 106
   emotions and, 89
   forces shaping, 29–31
   habitual, 96
   by young adults, 68–69
degrees, educational, 66–67
deliberate practice, 9
desires, 76–78, 99–100, 148
determination, 86–88
Dib, Allan, 145, 146–147
disabilities, 201
discrimination, 31–33, 236–237
Dixon, Matthew, 155–156
Doerr, John, 74, 78–80
Dominguez, Joe, 46
Drucker, Peter, 13, 79, 105–106
Duckworth, Angela, 86–88
Duhigg, Charles, 94
Dweck, Carol, 5, 6–7

Eagleman, David, 127
educational degrees, 66–67
effectiveness, 105–106, 186
Ekman, Paul, 140
Ellis, Keith, 74, 81–82

Elrod, Hal, 63, 72–73
emotions
   in conversations, 232, 234–235
   decision-making and, 89
   in families, 215
   finding purpose using, 55–56
   in goal-setting, 76–78
   microexpressions showing, 140
   as responses to stimulus, 29
   thinking and, 33
empathy. *See* compassion
Entrepreneurial Operating System (EOS), 192
entrepreneurship, 70–71. *See also* business
environment, 58, 96
Ericsson, Anders, 5, 8–10, 11, 87
Evans, Dave, 57–59
Evans, Nicholas, 230
experimentation, 59, 70–71, 174, 198
   in coaching, 239
   to impact lead measures, 195
   leadership and, 174, 178
   personality type and, 37
   when starting new business, 70–71
expertise. *See* better, getting
extroversion, 38–41

Faloon, Steve, 8
fear, 29, 38, 55
   of being misunderstood, 231
   of change, 163
   of conflict, 190–191
   of failure, 42
   focus and, 17
   managers' response to, 108
   ownership and, 30
   sales and, 135, 154
   in young adults, 69
feedback, 7, 11, 17, 85, 183, 184
feelings. *See* emotions
finances. *See* money
Financial Independence, Retire Early (FIRE) movement, 47
Fishburne, Tom, 145
fixed mindset, 6
flow state, 22
Flywheel effect, 198
Foa, Uriel, 139
focus, 103–112, 242. *See also* mindfulness
   by listing all tasks and next steps, 109–110
   in marketing, 150
   narrowing, 107–108, 111–112, 194
   on process, 118, 120
   reviewing past areas of, 118–119
   as secret to effectiveness, 105–106
Fogg, B. J., 83, 97–98, 244
Force Multipliers, 67
Ford, Henry, 144
Fowler, James, 213–215
Frankl, Viktor, 163
Franklin, Benjamin, 100, 144
FranklinCovey research, 175
Fredrickson, Barbara, 90–92
freedom, 46–50, 60–61
Friedman, Stewart, 177–178
friends. *See* relationships
Frisch, Michael B., 75–76

Gallwey, Timothy, 17–18
Gandhi, Indira, 113
Gandhi, Mahatma, 123
gender bias, 201
generosity, 213, 220–225
George, Elizabeth, 230
ghSMART company, 202
Gide, André, 164–165
Gilbert, Daniel, 50
Gitomer, Jeffery, 143–144, 153–154
giving. *See* generosity
Gladwell, Malcolm, 7, 217
goal-setting, 29, 74–82, 87, 90, 167–168
    better outcomes from, 30
    desires and, 76–78
    learning goals vs. performance goals, 240
    prioritizing goals, 78–80
    purpose and, 81–82
    for teams, 194–196
    values and, 75–76
    wishes as goals, 81–82
Godin, Seth, 120–121
Gottman, John, 217–219
Granovetter, Mark, 214
Grant, Adam, 221–222
Great Place to Work Institute, 176
Greenwald, Anthony, 31–33
Gregory, Emily, 227–228
Grenny, Joseph, 227–228
grief, 55, 56, 164, 171
grit, 86–88
Gross, Daniel, 200–202
Grove, Andy, 79
growth. *See* customers; influencing others; marketing; sales

growth mindset, 6–7, 87

habits, 93–102
    based on most important thing, 111–112
    based on relationships, 101–102
    cues for, 99–100
    of highly effective people, 100–102
    making easy/attractive, 99–100
    motivation and, 97
    self-control and, 95
    small changes leading to, 97–98
Hannah, Kristin, 230
Hansen, Morten, 12–14
happiness, 92. *See also* joy; purpose, finding
    money and, 48–50
    preceding success, 90–92
    relationships and, 212–213
Happiness House, 76
Harris, Paul, 36
Harter, James, 89
Harvard Negotiation Project, 231
Harvard Study of Adult Development, 212
Harvey, O. J., 234
Heath, Chip, 140–142
Heath, Dan, 140–142
Hedgehog Concept, 198
Heen, Sheila, 231–233
hiring, 199–208
    evaluations, 200–202, 206–208
    finding candidates, 202–203
    interviews, 202–205
    of minorities and people with disabilities, 201

Holt-Lunstad, Julianne, 212
honesty, in conversations, 227–228
hope, 91
hospitality, 224–225
Housel, Morgan, 48–50
Houston Symphony, 18
Huling, Jim, 194–196, 244
humor, 115, 154

ideas, stickiness of, 140–142
identity, 59–61, 232
IKEA effect, 30
Implicit Association Test, 32
improving. *See* better, getting
influencing others, 43, 133–144, 223
    changing their mind, 136–138
    by connecting, 138–140
    by making them feel important, 143–144
    role of managers in, 183–185
    with sticky ideas, 140–142
inspiration, 91
interest, hope, pride, amusement, inspiration, awe, 91
interviews, when hiring, 203–205
investing, 47, 49–52
irrationality, 29–31

Jackson, Phil, 238
James, Henry, 115
James, William, 144, 207
Jay, Meg, 63, 68
Ji, Maharaj, 17
jobs. *See* work

Jobs, Steve, 199
Jobs to Be Done (JTBD) framework, 128–130
joy, 14, 91, 235. *See also* happiness
    impermanence and, 171
    mindfulness and, 23
    progress and, 88–90
    purpose and, 54, 56

Kabat-Zinn, Jon, 19–21
Kagan, Noah, 63, 70–71
Kalbach, Jim, 128–130
Kareš, Jan, 8
Kaufman, Josh, 63, 66
Kegan, Robert, 163, 166–168
Keller, Gary, 111–112
Kelley, David, 115
Khalsa, Mahan, 196
Kimsey-House, Henry, 241–242
Kimsey-House, Karen, 241–242
King, Larry, 8–9
Klein, Gary, 96
Kleon, Austin, 118–119
Knight, Joe, 187–188
Knowledge Is Power Program, 11
Kornfield, Jack, 23
Kotter, John, 163, 168–170
Kouzes, James, 173–174, 176
Kramer, Steven, 88–90

Lahey, Lisa Laskow, 163, 166–168
Lambert, Craig, 22
Langer, Ellen, 15, 24, 140
language, role in finding purpose, 60–61
LaPorte, Danielle, 74, 76–78

Latham, Gary, 75, 185–186
Le Guin, Ursula K., 74
lead measures, 195
leadership, 172–180, 196.
    See also change; hiring; management; teams
    characteristics of good leaders, 173–174
    confronting facts, 197–198
    domains of life and, 177–178
    in great companies, 197
    leading change, 168–170, 174
    by managers, 183–185
    meetings of leadership team, 193
    transitions in, 64–65
    trust and, 175–180
learning, 1, 5, 12, 14, 17–18
Lee, Bruce, 78
Lencioni, Patrick, 190–191
Lewin, Kurt, 136
Lewis, Michael, 6, 199, 206–208
Lieber, Ron, 46
life, meaning in. *See* purpose, finding
life design, 57–59
Liljenquist, Katie, 221–222
listening, 101–102, 176, 222
    finding purpose by, 56–57
    in sales, 152, 160–161
lists, making, 115
Livingston, Robert, 236–237
Locke, Edwin, 185–186
Logitech, 125
Losada, Marcial, 91
love, 69, 91, 139, 180, 215, 216, 225

MacKenzie, Gordon, 116–117
management, 181–188
    evidence-based, 185–186
    feedback from, 184
    finances and, 187–188
    hospitality in, 224–225
    influencing others, 183–185
    new managers, 182–183
    by objectives (MBOs), 79
    responsibilities, 183
    starting new role in, 64–65
Mann, John David, 223
Map Framework, 197–198
marketing, 145–151. *See also* customers; sales
    laws of, 149–151
    for new business, 70–71
    nurturing cycle, 146–147
    owning word in prospect's mind, 150
    plan for, 146–147
    story-telling in, 148–149
Markey, Rob, 124–126
marriage, 217–219
Martin, Agnes, 119
Martinez, Tom, 11
mastery, 85
Mautz, Scott, 183–185
MBA (Master of Business Administration) degree, 66–67
McAdams, Dan, 140
McChesney, Chris, 194–196, 244
McCloskey, Robert, 116
McMillan, Ron, 227–228
McPherson, Gary, 11
meaning. *See* purpose, finding
measures, lead, 195

Meena, Rajveer, 8
meetings, 193, 195–196
MetLife, 92
Meyer, Danny, 224–225
Microsoft, 201
Miller, Caroline Adams, 75–76
Miller, Donald, 145, 148–149
mindfulness, 15–25, 29.
    See also focus
   change and, 25
   in coaching, 244–246
   defined, 15, 19
   flow state and, 22–23
   lack of, consequences of, 24
   reality and, 18
   seven pillars of, 21
   for stress reduction, 19–20
   in workplace, 17–18, 25
mindset, 6–7, 59, 87
minorities, 201, 236–237
mistakes, 7, 12, 30, 225
Modal Bias, 67
Moesta, Bob, 129
money, 44–52
   financial independence, 46–52
   goals and, 76
   investing, 47, 49–52
   management and, 187–188
   personal finance basics, 45–46
   psychology of, 48–50
   spending, 47–48
   time and, 46–50
Moore, Geoffrey, 130–132
morning routine, 72–73
motivation, 83–92
   habits and, 97
   happiness and, 90–92
   from morning activities, 72–73
   passion and perseverance, 86–88
   practice and, 11, 87
   progress and, 88–90
   rewards and, 84–85
   setbacks and, 89
Mullainathan, Sendhil, 236–237
multitasking, 33, 111
Mumford, George, 22

National Association of Colleges and Employers, 200–201
Neidert, Gregory, 134
Net Promoter Score (NPS), 124–126
Nettle, Daniel, 36, 37–39
networking, 153
Newcastle Personality Assessor, 39
North Star, finding, 54–56
Norton, Mike, 30

objectives and key results (OKRs), 79–80
120-item IP-IP-NEO Personality Inventory, 39
optimism, 34, 87, 92, 225.
    See also positivity
Orr, Julian, 142

Pang, Layman, 121
Papasan, Jay, 111–112
partners, romantic, 68–69
passion, 225
   motivation and, 86–88
   pairing with purpose, 13–14
patience, 21

Patterson, Kerry, 227–228
Patton, Bruce, 231–233
paying attention. *See* mindfulness
performance, improving.
 See better, getting
Perry, William, 166
perseverance, 86–88
personality, 36–43
 introversion, 39–41
 strengths, discovering
  own, 41–43
 traits of, 37–39
Peters, Tom, 114–115
Pink, Daniel, 84–85
Pool, Robert, 8–10
positioning, 149–150
positivity, 5, 34, 102.
 See also optimism
 in goal-setting, 75
 habits and, 98
 management and, 186
 in marriage, 219
 personality and, 38
 success and, 90–92
Posner, Barry, 173–174, 176
Power, Mark, 185
practice, 8–11, 85, 87
prejudice, 31–33, 236–237
pride, 91
prioritizing, 12–13, 27, 101, 106
 of goals, 78–80
 money and, 48
 for teams, 192–193
process, focusing on, 118, 120
progress. *See* creative work;
 focus; goal-setting; habits;
 motivation; starting

projects, 66–67, 114–115, 222
prospecting, 157–159
Purja, Nirmal, 8
purpose, finding, 53–61
 aligning with essential self, 54–55
 goal-setting and, 81–82
 helping customers at, 148
 by life design, 57–59
 by listening, 56–57
 motivation and, 85
 as ongoing process, 55
 passion and, 13–14
 role of language in, 60–61
 in work, 59–61

questions
 in coaching, 243–244
 for hiring interviews, 202, 204
 during sales calls, 160–161
quietness, 39–41

racism, 32–33, 236–237
Rackham, Neil, 160–161
Raz, Tahl, 70–71
Reference Levels, 67
referrals, 147
Reichheld, Fred, 124–126
Reis, Al, 145, 149–151
relationships, 211–219.
 See also conversations, difficult; generosity; teams
 connecting with others,
  138–140
 habits based on, 101–102
 happiness and, 212–213
 of managers with bosses, 184
 marriage, 217–219

partner selection by young
   adults, 69
shame and, 215–216
in social networks, 213–215
in teams, 43
vulnerability in, 215–217
winning friends, 143–144
repetition, 10, 12, 85, 92, 96, 99, 121. *See also* habits; practice
rewards, 84, 96, 115
Rifkin, Adam, 221
rituals, 72–73, 96, 218.
   See also habits
Robbins, Tony, 39
Robin, Vicki, 46
Rock, David, 27–29
Rogers, Everett 130
Roosevelt, Eleanor, 172
Rosenberg, Marshall, 233–235
Russell, Bill, 22
Russell Investments Group, 176

sales, 152–161
   attributes of star sales
      performers, 155–156
   importance of listening in, 152
   principles of, 153–154
   prospecting and new business
      development, 157–159
   using questions in, 160–161
Sandhal, Phillip, 241–242
Sarton, May, 119
S.A.V.E.R.S. (silence, affirmation, visualization, exercise, reading, and scribing), 72–73
Schulz, Marc, 212–213
Schwab, Charles, 144

Schwartz, Dan, 185
Science of People lab, 139
scoreboards, 195
Scott, Susan, 226, 229–231
self-awareness. *See* mindfulness
self-control, 95
Seligman, Martin, 75
Septien, Linda, 11
serenity, 91
Sethi, Ramit, 45
Shake Shack restaurant, 224
shame, 215–217
shipping creative work, 120–121
Sierra, Kathy, 126–128
Silsbee, Doug, 238, 244–245
Silver, Nan, 217–219
simplicity, 11, 28, 142
skills, 9, 10, 11, 13, 42
Smart, Brad, 202
Smart, Geoff, 202–204
Smith, Hyrum, 196
Smith, Melvin, 239–240
social mindbugs, 31–33
social networks, 213–215
social pain, 28
Solin, Dan, 46
solitude, 39–41
Spiek, Chris, 129
Stanier, Micheal Bungay, 243–244
starting, 63–73
   adult life, 68–69
   important activities in
      morning, 72–73
   new business, 70–71
   new job, 64–68
   new leadership role, 64–65
   new projects, 66–67

100 BEST BOOKS FOR WORK & LIFE **261**

Status Signals, 67
Steere, Douglas, 57
stickiness of ideas, 140–142
stocks. *See* investing
Stone, Douglas, 231–233
story-telling, 59, 228
    making ideas stick, 141–142
    in marketing messages, 148–149
    when prospecting, 158–159
Street, Randy, 202–204
strengths, discovering, 41–43
Stuart, Jim, 196
Switzler, Al, 227–228

talent, 10–12. *See also* hiring
    discovering own, 41–43
    focus on work instead of, 120–121
    mindset more important than, 7
    vs. practice, 8–9
tasks, listing all, 109–110
Taylor, Scott, 240
teams, 189–198, 206
    accountability on, 195
    developing and training, 186
    dysfunctions of, 190–191
    goals for, 194–196
    in great companies, 197
    meetings with, 193, 195–196
    priorities of, 192–193
    responsibilities for, 192
Tesich, Steve, 231
testimonials, 154
thanking, 7, 176
Thele, Scott, 194–196
thinking, 26–35.
    See also decision-making
    about money, 48–50
    brain, workings of, 27–29
    habit-based, 96
    modes of, 33–35
time, 106. *See also* prioritizing
    managing by saying no, 107–108
    money and, 46–50
    saving, 60
    for self, 102
    spending on what matters most, 111–112
    using effectively, 105–106
transitions. *See* change
transparency, 126, 176
Trout, Jack, 145, 149–151
trust, 102
    difficult conversations and, 228, 235
    influence and, 135
    leadership and, 175–177
    management and, 186, 188, 225
    marketing and, 148
    mindfulness and, 21, 23
    sales and, 153, 158
    on teams, 168, 190–191
truth, 34, 55, 227, 230
twenties, decisions made during, 68–69
Tyson, Neil deGrasse, 26
Tzu, Lao, 63

Ueshiba, Morihei, 232
Ulwick, Anthony, 129
Union Square Hospitality Group, 224, 225

university degrees, 66–67
Ury, William, 231
users. *See* customers
Uzzi, Brian, 214

value, 13, 30
Van Edwards, Vanessa, 138–140
Van Oosten, Ellen, 239–240
vocation. *See* purpose, finding
vulnerability, 140, 215–217

Waldinger, Robert, 212–213
Walker, Beverly, 194–196
Watkins, Michael, 63, 64
wealth. *See* money
Weinberg, Mike, 157–159
Welsh, Irvine, 119
Whitworth, Laura, 241–242
Whyte, David, 59–61
Wickman, Gino, 192–193
Wildly Important Goal (WIG), 194, 195
Wiseman, Liz, 196
wishes, goals as, 81–82
Wood, Wendy, 95–96, 98
Wooden, John, 5, 6, 11
work. *See also* business; creative work
    educational degrees and, 66–67
    finding purpose in, 59–61
    first ten years of, 68–69
    identity and, 59–61
    mindfulness at, 17–18, 25
    starting new job, 64–68
    transitions in leadership at, 64–65

working smarter, 29–31
    young adults and, 68–69
writing, learning from, 12

young people, starting adult life, 68–69

Zenji, Dogen, 15
Zhuo, Julie, 182–183
Ziglar, Zig, 83

About The Author

Todd Sattersten has over twenty years of experience in non-fiction publishing. He served as president of 800-CEO-READ (now Porchlight Books) and co-authored *The 100 Best Business Books of All Time*. As publisher and owner of Bard Press, he releases one book each year to help professionals excel at work and in life. His insights and recommendations have been featured in *Fortune*, *Business Week*, NPR, and *Harvard Business Review*. Todd lives in Portland, Oregon.

About Bard Press

Founded in 1995, Bard Press publishes business and personal development books. They specialize in publishing one book a year with carefully selected experts in their fields. This unique book creation process has produced over twenty national best sellers in the past thirty years, including multi-million copy bestsellers *The ONE Thing* and *The Little Red Book of Selling*. Their most recent titles include *When Everyone Leads* and *Give to Grow*. To learn more about Bard Press and their passion for books visit BardPress.com.

Post Credits

Thank you for making it all the way to the end!

The book ended up with a spare page, and I thought of how much I have always loved movies that give you a little bonus clip for watching through to the end of the credits. So, consider this the *100 Best Books* bonus scene.

When I started sharing the book, I was often asked "What did you learn from reading all of these amazing books?" This is a great question.

So, here are ten things I learned from reading the books in *100 Best Books for Work and Life*:

1. Self-improvement requires self-awareness. Self-awareness hinges on our ability to more clearly see our biases and perceptions.
2. Growth comes from believing that change is possible, and change is always possible. There is no limit to how good you can get.
3. Repeated daily focus will get you eighty percent of the way to your desired goal. Measuring your progress gives you extra energy for the journey.
4. Give people permission to do the things they have always wanted to do.
5. Someone has already thought really hard about the problem you are working on. Read four books and you will cut months off of your journey to getting better.
6. Time spent developing your coaching skills will benefit every relationship in your life.
7. "Being generous has never made anyone poor."
8. Contradictory advice isn't always wrong, it's often just the other side of the same coin.
9. Almost every situation is helped by listening more.
10. A different way to define the problem always leads to a different way to solve the problem.

Hmmm. A longer list of advice would make a great book ...

100 BEST BOOKS
FOR WORK & LIFE

100 BEST BOOKS BY CHAPTER

BETTER
- [ ] Mindset 6
- [ ] Peak 8
- [ ] The Talent Code 10
- [ ] Great at Work 12

CHANGE
- [ ] Managing Transitions ... 164
- [ ] Immunity to Change 166
- [ ] Leading Change 168
- [ ] When Things Fall Apart 170

COACHING
- [ ] Helping People Change 239
- [ ] Co-Active Coaching 241
- [ ] The Coaching Habit 243
- [ ] The Mindful Coach 244

CONVERSATIONS
- [ ] Crucial Conversations .. 227
- [ ] Fierce Conversations ... 229
- [ ] Difficult Conversations 231
- [ ] Nonviolent Communication.......... 233
- [ ] The Conversation 236

CREATIVE WORK
- [ ] The Project 50 114
- [ ] Orbiting the Giant Hairball 116
- [ ] Keep Going 118
- [ ] The Practice 120

CUSTOMERS
- [ ] The Ultimate Question 2.0 124
- [ ] Badass 126
- [ ] The Jobs to Be Done Playbook 128
- [ ] Crossing the Chasm 130

FOCUS
- [ ] The Effective Executive 105
- [ ] Get Everything Done .. 107
- [ ] Getting Things Done ... 109
- [ ] The ONE Thing 111

GOALS
- [ ] Creating Your Best Life 75
- [ ] The Desire Map 76
- [ ] Measure What Matters 78
- [ ] The Magic Lamp 81

GENEROSITY
- [ ] Give and Take 221
- [ ] The Go-Giver 223
- [ ] Setting the Table 224

HABITS
- [ ] Good Habits, Bad Habits 95
- [ ] Tiny Habits 97
- [ ] Atomic Habits 98
- [ ] The 7 Habits of Highly Effective People 100

HIRING
- [ ] Talent 200
- [ ] Who 202
- [ ] Work Rules! 204
- [ ] Moneyball 206

INFLUENCE
- [ ] Influence 134
- [ ] The Catalyst 136
- [ ] Captivate 138
- [ ] Made to Stick 140
- [ ] How to Win Friends and Influence People ... 143

LEADERSHIP
- [ ] The Leadership Challenge 173
- [ ] The Speed of Trust 175
- [ ] Total Leadership 177
- [ ] Reboot 179

MANAGING
- [ ] The Making of a Manager 182
- [ ] Leading from the Middle 183
- [ ] Becoming the Evidence-Based Manager 185
- [ ] Financial Intelligence ... 187

MARKETING
- [ ] The 1-Page Marketing Plan 146
- [ ] Building a Storybrand 2.0 148
- [ ] The 22 Immutable Laws of Marketing 149

MINDFULNESS
- [ ] The Inner Game of Work 17
- [ ] Full Catastrophe Living 19
- [ ] The Mindful Athlete 22
- [ ] Mindfulness 24

MONEY
- [ ] I Will Teach You to Be Rich 45
- [ ] Your Money or Your Life 46
- [ ] The Psychology of Money 48
- [ ] The Simple Path to Wealth 50

MOTIVATION
- [ ] Drive 84
- [ ] Grit 86
- [ ] The Progress Principle .. 88
- [ ] The Happiness Advantage 90

PERSONALITY
- [ ] Personality 37
- [ ] Quiet 39
- [ ] Now, Discover Your Strengths 41

PURPOSE
- [ ] Finding Your Own North Star 54
- [ ] Let Your Life Speak 56
- [ ] Designing Your Life 57
- [ ] Crossing the Unknown Sea 59

RELATIONSHIPS
- [ ] The Good Life 212
- [ ] Connected 213
- [ ] The Power of Vulnerability 215
- [ ] The Seven Principles for Making Marriage Work 217

SALES
- [ ] The Little Red Book of Selling 153
- [ ] The Challenger Sale 155
- [ ] New Sales. Simplified... 157
- [ ] The SPIN Selling Fieldbook 160

STARTING
- [ ] The First 90 Days 64
- [ ] The Personal MBA 66
- [ ] The Defining Decade .. 68
- [ ] Million Dollar Weekend 70
- [ ] The Miracle Morning ... 72

TEAMS
- [ ] The Five Dysfunctions of a Team 190
- [ ] Traction 192
- [ ] The 4 Disciplines of Execution 194
- [ ] Good to Great 196

THINKING
- [ ] Your Brain at Work 27
- [ ] Predictably Irrational ... 29
- [ ] Blindspot 31
- [ ] Six Thinking Hats 33